LOST DEESIDE

WITH SOUTH DONSIDE:
THE OLD PROVINCE OF MAR

Daniel MacCannell

BIRLINN

First published in 2011 by
Birlinn Limited
West Newington House
10 Newington Road
Edinburgh
EH9 1QS

www.birlinn.co.uk

ISBN: 978 1 84158 964 0

British Library Cataloguing-in-Publication Data
A catalogue record for this book is available from the British Library.

Design: Mark Blackadder

Printed and bound by Gutenberg Press Limited, Malta

CONTENTS

CHAPTER 1

INTRODUCTION

THE LOST FRONTIER

The successive ages of turnpike, railway and motor car have conditioned us to think of Deeside as a route: westward to the mountains, eastward to the sea. But in earlier times, the intensity of human settlement related not so much to this east–west axis as to the strategic passes that run from north to south, through the otherwise barely penetrable mountain range known as the Mounth. The now sleepy village of Kincardine O'Neil was in 1715 a bustling place, described as 'convenient for travellers, who are numerous, by reason of the great highrode south and north'.[1] Nor was the river itself much help, being navigable only for about a mile at its mouth, or just over 1 per cent of its length.

Historically there were up to fourteen Mounth passes, many with strange names including the Slug, Builg Mounth, Foggy Road, the Fungle and Corsedardar. Their precise number, and the minutiae of their routes, are debated. What is certain is that only three, the Cairnwell, Cairn a' Mount and the Slug, are useable by cars. The rest are tracks, trodden now by the more adventurous sorts of tourists, where drovers, migrant labourers, smugglers, highwaymen, pedlars, cattle raiders, Jacobites, Williamites, and medieval and ancient warriors went before. No fewer than twenty castles – some still inhabited, some ruinous, some known only by repute – were built principally or solely to guard these passes against hostile movements in either direction. They were not planned on a single occasion by a single evil genius, but

> arose, naturally and inevitably, out of the political and geographical circumstances . . . not in the east-to-west or blind-alley strategy of these narrowing valleys, but rather in the north and south or trans-versal strategy of the trunk roads leading across the Mounth towards Moravia [Moray]. On an east-to-west strategy the position of these castles is meaningless: they are 'at the back end of nowhere'.[2]

The lonely and still dangerous B974 Fettercairn–Banchory road follows the ancient Cairn a' Mount, the way taken by Edward I's army as they withdrew from the North-east in 1296, as well as the route the historical King Macbeth took northward to his doom two and a half centuries earlier. Ten thousand Covenanters arrived via the Causey Mounth in 1639, and the legions of Emperor Septimus Severus came in by Elsick Mounth in the early third century AD., fording the River Dee at Tilbouries and leaving behind the inaptly named Normandykes: Deeside's 106-acre exemplar of a Roman 'marching camp', one of six built in a chain from Stonehaven to Keith.

None of these incursions was an unmixed triumph. Deeside is the southern border of 'Up Here': that phrase still used by obstinate backwoods lairds to mean not the north or north-east of Scotland, but the 'real' North-east: Aberdeenshire and Banffshire, or the ancient mormaerdoms of Mar and Buchan, imagined as virtually a separate state, in both political and confessional terms. Beyond the Dee, we find ourselves on John R. Allan's 'Dark Side of the Moon', with the witches of Lumphanan, the fairies of Blelack House and the impenetrable secrets of the Society of the Horseman's Word. Visually, it astonishes: especially

Birse Castle was built around 1600 to guard the Fungle route through the mountains from Aboyne to Tarfside. Shown here as it looked in 1855, it is a 'lost ruin', fully restored beginning in 1905, and now inhabited.

when, after mile upon mile of silver birch, the trees' form and colour are echoed in some castle, astonishingly vertical, in pale grey, white, or pale pink; or a sudden bend in the road or break in the trees reveals the Dee herself, suddenly far below, shimmering curves through distant hills.

> We are apt to forget what we have already seen of the Dee, and incon-stantly exclaim: '*This* is the most beautiful spot in the Dee valley!' . . . for after all there is no fixed standard; cultured tastes differ; it is idle to attempt to place Beethoven, Mozart, and Wagner.[3]

Some of the woods have always been here; many more have been planted. They are an important cash crop in a region that is 'no' ideal' agriculturally, with frequent floods; unpredictable (but usually long and cold) winters; hoar-frosts in August; and a sandy, gravelly, thirsty soil intermixed with boulders of every size, from the merely inconvenient to the absolutely gigantic. Only a town-bred railway propagandist could have written with a straight face that Deeside was 'famed for excellent farming' in 1866.[4]

At a time when farm labourers were paid £2 a year, clearing the stones from fields on Deeside cost £6 an acre, even when explosives were used (and they usually were). Several of the largest drystone walls in the region were created not in the first instance to keep animals in or out, but because there was simply nowhere else to put all that unwanted rock. One such 'consumption' dyke, so called because it was created 'to "consume" the rocks and boulders littering the unimproved acres of the estate of Kingswells', is a third of a mile long, six feet high, and thirty feet thick.[5] In a touching Deeside wedding tradition of not so long ago, the groom would perambulate a field with stones tied on his back, and the bride would cut the cords to symbolise the sharing of burdens. Some tenant farmers in the early eighteenth century were required to build walls to the height of one ell (the old Scots yard of thirty-seven inches) using nothing other than field-stones found within the enclosure thus being made. Blasting also accompanied lake-drainage projects, with sometimes fatal results; and the Dee itself was widened by five feet using explosives, at Potarch, to facilitate the timber trade. It is perhaps unsurprising that this explosives-happy place also produced the man given overall command of Bonnie Prince Charlie's artillery.

Deeside is contrary. At least one historian has suggested that the region's ordinary people supported the cause of King Macbeth and his son Lulach the Fatuous; but not long thereafter, they adopted Malcolm III Canmore, slayer of both Macbeth and Lulach, as their particular and best-loved folk hero. Deeside preserved many of its precious artefacts when, in the rest of the country, Reformation zeal destroyed them – only to break, lose or obliterate great numbers of relics and whole structures during the nineteenth-century heyday of antiquarian preservation. In contrast to, say, mid-Wales, it has so far salvaged hardly a scrap of the railway that ensured its prosperity from 1853 to 1966. Deeside was royalist during the National Covenant period, and Jacobite at the Revolution, yet a key prop to Queen Victoria's rule when republicanism and Jacobitism both flared up again after the death of Prince Albert.

Part of this is readily explicable. As recently as the fourteenth century, three of the four largest estates on Lower Deeside – Durris, Drum, and Leys – were all royal hunting estates. The earldom of Mar followed them into royal ownership in 1435. In the medieval law of both Scotland and England, deer hunting (like mining) in effect belonged to the king, and could only be conducted with his permission; and in areas where these activities were major employers, royalist politics tended to follow, from the tin miners of Cornwall to the lead miners of the Derbyshire Peak to the ironworkers and charcoal-burners of the Forest of Dean. Likewise, throughout recorded history, when conflicts have arisen between Crown and nobles, or between Crown and commons, the folk of Deeside have understood their royals not as a political abstraction, but as a particular group of real people. Victoria's genius (if such it was) lay in the recognition of this fact; and her physical plantation of a Hanoverian hunting lodge on Upper Deeside, heartland of extremist loyalty to the House of Stuart, has probably done more to prolong the Anglo-Scottish Union than all the books and

The arms of the earldom of Mar as used by its largely absentee Royal Stewart landlords, c.1435–1565. The crest of two intertwined 'nessies' may represent the Dee and the Don, between which most of the earldom lay.

4

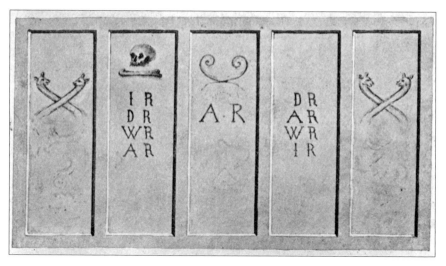

Twined serpents appear again in these now-vanished pew panels from the north side of the sixteenth-century kirk of Kintore, demolished in 1819.

laws ever written. When Marshall Lang, later Moderator of the General Assembly of the Church of Scotland, was invited to preach to George V and Queen Mary at Crathie Kirk in 1912, his brother Cosmo, then Archbishop of York and later of Canterbury, wrote him the following message from Balmoral:

[D]on't think you are addressing Kings and such like at all. Speak as if you were addressing an ordinary congregation of fair intelligence . . . Bow slightly when you shake hands with the King and Queen, address them as 'Sir' or 'Ma'am' with an *occasional* 'Your Majesty' thrown in, not too elaborately: and remember they are ordinary human beings: and everybody wants to be kind.[6]

The people of Deeside exhibit no unifying 'regional character', unless of course it is idiosyncrasy. From a very early date indeed, Deeside has been a refuge for outlaws and misfits of all kinds. The tone was set by Alexander Stewart, bastard son of the infamous 'Wolf of Badenoch'. Alexander acquired the earldom of Mar by a combination of treachery and force: he falsely imprisoned and almost certainly murdered the husband of Isabel, countess of Mar in her own right; forcibly married her; and from her extorted the title to the earldom, promising that it would pass to her Erskine relatives were she to die without issue. Isabel managed to avoid becoming pregnant, but the Son of the Wolf broke his promise, and possession being nine-tenths of the law, the Stewarts denied the Erskines their rights for another 200 years – by which time the lands and superiorities of the original earldom had been split among 150 new owners.

Deeside is a land of immigrants: from the Anglo-Norman lords of the lower

The hoopla surrounding Deeside's Victorian heritage can reach the realms of silliness. At worst, it has the potential to obscure or even erase other histories, newer as well as older. (Photo by Eleanor MacCannell)

No fewer than twelve triumphal arches were built all along Deeside for the royal visit of 8 September 1848. One of them was made entirely from heather, and another, entirely of stags' heads. This undated drawing may depict one such, in the background at right. The large building at centre is the Monaltrie Arms Hotel, Ballater. It was completely built over in 1860.

A temporary triumphal arch installed in Ballater to welcome King Edward VII.

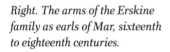

Above. The personal seal of Isabella, countess of Mar, c.1400.

Right. The arms of the Erskine family as earls of Mar, sixteenth to eighteenth centuries.

valley to the Speyside cattle rustlers and West Highland refugees of the upper reaches, to the scores of Bremners and Brebners – names indicating a medieval Brabant origin – to American loyalists fleeing the War of Independence, to centuries of Englishmen and Edinburghers who came to conquer (or shoot grouse) but put down roots. Today, they are joined by French, Poles, Indians, Germans, Canadians. So changed was the region between 1830 and 1870 that J.G. Michie, traumatised by the local extirpation of his Gaelic mother tongue, considered his own memories relics of a lost world, or even of a wholly bygone epoch of mankind. A common thread in Deeside's history is the taking of aliases by entire families and groups of families: MacDonalds become Ewans and Michies; MacGregors become Gregories, Griersons and Patullos; Stewarts become Dowies and Millers. Upper Deeside's leading family, the Farquharsons, adopted their name in place of McIntosh – and, some say, McIntosh in place of Shaw before that. At least one late-Victorian writer believed

> there was no dispersion of the races, the present inhabitants are in the main Vakomagoi, possessors of the same region for over 2,000 years. So that here, if anywhere, the true original Celtic blood is to be found, and the manners, games, customs, language prevailing here must, in good measure, derive from the very distant past.[7]

Few characterisations of the region could be less true.

Alongside continuous immigration and habitual secrecy there has been religious diversity. Pre-Christian beliefs and practices from 'Maying' to midsummer bonfires survived not just into medieval Catholicism but through the Reformation and well into the era of photography. Rowan trees at the doors of houses (including my own), planted in bygone days to ward off evil, are often the traveller's first, or only, clue to the remains of a cottage, or some wholly vanished small community, which existed here as recently as the nineteenth century. Just as pagan beliefs survived into the Christian era, so did Catholic ones survive the Reformation: in 1704, Calam Grierson erected a gigantic crucifix 'to be adored by all the neighbourhood' on his land near modern-day Ballater, and in 1718, Upper Deeside in general was described as a place where Presbyterian missionaries might as well 'make a speech to a horse' as reason with the people, 'gentry or commons'.[8] In contrast to Strathdon, however, the decapitation or forcible smothering of Presbyterian clergymen by local lairds was rare to non-existent. A hundred years later, mixed marriages were commonplace in Tullich and Glengairn, where even in Protestant schools, being Catholic or half-Catholic 'carried with it no stigma'.[9]

As we shall see, the region's Christian oddities go far beyond the mere presence of pockets of open Old Catholicism, however large. Mid-Deeside produced several notable Quakers and 'Brownists', but especially noteworthy are the hundreds, or thousands, of Deesiders who continued to *use* the Established Kirk after 1689, but who remained Episcopalian in spirit, and where circumstances suited them (e.g. America, Barbados or Oxford University), Episcopalian in practice. Two lairdly families whose principal lands faced each other across the Dee, the Burnetts of Leys and the Douglases of Tilquhillie, provided a bishop apiece to the see of Salisbury in the Church of England – at a time when, within Scotland, Anglicanism was still illegal. Claims that their castles were connected by a secret underwater tunnel are, like so many Deeside tales, utterly absurd yet also symptomatic of something or other.[10] Aside from the large prosperous village of Banchory-Ternan, salient of Kincardineshire and that 'other' Scotland lying to the south, Deeside is the edge-land and guarantor of the farther North-east's distinctive and arguably separate culture. 'A land of wonders and of happy people' it certainly is;[11] but Deeside is also a lost frontier.

The lost people, places and structures described in this book are all from the Christian era, and mostly from the high Middle Ages and since. The Romans will be mentioned in passing; the Vacomagoi, Taxaloi, and 'beaker people', not at all. As an historian, not an archaeologist, I would not presume to put my own spin (for such it would surely be) on the rich pre-history of the region, for which readers are referred especially to W. Douglas Simpson's *The Province of Mar*

The spa town of Ballater, seen here in 1856 and c.1890, was founded by the Jacobite
Francis Farquharson of Monaltrie. Susan Carnegie praised the project in verses of 1782:
'When ill-got wealth and Tyrant power / Shall cease to dazzle or devour . . ./ Our
children's children shall revere thy plan / And praise Monaltrie as the friend of Man.'
These photos shows the third (wooden) and fourth (current, stone) bridges of Ballater; the
first bridge, built of stone in 1783, was a hundred yards to the east and right. The
'centrical' church, serving the dwindling populations of the three parishes of Glen Muick,
Tullich and Glengairn, was also rebuilt. The version standing in 1856 was the first, dating
from 1798–1800, with a spire made largely of wood. The current church is from 1873–74.

Col. Francis Farquharson of Monaltrie (1710–90). His original inn at Pannanich Wells vanished without trace by 1962, but not before it ruined the rival wells of Poldow or Poll-dubh in Logie-Coldstone.

(1944), Alex Woolf's *From Pictland to Alba* (2007), and *Grampian's Past* (1996) by Ian Shepherd and Moira Greig. The cultural unity of Mar was, however, extremely ancient. The province acted as a 'buffer state' between North and South even before Scotland came together as a united monarchy. Alexander Keith's manuscript 'View of the Diocese of Aberdeen', written about 1732, claimed the Dee as a border between the Picts and the ancient Scots. Be that as it may, in more recent epochs it was the wild men of Moray who were most feared, most of the time.

Legally, the earldom of Mar dates back only to 1404; historically, its continuous existence can be traced to the 1130s. It is now usually accepted as Scotland's oldest earldom, but as a pre-feudal territorial title, it is much older still. Its original line of rulers had no surnames at any point before they died out, and no names at all, so far as history records, until one of them, Donald, son of Emhin, son of Cainnech, travels to Ireland and is killed fighting the Danes at the battle of Clontarf (1014). They are, indeed, 'shadowy figures dimmed by the mists of years'.[12]

Since the demise of the old line of Celtic mormaers and earls in the 1370s, fewer such difficulties present themselves. On mid-Deeside, the sphere of influence of the Gordons of Aboyne extended almost to the Don, where it was blocked by their most hated rivals, the Forbeses; whereas from Upper Deeside, the Farquharsons' influence reached down the Cairnwell Mounth and far into Perthshire. On the lower reaches of the river, the most important territorial magnates were the Irvines of Drum (and elsewhere); the Frasers of Durris; and the Douglases and Burnetts already mentioned. About the 'lost world' of these

Arms of the Celtic earls of Mar, as shown in the fourteenth-century Wapenboek Gelre.

families and their various triumphs, tragedies and obsessions, we shall be hearing a great deal.

Mar was divided into five parts. Two are now considered to be in the Highlands: Braemar, west of the River Gairn, and Cromar, stretching from the Gairn to the Dinnet Burn. East of Dinnet, the borders are less clear-cut, but the Strathdee district certainly includes the town and castle of Aboyne, and the Midmar district, Echt, Skene, and of course Midmar Castle itself. The fifth portion was the city of Aberdeen, which has been dealt with by other books in this series, and its immediate environs. The relative unimportance of the shire boundaries, in Scotland as compared to England, is very obvious here. Five Deeside parishes, all south of the river, historically lay in or mostly in Kincardineshire. These are (from west to east) Strachan, Durris, Maryculter, Banchory-Devenick, and Nigg. The section of Banchory-Devenick called 'Half Banchory', however, was in Aberdeenshire. Conversely, a small part of Aberdeenshire's Drumoak parish was in Kincardineshire. Banchory-Ternan was at first in Aberdeenshire, but was detached and given to Kincardineshire by act of the Scots Parliament in 1646.

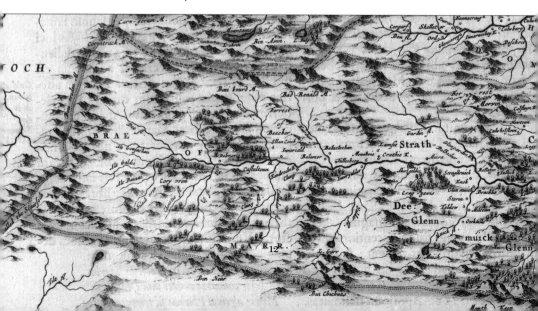

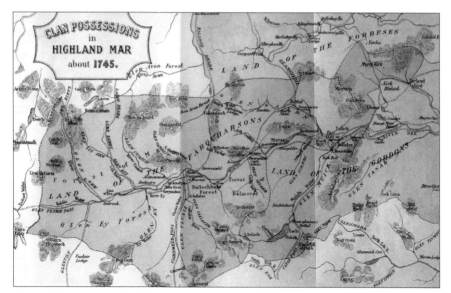

Above. This map was clearly intended to show broad spheres of influence only, ignoring as it does the local landholdings of various other families including Stewarts, MacDonalds, MacGregors and Mackenzies. A marked characteristic of Deeside before Culloden is, in fact, how very numerous the lairds were and how small their lands. The parish of Crathie alone had eighteen proprietors in 1635. The Farquharsons, too, were 'remarkable' for the number of their independent landed branches, among whom Invercauld 'was no more than . . . primus inter pares' (J.G. Michie).

Below. 'Marr' by Joan Blaeu, 1654. Almost a century later, Herman Moll got the position of Banchory-Devenick right, but placed Banchory-Ternan a dozen miles too far east, and on the wrong river. Indeed, so much misinformation about the region has been published over the centuries that I cannot hope entirely to avoid repeating some. I can only hope that this book will tend to diminish, rather than increase, the net amount of hogwash in circulation.

CHAPTER 2

MEANINGS

THE LOST LANGUAGE:
DEESIDE GAELIC

As already mentioned, the Mounth and to some extent the River Dee itself amounted to a formidable obstacle to north–south communication, and early Deeside can be thought of as a frontier area. However, the region was also home to a second frontier, albeit a continually shifting one: the border between the Gaelic language and the Scots form of English. Until some time in the 1100s, it is believed Gaelic was spoken in all parts of Deeside and throughout Aberdeenshire, even on the coasts. The advancing Scots speech won out in Lower Deeside by the sixteenth century, and perhaps as far west as Dinnet Moor. The early modern privy council, though not always the best observers of the realities of life in remote districts, considered the border between the languages to be Culblean Hill, just west of Loch Kinnord between Aboyne and Ballater. Nineteenth-century observers in effect agreed, but specified that the boundary line was not the hill, but the nearby Burn of Dinnet, which flows out of Loch Kinnord. The modern sign on precisely this stretch of the A93 which announces to westbound motorists that they are entering the Highlands is, in this respect, correct – or at least reflective of a very old governmental tradition. Other sources, however, suggest that as recently as 1769, the 'language barrier' began a little farther east, within the district known anciently as the Howe of Cromar, which includes the modern settlements of Logie-Coldstone, Coull and Tarland.

During the 900-year period over which an almost wholly Gaelic-speaking Deeside became almost wholly English-speaking, there were at times more Gaelic-speakers on the northern side of the river than the southern. In Birse – which seems very Highland-like today, with its sparse population and rough-hewn log porticoes – in 1792, no Gaelic was spoken except by incomers to the parish. This has sometimes been put down to the greater influence of the English-speaking Gordons as resident landowners on the southern banks of the river, perhaps especially in Glen Tanar and Glen Muick. Their principal seat on Deeside prior to the seventeenth-century building or rebuilding of Aboyne Castle was the mansion house of Kandychyle (variously spelled Candacorl, Canakyle, Ceann-na-Coille, Kean-na-Kyll, Candecaill, Chandakailzie, and so forth), which guarded the strategic Mounth Keen pass, and which was where the first marquess of Huntly was born.[1] The mansion itself has now utterly vanished but is recollected in the name of the farm called Deecastle, where some interesting early seventeenth-century barns remain. Among the north-bank landlords, on the other hand, there were many Gaels as well as absentees, the Farquharsons in particular being noted for bilingualism – where they were not monoglot Gaelic-speakers.

In the seventeenth century, Scottish Gaelic was usually called the Irish language and those who spoke it were increasingly thought of as existing outside of 'decent' Scottish society. In 1690, 'Irish'-language Bibles were printed, and in or by 1706 these had been provided to Upper Deeside's five westernmost, bilingual, Presbyterian churches: Braemar, Crathie, Glen Muick, Tullich and Glengairn (as well as the neighbouring Upper Donside parish of Strathdon-and-Corgarff). It was found, however, that the Deeside dialect was sufficiently different from the west-coast Gaelic used in preparing these Bibles that they were of little use. By 1713, the provision of Gaelic printed religious books to Deeside parishes was frowned upon, and from 1722 – in the wake of the near-

Crathie Kirk as it appeared between 1804 and 1893.

success of the Jacobite Rebellion of 1715 – missionary schoolmasters working among Gaelic-speaking Deesiders quite aggressively sought not to cater to their language but to eliminate it. Of course, some teaching in Gaelic remained necessary 'since the strategy of the language's eradication stalled on an inability in the first instance to communicate'.[2] It persisted in oral use in church services for another century: Braemar ministers were removed for not knowing enough Gaelic in 1739 and 1795.

A campaign for continued Gaelic church services on Deeside east of Crathie was fought, and lost, at the turn of the nineteenth century. In 1790, Gaelic-speakers from the Ballater area were officially advised to go to Crathie Kirk in the next parish, rather than continuing to lobby for Gaelic services where they were. The language was last used in church in Ballater in 1809.

The schoolchildren of Glen Muick could not speak any English in 1712, but all of them could in 1725. Three generations after that, Gaelic had become nearly extinct in Glen Muick (a lone bilingual speaker was reported in 1832), as well as in Logie-Coldstone. It was still dominant in nineteenth-century Braemar, however, even in the town, which didn't acquire its first English-speaking resident until 1782. Here, at Deeside's extreme western end, it was a case not of Gaelic's collapse but of the advance of English – used not least by English tourists – amid Gaelic survival. Much of the credit for this survival is due to a lone teacher named McMurich, who contrived to teach Braemar schoolchildren in Gaelic through the period of severest condemnation of the practice, and until the language became tolerated again – or even somewhat fashionable – in the early nineteenth century. Braemar people were said mostly to understand spoken English in 1794, and to be fully bilingual in Gaelic and English by the early 1840s. Measuring who could and who could not speak English was not an exact science, of course:

> It was no unusual thing to find a boy or girl with a good ear who could glibly enough run over whole pages of the Shorter Catechism without comprehending the import of a single sentence, or even the meaning of a single word.[3]

Then again, schooling was more or less a disaster in many parts of the region, even purely English-speaking ones. Teachers were derided as 'the laird's ground officer', were supported in part by the proceeds of cock-fighting organised for the purpose, and given to 'coarse jokes'.[4] This was in the 1830s, but even a hundred years later cruelty and irregularity abounded. Chrissie Gibson remembers that for being *one minute* late to school – after a three-and-a-half mile walk in the depths of winter – she was strapped so hard on her hands that they never worked properly again. No medical treatment was provided by the school, and at the end of the day, Gibson's blood literally froze in her gloves on the way home. Despite a complaint from the family doctor, who feared gangrene might set in, nothing happened to the teacher. Indeed, as Gibson remembers it, teachers 'seemed to be immune from prosecution in those days for anything short of murder'.[5] All children had to leave school on the day they turned fourteen, regardless of where this fell in the school year. The teachers of North-east Scotland were forty times more likely to have a university degree than teachers elsewhere in the country (85 per cent versus 2 per cent in 1875), but this does nothing to excuse brutality; rather the reverse.

By 1908, Braemar village was the dividing line between the languages, with Gaelic in routine, daily, use only west of that point. However, two sisters living within the town, Jess and Mary MacDonald, still spoke it in 1951. Writing in 1850, the brilliant naturalist William MacGillivray predicted that Gaelic would be extinct on Deeside by the year 2000. In point of fact, its last Gaelic-speaking community – unconquerable Inverey, the river's westernmost settlement – ceased to be so some time between 1930 and 1950. Even MacGillivray could not have predicted the emergence of broadcasting, until recently the great enemy of small languages everywhere.

The Deeside speech which was considered incompatible with the Gaelic Bible in 1706, and called a 'barbarous dialect' of Gaelic in the 1790s, contained a number of odd pronunciations, as well as a now-unknown number of whole words not used elsewhere. Colin McIntosh, from Dalgowan, reported the local tradition that the Braemar dialect was 'a doggerel Gaelic' brought into the area by outlaws 'fae different parts o the country an it wis a bit mixed up'.[6] It is now reckoned to have been more similar to Atholl Gaelic than to that of Badenoch, Nairn, Moray, or elsewhere. This may have been due to the unifying influence of the Farquharson estates, which since the seventeenth century have stretched from Birse to Braemar, then south through Glen Shee towards Blairgowrie in Perthshire along the Cairnwell Mounth, roughly the north–south-running part of the modern A93.

The last speaker of the dialect, Jean (McDonald) Bain who was brought up at Claybokie, Inverey, from the age of eight, died in Crathie in the early 1980s. Mrs Bain never sought publicity for herself, perhaps living by the local proverb: *Rud nach bean dhuit, na bean da* ('The thing that doesn't touch you, don't touch it').[7] She was discovered by Gaelic scholars quite by accident in her mid eighties. Fortunately, sound recordings of her were made by Dr Adam Watson, and these are held by the University of Aberdeen.[8]

Meanwhile, nostalgic 'Highlandism' has been pushing in the opposite direction. Even as Deeside Gaelic died out as a *spoken* language, in the end completely, it has slowly been expanding its range as a language of place-names. Dunecht, for instance, is a double 'improvement': from 1705 until 1818, the mansion house of the Echt barony was called Housedale. When Housedale was superseded in 1820 by a new building with pretensions to castle-hood, Gaelic *dún* meaning 'fort' was combined with the name of the barony and thus 'Dunecht House' was born. Soon after, the nearby village of Waterton was renamed Dunecht to reinforce this. It cannot have been universally or immediately

Brackley (now House of Glen Muick) and House of Glen Muick (since destroyed by fire), about 1905.

18

popular, however, for the Post Office continued to refer to Dunecht village as 'Waterton of Echt' in postmarks after the introduction of adhesive postage stamps, which did not occur until 1840.

The same architect responsible for Dunecht House created Banchory House in Banchory-Devenick, obliterating a 1620s house of the same name. The newer structure has since been renamed 'Beannachar' – never mind that the experts cannot agree whether the name 'Banchory' itself is Scots Gaelic, Irish or Welsh in origin. The farm previously called Banchory-Hillock was, some time before 1921, renamed 'Drumthwacket' after a comic character in a Walter Scott novel. Brackley, another Deeside property that had been important in its own right for centuries, took on the name 'House of Glen Muick' in 1947, when and because the actual House of Glen Muick – another *ersatz* Tudor manor dating back only to 1898 – was destroyed in a fire. Just twenty years later, the ordnance surveyors found 'no trace or local knowledge of an old castle at the modern house formerly known as Brackley, now called the House of Glen Muick'.[9] As we shall see again and again, the speed with which local knowledge disappears can be astonishing.

The most irritating case of Gaelicisation occurs at Braemar. One wonders immediately why a village should be given the exact same name as a surrounding district large enough to contain the European countries of Lichtenstein, San Marino and Andorra – probably with room for a second San

Detail of Joan Blaeu's 1654 map showing 'Inner-ey' to 'Casteltoun' along the 'Die River'.

Marino left over. In fact, 'Braemar' was two villages, known from the Reformation until 1870 as Castletown and Auchendryne. Separated from each other by the Clunie Water, Auchendryne was Catholic (at least following the conversion of its Farquharson lairds about the time of James VII) and Castletown or Castleton was Protestant. The name 'Braemar' cannot have been popular initially; almost thirty years after the 'rebranding', it was reported that

The Invercauld Arms Hotel, Castletown, before its extensions and 'baronialisation' covered over the the spot where the Jacobites' standard was unfurled in 1715. As of 1925, a brass plaque on the outside of the building commemorated the raising of the standard, but this was gone by 1967.

The same hotel about 1900.

the name Castletown is 'now frequently applied to both portions'[10] – as, indeed, it had been among map-readers in the 1650s, when the cartographer Joan Blaeu knew it as 'Casteltoun' only. We must not be too indignant about any of this, however, for before the Reformation the settlement was called Kindrochit and the parish, St Andrews.

Braemar's rival Fife Arms Hotel before and after its late-Victorian expansion and remodelling.

LOST CLOTHING

When the English poet John Taylor visited his friend the earl of Mar in Braemar in 1618, he saw lords, ladies, knights, esquires and others to the number of 1,400 or 1,500, all wearing tartan; and 'all and every man in generall in one habit, as if Licurgus [of Sparta] had beene there and made Lawes of Equalitie'.[11] About 500 of the men were detached to circle around and drive deer toward the main party, where about eighty animals were killed with 'strong Irish Grey-hounds' and all manner of military weapons – from arquebuses, to bows and arrows, to swords and bucklers – in what Taylor termed 'The Calydonian anuall peacefull warre'.[12] Peacefulness notwithstanding, he was bruised all over and had to stay eight days afterward in Edinburgh recovering. The Highlanders considered it an insult for anyone not to wear Highland garb, and the earl provided Taylor with the correct gear. 'The authority of the chief, however great,' the earl of Selkirk pointed out two centuries later, 'was not of that absolute kind which has sometimes been imagined . . . [T]he meanest expected to be treated as a gentleman, and almost as an equal.'[13]

Officers and sergeants of the Gordon Highlanders in the mid 1820s.

Towns had a very different form of social organisation, but plaids and 'blew bonnets' were sufficiently popular among Aberdeen's mercantile elite that wearing them had to be prohibited many times, notably in 1576, 1580 and 1611. Penalties included a £5 fine or, if the offenders were females, being taken for 'harlottes'. This is odd indeed, given that in the southern Lowlands, the main sartorial 'crime' was dressing *above* one's station, not beneath it; or as in this case, altogether outside it.

For wearing a kilt during the validity of the diskilting act (1748–1782), the penalty was six months' imprisonment without bail for a first offence, and for a second, transportation to the plantations. Aberdeenshire's variant of the law allowed the prison term to be altered to forced enlistment in the army, at the judge's option. Prior to the nineteenth century, peacetime enlistment in the British Army was for life; and the inherent cruelty of the law was enhanced by its selective, even capricious enforcement. In Braemar in the summer of 1749 alone, one man was arrested, judicially examined and released, on the grounds that his 'plaid' was just a blanket, while another was 'shot while trying to escape'.

When once again allowed, Highland dress was worn in various combinations with Lowland dress, sometimes to 'ridiculous' effect. Tartan plaids were still worn in Leochel-Cushnie in the 1790s, but George Adams reported from Kintore at the same date that, within the last fifty years, people there had stopped weaving their own plaids (which were not necessarily tartan to begin with) and

Many illustrations from the 1850s, including this one by Keith and Gibb, indicate that Highland and Lowland dress were seen in most Deeside towns, though not usually combined in one individual. The bridge at Banchory-Ternan is seen here not long after the replacement of its wooden span with an iron one, due to 1829 flood damage.

started using cloth bought from Aberdeen. 'It would probably give nearly as much trouble to make the people of Morven return to the kilt to-day,' Col. C.G. Gardyne wrote in 1900, 'as it took to make their grandfathers leave it off!'[14]

'Plaid' carried a number of meanings,

> from a horse-blanket to a shawl worn by a lady. It also referred to the cloth itself, sometimes known as 'plaiding', a strong, woollen cloth, identified by one writer at the end of the eighteenth century as flannel. Tartan sometimes meant a self-coloured cloth, and was so described by the Army as late as the eighteenth century. Thus two names for fabrics became a garment and a peculiar arrangement of coloured checks and stripes, as if the whole question of Highland dress was not complicated enough![15]

The blue bonnet's best days were also behind it by 1807, when it was reported that only the elderly still wore it in Kincardineshire. Its replacement was somewhat surprising:

> By 1840, men of all classes wore top hats at one time or another. Middle-class children wore them to school; the clergy, the lawyers, the tradesmen, all wore them. Postmen and policemen wore them. No one of whatsoever class could attend a funeral without a lum [chimney] hat.[16]

Throughout the Deeside region as in the city of Aberdeen, stocking-knitting was one of the major crafts, amounting to an important export industry in the seventeenth and eighteenth centuries. It was a 'cottage industry' in the literal sense. On prearranged 'factory days', the Aberdeen hosiers would visit the hinterland, handing out their combed wool (some of which was imported from England, and some from Shetland) and collecting the finished stockings made since their last visit. 'Mitts' were also knitted in Echt. In eighteenth-century Maryculter, the workforce consisted of females aged seven and up. In Kemnay, it was reported, stocking-knitting was the usual work of women, who did agricultural work only at harvest time; the weekly profit of this activity being up to 2s 2d per person. In Cluny, it was 2s 6d, and in Leochel-Cushnie, as much as 3s. The very finest pairs sold for as much as three guineas in the eighteenth century, and one pair, presented by the earl Marischal to the Tsarina of Russia, was valued at five guineas. Though the work was dominated by women, it was not exclusive to them: old men and boys of Kemnay and Leochel-Cushnie also took part. The retail value of knitted goods from the Kincardineshire side of the river alone was estimated at £120,000 per year, of which perhaps a third was spent on raw wool. Much of the rest ended up in the pockets of the workforce. George Brown dismissed the late eighteenth-century inhabitants of Glen Muick, Tullich and Glengairn for their general sloth, but this failed to square with his own comment that, instead of doing piece-work for the Aberdeen stocking manufacturers like most Deeside women, the women of these areas made tartan cloth which they retailed themselves at 2s to 2s 6d the ell.

In Strachan, stocking-making was the 'chief' work of women (but only women) in the 1790s, and was still performed in individuals' homes half a century later, despite the arrival of a woollen mill. Leochel-Cushnie was not so lucky: by 1843, its women workers (only) had been herded together into a factory owned by Messrs Hadden of Aberdeen. This was no doubt a response to increased competition from Jersey, Guernsey and Germany, as well as the recent loss of the American market, which severely threatened the trade throughout Aberdeenshire and Kincardineshire. Even so, in the South Donside parish of Tough in the 1840s, home-based worsted stocking-knitting 'at which they labour with the utmost diligence' was still prevalent among the women, who produced 3,000 'excellent' pairs annually, earning 3½d to 4d per pair. The writing was on the wall, however. From Coull around the same time, it was reported that, though stocking-knitting was not extinct, its profits 'are now become extremely small'.[17]

One of the region's related lost arts is the full range of natural dyeing. Birch bark, oak bark, yellow lichen, heather, blaeberry, broom, bracken root, bramble, dandelions, acorns and other local vegetation were once used to create an array of colours from black and brown to orange and magenta – though undyed 'hodden grey' cloth remained cheap and popular.

LOST EXPLANATION:
THE FARQUHARSON FAMILY

With the collapse and fragmentation of the old Celtic earldom of Mar at the end of the fourteenth century, a power vacuum was created, comparable to 'the Balkanisation of Eastern Europe after the fall of the Austrian empire in 1918'.[18] One of the legacies of this was the enduring regional feud between the Gordons and Forbeses. The real winner of this feud, as is so often the case, was a clan that largely declined to participate in it. I could hardly provide a better comment than W.M. Farquharson-Lang's, that

The map of West Aberdeenshire in the seventeenth and eighteenth centuries became like a jigsaw puzzle, each piece adding yet another property to some branch of the Farquharson clan, until about 1850 when the picture was complete and the whole area was virtually Farquharson territory.[19]

In fact, the Farquharsons' peak of territorial influence may have been reached about 1820; in any case, we are fortunate that they are also one of Scotland's most interesting families.

Poachers turned gamekeepers in an almost literal sense, the first Farquharsons seem to have been fifteenth-century McIntosh raiders from Rothiemurchus who were 'turned' by the earls of Mar. Thereafter, largely with success, they guarded the Mar region's mountainous western flank ('such mountaines, that Shooters Hill . . . or Malverne hilles, are but Mole-hilles in comparison'[20]) against their former compatriots. They continued to be styled 'Farquharson *alias* McIntosh' into the seventeenth century, at which time they were still paid large sums of central-government cash 'to defend Angus, Mearns, Aberdeen and Banff from the depredations of the MacGregor caterans'.[21]

Not all the branches of the family were vassals of the earldom of Mar, however: in 1579, Donald Farquharson moved from Castletown of Braemar to Tillygarmond, a hitherto unimportant property halfway between the family's later acquisitions of Finzean and Blackhall, and where their feudal superior was the bishop of Aberdeen. These Farquharsons were unbelievably fecund and prominent Stuart loyalists. The legend that the Finzean Farquharsons descended from a clever miller (or even the selfsame 'Jolly Miller' of the eighteenth-century songbooks) who tricked the 'real' laird out of his property is obviously fictitious – though perhaps not as ridiculous as the legend that the first Farquharson of Invercauld was a 'poor basket maker' who bartered his wares for meal. The Finzean lairdship was created specifically for Robert Farquharson, son of the laird of Tillygarmond, in 1609. But like many such tales it may conceal a deeper truth. In common with their clansmen higher up the Dee, the Finzean family pursued a precociously practical and un-snobbish policy of intermarrying with the clergy, university professors and the higher professions; they educated their children in Scotland rather than England or the Continent, and at good but not always the 'best' schools; and they lived on their estates and, for the most part, within their means. They were, in short, 'middle class' before such a thing can properly be said to have existed, and they remained decidedly so even after the erection of 'the towns and lands of Finzean' into a barony by Queen Anne in 1708. The last piece of their Birse jigsaw, Tillyfruskie, a still-standing 'Ha' Hoose' built in 1733, was acquired from the Ochterlonys in 1759 after David Ochterlony died at the battle of Quebec.

Between 1814 and 1822, in the Indian Summer of their mini-empire, the Finzean Farquharsons controlled no less than 45,000 acres on Deeside: mostly in Birse, Strachan, Lumphanan and Migvie. All of this was nearly lost, due to the perfect storm of activity and inactivity which characterised the eighth laird, Archibald, a *bon viveur* in the true Regency mould. In contrast to his predecessors, the 'Wild Laird' lived large on the British stage. He entered parliament, where he did nothing more useful than foment a riot in Elgin on election day, 1820, arguably the last instance of clan warfare. He created a racecourse on the neighbouring estate of Blackhall, which he had acquired through marriage; threw extravagant parties; fought and lost various ill-advised lawsuits (one of them reaching the House of Lords); sold Blackhall at a loss; and made ridiculous wagers such as who could crawl farthest along his giant holly hedge. Perhaps his greatest stunt was putting powerful laxatives in the tea at a meeting of a Banchory temperance society, a crime for which he was duly convicted and fined. Despite heavy drinking that probably hastened his early death (at 47), his wife recorded – on his tombstone, no less – the 'unbroken conjugal affection that subsisted between them for 26 years'.

This conjugal affection having produced no children, the 'Wild Laird' was succeeded by an elderly and childless Roman Catholic uncle, with whom the original, sixteenth-century line ended. Though still related to the original stock, the apparent unbroken Farquharson ownership of Finzean has been the result of at least two strategic surname changes (as the case has also been at Invercauld). Distressingly, Finzean House mostly burned in 1954. At that time, it was occupied by Violet Hay, the much younger widow of Joseph Farquharson RA, the twelfth laird, a highly accomplished and successful landscape painter, who was close friends with America's greatest portrait painter, John Singer Sargent. Along with all of her husband's paintings that had not gone into museums or private ownership elsewhere, Violet lost two priceless letters written by Robert Burns to the tenth laird's father-in-law. Even so, 'it was her wish to continue to live in the remaining part of the house surrounded by the charred ruins of the old building'. She was partly successful in this; the ruins were rebuilt more or less in the style of the old house, which had been constructed in several phases from 1686 to the 1850s. But Violet kept strictly to her own part – for another seventeen years.[22]

There have been, as I mentioned in passing, many other branches of this accomplished family resident in the area. They wisely pursued a policy of peace with the equally powerful Gordons: acquiring Balmoral from them lawfully c.1660, and selling Craigmyle to them in 1752. The principal chief of the clan, as it was determined by law in the 1940s, is the laird of Invercauld. About the Invercaulds, and Col. John Farquharson of Inverey (Jacobite and legendary folk hero), and Francis Farquharson of Monaltrie (Jacobite and prodigious 'improver'), and the others, we shall hear more in due course.

THE GREAT LOST CAUSE:
DEESIDE AND STUART LOYALISM

It seems on the face of it puzzling that one of the most important battles that took place on the 'lost frontier' in the immediate aftermath of the Protestant Reformation was fought between two Catholics: Mary, Queen of Scots, and the 4th earl of Huntly. Huntly lived through his forces' crushing defeat on the field of Corrichie, 28 October 1562, only to die of a stroke before leaving the field. Graves in the known, general area of the battle – on the Burn of Corrichie halfway between Meikle Tap and the Hill of Fare – are now accepted as the exact position of the Gordons' last stand, though the originally scrubby, boggy battlefield has recently been planted with larch and spruce trees. The night before the battle, Huntly with a thousand followers had camped at Cullerlie, south of the Loch of Skene between Echt and Garlogie, and Mary's forces, numbering two thousand, in and around Garlogie itself. Huntly's entire plan and execution of the campaign suggest that he saw himself as a prince, a rival authority to the Crown in the region, certainly more than a mere nobleman. The Crown recognised this too: Huntly was embalmed, and his pickled remains sent to Edinburgh 'to "hear" the sentence of forfeiture passed on the noble house of Gordon and "see" the family's armorial bearings struck from the Heralds' Roll'.[23] In the event, the Corrichie campaign was the last serious threat to the authority of the House of Stuart to emerge in or from Deeside before the Williamite Revolution.

The royal victory at Corrichie has been ascribed to the then rare presence of 120 highly trained hand-gunners on the Marian side – although this was a matter of tactical proficiency as much as technology, since bows and arrows told against the same sort of gunpowder weapons nine years later at Craibstone. Huntly, hitherto the most powerful man in the North-east, in effect wanted to turn the Deeside frontier south: to make the whole region north of the Mounth a bastion of Counter-Reformation Catholicism, perhaps as a prelude to the reconquest of the remainder of Scotland for Rome. He hoped that the queen would join him in this project. But Mary, though she remained a Catholic herself, had consented to the establishment of Protestantism fourteen months earlier, and now preferred the advice of her illegitimate half-brother, James Stewart, earl of Mar. Mar was a not-very-extreme Protestant and probably would have been called an Episcopalian had he lived a generation later. John Knox's *Book of Common Order* did not yet exist, so Scottish Protestants used the 1552 English *Book of Common Prayer*, which they adopted officially in 1557. Not long after this, the queen became convinced that peace and friendship with Protestant England was the way forward for Scotland.

When Mary and Mar came to visit Aberdeenshire a curious cat-and-mouse game began. First, Huntly's third son Sir John Gordon, already an outlaw, plotted to 'rescue' the queen from the Protestant faction. Escaping his clutches, the queen announced that as well as Mar, the earldom of Moray and keepership of Inverness Castle would be transferred from the Gordon interest to her brother. The Gordons became restive, and then shocked, as Mary went on to hang the existing keeper of Inverness, and demand that Huntly surrender three of his castles including Huntly itself. On this last point, he refused, and an even more serious conflict became inevitable when Huntly called up his armed retinue. The weakness of Huntly's position, however, is shown by the fact that the army thus raised to oppose the queen consisted almost entirely of his Gordon kin; while their traditional feudal underlings including Grants and Leslies – not to mention the Gordons of Haddo – came out against them. Thereafter, and until the wreck of the House of Stuart in the eighteenth century, Deeside would remain divided in religious faith, but nearly united in its support for the Stuart monarchy.

The National Covenant of 1638 was an inherently vague document. Some part of its seemingly immense popularity may be attributed to the fact that there was so little in it that even a royalist could object to. It was traditionalist: describing itself, first, as a successor document to the Confession of Faith signed by James VI in 1580, and to the 'general band for the maintenance of the true religion, and the King's person' of 1590. It went on to assert that its current purpose was 'to maintain the said true religion, and the King's Majesty, according to the confession aforesaid, and Acts of Parliament'. This was followed by 600-word attack upon the Pope and Roman Catholicism – which, due to its repeated use of 'his' (meaning the Pope) and its general level of doctrinal detail, no reasonable person could have mistaken for an attack on Episcopalianism. After this came an 800-word affirmation of the subscribers' own Protestantism, laden with praise for various specific laws of James VI and confirmations of loyalty to his son. Finally, the actual oath sworn specified that

> we have no intention or desire to attempt anything that may turn to
> the dishonour of God or the diminution of the King's greatness and

authority; but on the contrary we promise and swear that we shall to the utmost of our power, with our means and lives, stand to the defence of our dread Sovereign the King's Majesty, his person and authority, in the defence and preservation of the aforesaid true religion, liberties and laws of the kingdom; as also to the mutual defence and assistance every one of us of another, in the same cause of maintaining the true religion and His Majesty's authority, with our best counsels, our bodies, means and whole power, against all sorts of persons whatsoever[.]

Altogether, the document suggested not a revolution-in-progress or even mere nationalist anger, but rather that there was a Popish plot against Great Britain. Generally speaking, opposition was not to the Covenant *per se* but to the subsequent specific behaviour of the Covenanting regime; which explains why southern Lowland noblemen like the earl of Glencairn and the marquess of Montrose, and even King Charles II, could sign the Covenant one year and oppose the Covenanters the next. As much as we may recoil today from the groundless anti-Catholic bigotry being expressed, the National Covenant was a

Political/heraldic playing cards, identifying the marquess of Montrose with the knave of clubs, and the earl of Glencairn with the three of spades.

document of its time in that respect. If you had replaced 'True Religion' with 'our British way of life' and 'Pope' with 'Politburo', most people would have signed it in 1955.

Deeside stands apart in this, however. The centre of non-violent resistance to the National Covenant was Aberdeen, where the 'Aberdeen Doctors' – a group of academics and moderate ministers that included John Forbes of Corse, Alexander Scrogie, William Leslie, William Guild, Robert Barron, James Sibbald, Alexander Ross and possibly Patrick Dun – fought a vigorous pamphlet war against the Covenanting movement from its inception. (William Guild later defected and swore the Covenant, but refused to condemn bishops, and when asked to swear it *unconditionally*, he temporarily fled to the Continent.) The city's two universities were extremely well integrated with their hinterland, their teaching staff boasting a rate of intermarriage with the daughters of the local landed gentry that would have made Oxbridge dons' eyes pop in that, or any other time. Forbes of Corse, leader of the Doctors and 'one of the ablest and most learned theologians whom Scotland produced between the Reformation and the Disruption',[24] can at a stretch be counted as a Deeside laird in his own right, as well as a bishop's son. Sibbald was from an ancient Kincardineshire family. Dun owned the lands of Ferryhill. Barron and Leslie were from outside the North-east originally but had lived there for twenty years and thirty-five years, respectively. Their position was generally tolerant and, by the standards of the time, practically ecumenical, and strongly favoured royal supremacy over the Church. Whether the Doctors' opinions on these matters were more the cause, or the effect, of local public opinion is an enduring 'chicken-and-egg' problem for which we have no space here. The fact remains that Deeside's leading Protestants consistently favoured the king's cause in the Civil Wars, the right of Protestant bishops to exist, and the rights of their Catholic neighbours to life, liberty and property. Dr Barry Robertson has successfully argued that 'the traditional idea of Aberdeen being staunchly and unequivocally Royalist is misleading', and indeed there were some influential native Covenanters in the vicinity, including the city bailie Patrick Leslie and the ministers of Kinnellar and both Banchorys. But other than Burnett of Leys (who later turned his coat and supported the king's cause) and others who can be counted on one hand, the Deeside lairds either opposed or ignored the Covenanting movement. Conversely, Glen Muick, Glen Tanar and Strathdee were notably fruitful recruiting grounds for the royalist rank and file, and several ministers of Birse were as strongly opposed to the National Covenant as were the more famous Doctors. Nor should we forget that the Aberdeen Town Council unanimously refused to take the Covenant in March 1638 and again in July. When a huge army of Covenanters from the south came up over the Causey Mounth in 1639 to attack Aberdeen, it was Viscount Aboyne who defended the city's Brig o' Dee in a battle lasting two days – sadly, within hours of a peace treaty being signed down on the English border.

The Braes of Mar was one of six areas of the country named as particularly disaffected to the Covenant in June of the following year. In revenge for this, many lairds were gaoled; and in 1644, the earl of Argyll's Covenanters pillaged and burnt houses, felled woodlands, and allegedly stole or ate every 'four futtet beist' in Abergeldie, Aboyne, Coull, Cromar and Drum. Along the banks of the Dee, in stark contrast to Scotland's Central Belt, it was not Laudian Anglicanism, but Covenanting, that was experienced as a mean-spirited and fundamentally alien imposition.

One wonders how much has changed. On my first visit to the region I saw a group of Aberdeen City football fans attacking a smaller group of visiting Glasgow Rangers supporters. A man on the sidelines was cheering the Aberdonians on, and I had the temerity to ask him why – probably in terms that suggested the enmity was some kind of extension of Glasgow's own internal

Portrait in oils of Patrick Dun by George Jamesone (1631). This painting was destroyed in a fire in Aberdeen Grammar School in 1986.

Aberdeen's sixteenth-century Brig o' Dee, seen here in 1894.

conflict. 'We don't hate them because they are Protestants,' he replied. '*We* are Protestants. We hate them because they are *bigots*.' The North-east earned a special place in my heart that day.

Even militant Covenanters could agree that the House of Stuart was a distinctively Scottish possession with some degree of value; and when Charles I was unilaterally executed by the English Roundheads in 1649, it caused an immediate breach between the two nations' respective puritan strongmen. Charles II was proclaimed king in Scotland six days later, and not merely king of Scotland but of England and Ireland too. Beginning in 1650, Oliver Cromwell's forces invaded Scotland, wiping out the Scots army at Dunbar, sacking Dundee (where a thousand men, women and children were put to the sword), introducing English laws, and pursuing a general policy of union through force. For the next four years, guerrilla opposition to Cromwell's invasion was orchestrated by the mysterious Col. William Cunningham, 8th earl of Glencairn, a touchy man who once fought a duel against his superior officer Sir George Monro, badly wounding him. In classic guerrilla style, Glencairn's forces avoided head-to-head fights with the English army, preferring to harry the invaders with long-range raids as far off as Falkland, stealing horses and supplies and bringing new royalist recruits, including many Lowlanders, back to their bases in the central Highlands. So popular was the royalist cause among ordinary Scots by this point that even people whose goods were plundered by

Glencairn's troops refused to cooperate with the English occupying authorities seeking to recover them.

Oddly, Montrose and Glencairn, Scotland's two greatest royalist guerrilla leaders of the wider period, never fought side by side, only against each other. Glencairn was in some respects Montrose's mirror image politically: having been a strong royalist in 1639 when Montrose was a Covenanter; an advocate of neutrality in 1643; and a Covenanter by 1645, when Montrose (by now the country's leading royalist) virtually annihilated Glencairn's regiment and others at the battle of Kilsyth. Montrose was captured by the Covenanters and executed in 1650, but conflicts within the Scottish royalist party on a national scale persisted; these divisions eventually led to the collapse, in September 1654, of the Glencairn Uprising, a war now remembered chiefly by military historians.

It was not a minor war by the standards of the time, involving 5,000 to 10,000 royalist troops (including 'a piratical band of musketeers who called themselves "Cravattes" . . . a common corruption of Croats'[25]) and up to 15,000 Cromwellians. Because it is rightly conceived of as a guerrilla war, however, its main pitched battle is even more forgotten than the war itself. This was fought on Upper Deeside around that portion of the old king's highway that still survives under the name of the Pass of Ballater (B972). In 1654, however, it was called the Pass of Tullich, for reasons that will be explained in *Lost position: three towns that moved* (see pp. 185–6). On 10 February in that year, eight companies of foot, six troops of horse and three troops of dragoons (or up to a thousand men) from the Cromwellian occupying force in Aberdeen were led westward up Deeside by Col. Thomas Morgan. At Tullich they found a royalist force of about 1,500 men. The latter sought to decline battle but were too slow in withdrawing, and a brisk encounter ensued, with the English horsemen chasing the main body of the royalists, and other royalists firing down onto the former from the icy walls of the pass, largely with bows and arrows. In the end, no more than a tenth of the combatants were killed on either side.

As with so much Deeside lore (see *Lost in the retelling*, pp. 53–9), various embellishments have been made to this event, the most dramatic perhaps being that the battle was a resounding victory for Clan Cameron – in 1652 – over the English general Robert Lilburne, Baptist brother of the Leveller leader, John Lilburne. There is no evidence that Gen. Lilburne or any other person above the rank of colonel was present, or indeed that victory was achieved by either side; nor is the site currently acknowledged by the UK Battlefields Resource Centre created by the Battlefields Trust. The Camerons also claim to have won three more pitched battles against the occupiers, but these have not seemingly

The battle of the Pass of Tullich (the modern B972, now called the Pass of Ballater), fought on 10 February 1654, is supposed to have been the last British battle in which the longbow was used. Longbows made of yew were also deployed by the royalist left wing at the battle of Tippermuir.

The Pass of Tullich in the mid nineteenth century.

made their mark outside of Cameron circles. The earl of Glencairn survived the battle, the war, and a period of imprisonment in Edinburgh, living to see the collapse of the hated English Republic in 1659–60 and his own elevation to the lord chancellorship of Scotland. He died in bed.

Stuart loyalism ran in families. The Jacobite 'Black Colonel', John Farquharson of Inverey, was the son of the royalist William *maol* Farquharson, who according to one source invited the earl of Glencairn's guerrilla army to Deeside where they remained for four or five weeks. Between the end of the Glencairn Uprising in 1654 and the outbreak of the first Jacobite Uprising in 1689, the younger Inverey served alongside the future Jacobite general Lord Dundee, quashing a new Covenanting rebellion. John of Inverey's son, Peter, was out in the '15. The Irvines of Drum, a far more prominent family in the east of the valley than the Invereys were in the west, were likewise royalist at mid-century and Jacobite at its end. Moreover, despite the many differences between them, the same two families organised a joint raid on Deeside Covenanters' quarters in 1646, capturing seventy prisoners, many horses, and a significant amount of booty. The Gordons of Blelack also boasted a continuous royalist and Jacobite history from 1638 to 1746. Similar examples all along Deeside could be given. Historians tend to ignore the relatively quiet period after 1660, and as a result tend to perceive royalism and Jacobitism as distinct from each other in a way that the families participating in these movements did not. In a Jacobite pamphlet of 1714, King's College graduate and Episcopal minister Robert Calder prayed in terms that would not have missed the mark in 1642: 'From religious Rebels . . . holy Cheats . . . railing Preachers, scandalous Scriblers, slandering Scoundrels . . . Good Lord deliver Us.'[26]

Deeside was virtually the first stop for 'Bonnie Dundee' when he set out to raise the clans for James VII in April 1689. He arrived via the Cairn a' Mount route, staying either at the Feughside Inn or a now-vanished inn at Cuttieshillock. Hearing that the enemy dragoons were close behind, Dundee faked a return to the south – probably via the Fungle – and instead crept past Glen Tanar to Upper Deeside along the south side of the river. He was well received: the old earl of Mar, the local man most likely to oppose him, had just died, and 'Jacobite Farquharsons then overran the entire Braemar area'.[27] Abergeldie Castle, garrisoned by the Williamites, was besieged by the Black Colonel. In July, the Jacobite army, though slightly outnumbered, heavily defeated Gen. Mackay's Williamite army at Killiecrankie. Lord Dundee was shot and killed at the hour of victory, however, and the first Jacobite Uprising slowly subsided.

The lowland parts of Deeside, beyond the Farquharsons' territory, shared in the Jacobite movement in much the same way as lowland Aberdeenshire. Capt. John Burnet, a Woolwich graduate who had overall charge of the Jacobite artillery in the '45, was from Campfield, a mile or two south-east of Torphins. In the same rebellion – one of five that took place – Alexander Irvine of Drum served as a gentleman volunteer in Pitsligo's Horse. Two of Drum's servants, James Adamson and Robert Hendry, served in the ranks. Robert Forbes of Corse was a captain in the Duke of Perth's Regiment. The Forbeses of Corse might be called 'middle class' in much the same way as the Farquharsons – and intellectual with it. But Perth's Regiment was a particularly 'democratic' unit whose officer corps, in addition to the expected lairds, merchants, and lawyers, included two farmers, a coffee-house keeper, a shoemaker, a weaver and a wheelwright.

Of the five Jacobite rebellions, that of 1715 involved the most people and came closest to success. In the '15 and its immediate aftermath, no fewer than four ministers of the Established Church on Deeside proper, plus the minister of Alford, were either openly Jacobite or accused of Jacobitism. Their parishes were Coull, Lumphanan, Durris and Maryculter, or about one Deeside parish in four. Their Jacobitism is all the more surprising given the strong association of the movement with Episcopalianism. It begs the question of just how Presbyterian the Kirk on Deeside had become by the eighteenth century. Officially, the Kirk had been Episcopalian from James VI's days until the Covenanting revolution, and again from the Restoration until the Williamite Revolution. So during the initial Jacobite Uprising of 1689, sparked by the overthrow of James ('Jacobus') VII by the Williamites, a clergyman of the Church of Scotland might well be an Episcopalian in a completely unproblematic way. With the uprising defeated and Presbyterianism established, the Comprehension Act of 1690 allowed Episcopalian ministers to retain their parish churches, but only if they swore allegiance to William and Mary and took no role in the governance of the Church as a whole. With the passage of time, this position would have become increasingly difficult; yet it can be seen that on Deeside, many ministers – and other Kirk members – remained much less like Presbyterians than the name on the tin would suggest. The incumbent of Peterculter, the Rev. John Irvine, was removed in 1695 for refusing to swear allegiance to King William, and the minister of Strachan remained an avowed Episcopalian until his death in 1704. At Nigg, the Rev. Richard Maitland 'after being 40 years Episcopal minister . . . was ejected, 1710'.[28] When the dowager lady of Blelack famously cursed the Presbyterian minister of Logie-Coldstone for preaching against the Jacobites, she was actually in his church attending services at the time.

One eighteenth-century minister of Cluny strongly denied the presence of any Catholics in his parish, but noted that someone was continuing to patronise the Tipper Castle Well with 'rags, threads and small oblations in money',[29] as Catholics had done in the Middle Ages (and as Protestants had been strictly forbidden to do since 1581, on pain of up to £100 fine or one month's imprisonment, and possible prosecution for witchcraft). The minister of Nigg, David Cruden, defended the similar patronage of Downy-well as 'the remains of some superstitious respect to the fountain, and retreat of a reputed saint, gone into an innocent amusement'.[30] (It has since been destroyed by erosion.) One wealthy London merchant, who had begun his career as a poor cowherd in Durris, perpetually endowed a midsummer bonfire on the hill of Cairnshea, an instruction 'still carefully carried out' – by the Protestant parish kirk – more than a hundred years after his death:[31] this at a time when, in the southern Lowlands, such 'rags of Popery' were strongly forbidden and severely punished. Indeed, in most *other* places, the Reformed Kirk earned its reputation for

> vigorous repression of festivity hardly to be surpassed by any other Protestant church. From 1560 on, the authorities of the kirk from local session to General Assembly waged a stern and unremitting campaign against the celebration of Yule, Easter, May Day, Midsummer, and saints' days; against feasting, whether at marriages or wakes; against Sunday sports and dancing and guising . . . Modern observers generally credit their campaign with remarkable success; certainly the popular image of Scotland after the Reformation is grim and joyless – and with some reason.[32]

'May Wallie' on the Leuchar Burn at Culter, a Beltane festival that seems to have been performed without interruption from medieval times to the 1940s or '50s. This 'was a practice probably rooted in Celtic veneration of water, which early Christian missionaries incorporated into the Roman faith by blessing the wells and naming them for Christ or the saints. The magical healing customarily associated with particular springs was simply transferred to their saints. By one estimate there were more than six hundred such wells in late medieval Scotland' (Margo Todd).

Auld Yule, abolished by act of parliament in Scotland in 1592, was still so popular in Glen Tanar centuries later that school had to close on that day due to lack of interest; and Yuletide shooting matches at Banchory-Ternan continued into an era where the prizes included eight-day clocks (invented *c*.1670). The parish kirk of Banchory-Devenick, meanwhile, went through Episcopalianism and out the other side, adopting in 1712 the feasts, fasts and liturgy of the Church of England. At the time of the 1719 Rebellion, the Jacobite claimant to the throne, James VIII and III, wrote to John Farquharson of Invercauld, stating that Anglicans have 'reason to be assured of . . . particular favour as well as protection' in the event of a Jacobite victory, and that the exiled monarch 'thinks the Interest of the Church of England and that of the [Stuart] Crown to be the same'.[33] As a propaganda line, this would hardly have been taken unless James was quite sure Invercauld was an Anglican himself.

The battle of Culloden is becoming an historical black hole: the single point into which the whole 77-year history of active Jacobitism now threatens to collapse, bending wildly out of shape even as it disappears. Artist Andrew

There seem to be no pictures of Blelack House, destroyed in response to its owner's active Jacobitism. However, Blelack was roughly the same age and size as Balnacraig, in Birse, shown here. Since this photo was taken (1921), Balnacraig's chapel wing was heavily remodelled, losing its rare 'dool chamber', conveniently near a priest hole, where family members were taken when about to die. It also acquired a 'saddle' roof which tends to spoil the symmetry of the whole compound.

Crummy is to be commended for bucking this trend with his magnificent, recently completed tapestry depicting Prestonpans, a Jacobite triumph. Yet, so much is Culloden commemorated that most Jacobite victories have been nearly forgotten. Foremost among these was the battle of Inverurie, 23 December 1745, in which Lord Lewis Gordon's Jacobites crushed the government forces of MacLeod of MacLeod and Munro of Culcairn, thereby securing 'most of the country from Aberdeen to the River Spey for the Prince'.[34] As with the Duke of Perth's, Lewis Gordon's officers were a mixed bag: the captains included three farmers, one from Auchlossan named David Lumsden, as well as the Deeside lairds Charles Gordon of Blelack and Patrick Duguid of Auchinhove.

According to legend, a Jacobite soldier named Malcolm, who had been Duguid's servant, hid 50,000 silver merks in a man's boot somewhere near Auchinhove after the '45. Some 2,000 Queen Anne shillings were indeed found there c.1790 by two children, but given the date of the coins, they are likely to date from the '15, which was sparked off by the importation of the House of Hanover on Queen Anne's death. That earlier rebellion was supported by both Robert Duguid of Auchinhove and his brother Alexander. In any case, the supposed total amount of the treasure is highly improbable: the sheer bulk (not to mention weight) of 50,000 one-merk or shilling coins, each about the size of a modern 10p piece, would have overwhelmed the largest man's boot of that, or any other time. The castle of Auchinhove, probably built between 1550 and 1600, was destroyed in the '45 and its remains incorporated into farm steadings, themselves now ruined. As a residence, it was replaced by a substantial 'cottage', which had passed to the Farquharsons of Finzean by 1823 when they were using

Queen Anne shilling, shown at actual size. One superior feature of the old pound of 240 pence was that it could be divided into thirds. These were half-merks (6s 8d), the merk being 13s 4d or exactly two-thirds of a pound. The Scots merk coin was similar in size to the English shilling because after 1603, the Scots pound was worth just 1s 8d sterling.

it as a dower house.

None of Perth's, Pitsligo's and Gordon's regiments can really be described as a Deeside unit, however; that honour goes to Monaltrie's, which fought at Falkirk and on the right wing at Culloden. A total of 300 men served. Among those whose names and addresses have survived, half are from Upper Deeside, the proportion being the same for officers and other ranks. A third of the officers were Farquharsons from Tarland (allegedly the 'Rough Tykes of Tarland' commemorated in a bagpipe tune of that name); others were from Gairnside and Balmoral. Officers and men alike came from Tullich, Glen Muick and Monaltrie; Crathie, Durris, and several of the villages of Lower Deeside were also represented.

The regiment's leader was Upper Deeside's leading 'improver', Francis Farquharson of Monaltrie, whose exemplary career of road-building was merely interrupted, not stopped, by the rebellion and his subsequent sixteen- or eighteen-year imprisonment in England. Clearly, the widespread modern idea of the Jacobite officer as allergic to change in any form does nothing to explain such a figure as Francis, who also founded Ballater as a spa town (the immediate area's previous centre having been the just-now-reviving 'ghost town' of Tullich: see *Lost position*, pp. 185–6). I cannot prove or disprove a recent claim that he did so 'primarily to receive his former Jacobite friends'.[35] The Monaltrie that Francis was 'of', built in 1704, was west of Balmoral and burned in or shortly after the '45. Still standing and in use as a farmhouse in 1967, it should not be confused with Monaltrie House, his 1782 mansion at Ballater, designed by James Robertson and also sometimes known as Ballater House or Tullich Lodge. Though I have heard nothing as to whether Francis was or was not a Freemason, his successors at Monaltrie were proudly so. During the earl of Aboyne's tenure as Provincial Grand Master Mason of Aberdeenshire, William Farquharson of Monaltrie had his portrait painted wearing a masonic collar which astonishes by its size. Archibald Farquharson MP, the 'Wild Laird' of Finzean, led a procession of the St Dardinius Lodge of Freemasons to the opening of the new kirk at Banchory-Ternan in 1824. Capt. James Farquharson of Monaltrie, for his part, laid the foundation stone of the third Bridge of Gairn in 1856 – or as his inscription would have it, 'the year of masonry 5860'. A.A. Cormack has written that Aberdeenshire Freemasons 'were notoriously Episcopalian and Jacobite' in the late eighteenth century[36] and thus far, the circumstantial evidence from Deeside has suggested nothing to contradict this.

Moir of Stoneywood's Jacobite regiment was a city of Aberdeen unit, but was brigaded with Monaltrie's and had a company commanded by another alleged Mason, Patrick Byres of Tonley. Byres's title derives from the Tonley

*William
Farquharson
of Monaltrie
(1754–1828).*

five miles east of Cushnie, one of two Tonleys on Deeside. In light of the eighteenth-century Dee valley's sometimes vague border between Highland and Lowland customs, it is interesting to note that Tonley's was the only company of this regiment with a piper. (The city of Aberdeen had dispensed with pipe music as early as 1630, as being 'incivill' and 'often fund fault with als weill be sundrie nichtbouris of the toun as be strangeris'.[37]) David Adie of Easter Echt – great-grandson of painter George Jamesone, the 'Scottish Van Dyck' – was out in the '15. Other notable Deeside families not mentioned above whose members took part in one or more of the rebellions included Farquharson of Whitehouse, Farquharson of Balmoral, Gordon of Birkhall, Gordon of Abergeldie, Gordon of Coldstone, Gordon of Hallhead, Irvine of Kingcausie, Fleming of Auchintoul, Innes of Balnacraig, Lumsden of Cushnie, Menzies of Pitfodels, Grierson of

Hallhead, drawn by James Giles. Built in the Restoration period, Hallhead was used for many years as a farmhouse, and by the time this drawing was made in the early 1840s, it was described as 'fast going to decay'. It was restored in 2002.

Remains of the Chapel of Dalfad, Glengairn, before 1909.

Dalfad, and McGregor of Inverenzie. A Gordon of Pronie also took part in the '45, but sources disagree on whether this was the same person as Gordon of Blelack. The Menzies family was perhaps disproportionately represented, with the head of the house and five of his sons all seeing combat.

Though they were not from Deeside, Lt-Col. Laurence Oliphant of Gask and his son, 'ideological Episcopalian Jacobites of undiluted vigour and a distinctly Scottish world view',[38] hid out at Birkhall after Culloden. Using the aliases 'Mr White' and 'Mr Brown', they were protected by the Jacobite owners, Joseph and Elizabeth Gordon – not 'for twenty years', as it is remembered in the district, but for something less than seven months. The story that they escaped to Sweden is also questionable, as the elder Gask was definitely living in France between 1755 and 1763. Ebenezer Oliphant, his brother, was a professional silversmith who made Bonnie Prince Charlie's travelling cutlery set.

John Farquharson of Invercauld was lukewarm to the Jacobite cause in 1715, and opposed the '45, but his much more famous 22-year-old daughter did not. Due to her marriage to the McIntosh of McIntosh, she had left the Mar region, but apparently she returned in time for the battle of Inverurie, dressed (without any intent to deceive) in male clothes, and leading a 300-strong regiment which she herself had raised. She also recruited 600 Deesiders, to be commanded by John Gordon of Avochie. She and her men saved the Young Pretender from capture at Moy Hall on the night of 16–17 February 1746. According to different versions of the tale, 'Colonel Anne' McIntosh captured her own brother in December 1745, or her own husband in March 1746. Perhaps she did both. Surprisingly, Anne and her marriage both survived the battle of Culloden and she lived for another forty-one years.

The example of the clergymen reminds us that not all Jacobitism was of a military character, however. It was a fully formed political ideology and, arguably, a mindset that – among other things – valued beauty. Capt. Patrick Byres of Tonley's son, James, was a famous architect, antiquarian, and designer, a patron of the young artist Henry Raeburn, and a close friend of the considerably more famous designer Giambattista Piranesi. James Byres's designs for buildings were mostly not executed, yet *Apollo* magazine recently described them as 'some of the most beautiful architectural drawings in Britain'.[39] Byres's 'austere and beautifully detailed' mausoleum for Eliza Fraser of Castle Fraser, in the Cluny kirkyard, is 'the only free-standing building by Byres which is known to survive'.[40] The infinitely more famous Adam family of architects worried that Byres might put them out of business, were he ever to return from Rome (where the whole Byres family had fled, probably via Sweden and France, after the collapse of the '45). In response to Whig/Hanoverian theories claiming

Eliza Fraser's mausoleum at Cluny, the only complete building design by architect James Byres of Tonley known to have been executed. (Photo by David Walker)

that the essential, true Scottish culture was an *Edinburgh* culture derived from England and ultimately from the Roman Empire, Byres came to associate the Jacobites with the Etruscans: an earlier people of Italy whom the Romans barbarically subjugated.

Poetry, theatre, dance, and song were part and parcel of a Stuart loyalist culture shared by Jacobites of all classes and nationalities. John Skinner, an Episcopal minister born at Balfour in Birse and educated at Echt, is better remembered as a poet and songwriter; his chapel was burned down by the government due to alleged Jacobitism in 1746. James Irvine of Drum moved to Rome, and spent most of the rest of his life as a successful art dealer in Italy. John Bruce from Braemar was a 'celebrated' violin player and a 'warm Jacobite'.[41] John Pate, a prominent English opera singer, was 'dismissed from the playhouse on the lord chamberlain's orders after . . . involvement in a Jacobite celebration at the Dog tavern, Drury Lane, which ended in a riot' in April 1695.[42] Also present on that occasion was the noted actor Cardell Goodman, who had been mixed up in a plot to kidnap William III in the previous year. The Midmar poet William Meston, who tutored the younger Oliphant of Gask and 'accompanied the Earl Marischal with drawn sword to proclaim the Old Chevalier at the Cross of Aberdeen', will be discussed further in *Lost literature*, pp. 69–70 below. The Irish playwright William Philips dedicated a 1698 play to the Jacobite 2nd duke of Ormond. The early cartoonist Isaac Crookshanks and the painter E.F. Cunningham were both sons of Jacobite

A contemporary satirical print, showing the aftermath of the Jacobite victory of Prestonpans. 'Your [sic] ye first General that ever was ye Messenger of his own Defeat', the shocked border guard tells a fleeing Sir John Cope, who holds a broken field-marshal's baton. The Jacobite song commemorating Cope's defeat, 'Hey Johnnie Cope are ye walkin' yet?', was played by the Aberdeen City Band at the formal opening of the Deeside Railway in 1853.

veterans of the '45. Similar examples could be multiplied, but it is interesting to note on the local front that John Ross, the notoriously Jacobite ferry-boatman of Waterside of Birse, sired a whole dynasty of well-respected Aberdeen architects including William Ross, designer of Union Bridge, and Lord Provost James Matthews. I find it hard to disagree with Murray Pittock's recent comment, that Jacobitism was 'a political and cultural movement . . . far more interesting than the dynasty which it was its ostensible purpose to restore'.[43]

The elder Ross was not the only Jacobite boatman: Ewan MacDonald, one of just two adult males to survive the Glencoe Massacre in 1692, came to Deeside for his health under an assumed name (as so many others had before) and became the ferryman of Inchbare. Overshadowed no doubt by the horror of Glencoe, one of the less-remembered atrocities of the Jacobite War of the 1680s and '90s was perpetrated on Deeside by General Mackay – who once, with 'great self-complacency . . . determined that no Scotsman, except himself, had any regard for the public good'.[44] Unable to defeat the local Jacobites led by Col. John Farquharson of Inverey, Mackay lashed out at the civilian population and by his own account burned '12 miles of a very fertile Highland country; at least 12[00] or 1400 houses', leaving orders that none be allowed to rebuild unless they swore allegiance to William and Mary.[45] Abergeldie and Strathdee were particularly hard-hit. Inverey's own 'castle' (an ordinary unfortified laird's house of c.1640) was 'blown up' (burned down) by the redcoats at about this time – though of course, no tale being too tall for the Black Colonel's legend, there are those who insist that the mighty 'explosion' was a trap *he* set for *them*. No one would dispute, however, that Col. Farquharson escaped their clutches on that day, and all the rest of his life.

As with everything else on Deeside, commemoration of Stuart loyalism has been a mixed bag. I have already alluded to the building of a hotel dining room over the spot where the Jacobite standard of 1715 was first unfurled. At another extreme, in 1949, Capt. and Mrs Farquharson transformed a former Presbyterian church in Braemar village into a festival theatre (of all things), complete with figurative painted glass and an Italianate Jacobite mural by James Speirs. Though the building is now a pair of flats, the murals apparently remain intact.

Perhaps the greatest possible memorial to Jacobite resilience is the area itself. In the absence of the tireless road-building, town-building and other development efforts of the Jacobite Farquharson of Monaltrie, the Ballater area might not have proved attractive to the new dynasty's favourite daughter. And without her influence and approval, the entire further touristic and economic development of the region would have been at best a slower and more difficult process, and at worst a dead letter.

LOST CONNECTION:
DEESIDE AND THE WEST INDIES

There is a small rural community called Deeside in the parish of St Catherine, Jamaica, about twenty-five miles from Kingston. Perhaps its name refers to that other Deeside in the north-west of England; perhaps not. But one of the most surprising and quite unremembered features of our region in the eighteenth and nineteenth centuries was the apparent depth of its connection to the Caribbean.

In late eighteenth-century Maryculter, there was a school attended by '20 to 26 young gentlemen, some from the West Indies and America, and others from England'.[46] Described as an academy, it was founded by the Rev. John Glennie and run by two of his sons. At about the same date, the parish poor of Kemnay were getting £10 a year from a Mr Anderson of the island of St Christopher, 'who was once a beggar boy, and educated in this parish at public expense'.[47] Also at this time, a £400 bequest from Tullich-born Mrs Elizabeth Farquharson of Jamaica, plus £200 interest earned since her death, was eagerly anticipated in Tullich. We do not know when or if it was received, but it would not in any case have saved this lost community from its fate (see *Lost position*, pp. 185–6). Gen. James Alexander Farquharson, born on Upper Deeside, was twice governor of St Lucia in the 1830s.

Long before the national provision of medical care and before even the full development of a cash economy, Deeside lairds and clergymen gave financial backing to doctors who would treat the poor for free. In Cromar from 1792, this duty fell to Jonathan Troup MA, 'lately from the West Indies'.[48] Dr Gilbert Ramsay, a native of Birse and rector of the Anglican parish of Christ Church, Barbados, gave £500 for the establishment of a free school in Birse, and the interest on another £500 (or £25 per annum) to the poor of the parish in 1732. Clearly a very wealthy man, he also endowed a professorship of Oriental Languages at Marischal College, Aberdeen, and eight studentships there. Isaac Robertson of Grenada left Birse another £20 in 1789. These bequests were significant: though there were still about fifty poor people in the parish in 1792, not counting three Chelsea Pensioners, Joseph Smith reported that there was no illiteracy and that 'None ever died of want',[49] despite the near-famine that accompanied the loss of the American colonies in 1783.

It would probably not be amiss here to mention that Dr Alexander Garden of Charleston, South Carolina (see *Lost heroes of the scientific revolution*, pp. 131–2) returned to his native Birse as a refugee from the American Revolution. Garden was not the parish's only loyalist returnee – nor was loyalism the only attitude expressed there: one entire, large and prosperous family upped stakes in favour of post-Revolutionary Philadelphia. While South Carolina is not of course in the West Indies, the politics of American independence have long obscured deep connections and similarities between the British Caribbean and the American slave states. Charleston, North America's largest port south of Philadelphia in these years, was founded in large part by Barbadians in the 1670s, and was sometimes referred to as 'in the West Indies' for some time thereafter.

Certainly, Aberdeenshire played a prominent role in abolitionism, making it a 'genuinely British political movement', and people of all ranks including the naturalist laird Alexander Thomson of Banchory-Devenick contributed not-inconsiderable sums to the cause; £200 was raised locally between 1825 and 1831.[50] Yet, large as this sum was in terms of how many abolitionist pamphlets and public lectures it could buy, it pales into insignificance beside the vast amounts lavished on Deeside's poor by Scots residing in the West Indies, as mentioned in my far-from-exhaustive list above. While these people may or may not have been slave-owners, the West Indian colonies themselves depended on slavery for their prosperity to some degree. In any case, the British Empire's ending of the slave trade (1807) and of slavery itself (1833) seemingly did little to check North-east Scots' interest in the Caribbean region, and six emigrant ships left Aberdeen for the West Indies in 1829–39 alone. For what it's worth, a contemporary columnist calling himself 'Africanus' stated of slavery that 'There is certainly no description of men, in this kingdom, so little interested in this odious traffic as the people of Scotland'.[51]

There were other, less intentional emigrants. These included men sentenced to transportation (see *Lost people*, p. 101 below) but also soldiers. The 2nd Battalion of the Black Watch raised on Deeside during the Seven Years War served, in part, in the West Indies. 'This resulted in the capture of Guadeloupe but was not altogether a success and a great many men were lost by fever and sickness . . . This was a severe initiation for the new recruits who had been herding sheep [perhaps!] on their native hills nine months before.'[52] After several years serving on the North American mainland, they returned to the Caribbean, launching attacks on Martinique and Cuba and capturing Havana. Recruits from Upper Deeside's Monaltrie estate must have been quite numerous at the time, for the hamlet called Street of Monaltrie was built for the survivors upon their return, near the later milestone 51 on the south side of the A93. No trace of this settlement can now be seen.

Survivors of West Indian military service were lucky indeed. In Jamaica in the six months to Christmas, 1819, the Gordon Highlanders (who would not have numbered more than 1,000 to begin with) lost 285 officers and men, 34 wives and 31 children, all to yellow fever. A full century of medical improvements after the Black Watch's first horrifying visit, yellow fever remained particularly lethal, killing 8.3 per cent of the British soldiers stationed in Newcastle Barracks, Jamaica, in 1857.

The connection between Deeside and the West Indies continued well into the twentieth century. During the Second World War, second only to the Canadians, British Hondurans were called 'foremost in the prosecution' of forestry in Aberdeenshire.[53] William Miller Macmillan (1885–1974), already an influential if controversial sociologist of southern Africa, witnessed conditions on the island of St Kitts that led him to write the highly regarded book *Warning from the West Indies* in 1935 in a cottage on the Finzean estate. The colourful 11th laird of Finzean, Robert Farquharson, Radical Liberal MP for West Aberdeenshire for twenty-six years, would no doubt have approved, had he lived. And as of 1959, there were as many Aberdeen University graduates residing in Jamaica as in the whole of continental Europe. All this is the more surprising, given that the ethnically West Indian population of Deeside today is less than one-twentieth of the British average.

LOST LORE:
DEESIDE GIANTS

The kelpies and were-seals so common in the mythology of other parts of Scotland are strangely under-represented in Deeside folk tales, almost as if the non-navigability of the river repelled the supernatural itself. The exception proving the rule is the kelpie of Inchbare, who molested the Inchbare ferrymen until the Potarch Bridge was built there, or so the ferrymen said. It is entirely possible that this legend was imported wholesale by the aforementioned Ewan MacDonald, an immigrant from the west coast, and perpetuated by his family members who succeeded him as ferrymen. The 'wee folk' are also known, and rather better. However, on Deeside it is legends of giants that are met with again and again, and which seem to keep proliferating. These, it has in common with other heavily forested and remote areas worldwide, from the Yeti of Tibet to the Wendigo of Manitoba to Wisconsin's Paul Bunyan – though the latter's 'folk' legend may have been invented from whole cloth by James Pittendrigh MacGillivray (1856–1938), a sculptor and author from Inverurie.

It has sometimes been claimed that the Durward family were giants who constructed a stone footpath through the swamps between their two castles of Coull and Migvie, a distance of seven miles. Finlay *mór* Farquharson, a more recent but equally historical figure (he was deputy royal standard-bearer at the battle of Pinkie), is said to have bested a giant in an impromptu wrestling match in Ballochbuie Forest. The Devil, in Mar stories, is almost always enormous, whether he is building Kildrummy Castle or kicking Corse Castle down. The Black Colonel is remembered for his eighteen-foot stride; his son Balmoral the Brave for his three-foot-long dirk; and the colonel's henchman, Alastair MacDougall, as a man of 'colossal bulk' and 'elephantine tread' who, when in need of firewood, would pull a birch tree up by the roots with one hand.[54] Many stories are told of a giant weaver, Muckle Fleeman, who lived in the now-vanished village of Greystone in the late sixteenth century. Unassisted, Fleeman was supposed to have taken up an enormous flat stone and placed it across the Girnock, where it served as a bridge for people of ordinary size for two hundred years. And the priest John Avignon, alias Owenson, used a giant cross to vanquish something 'loathsome, black, shapeless, monstrous, huge' which used to roll 'huge stones' down from the top of Creag an Fhuathais.[55]

Some of Mar's 'giants' may be rooted in biological fact. In Upper Donside a century ago, it was said 'that anyone under 5 feet 11 inches was a "sharger"',[56] puny, thin and stunted. Long before that, six-footers were commonplace in the parishes of Tough and Midmar, and in 1790s Maryculter, men frequently

Though not exceptionally tall, Aboyne's Victorian strongman Donald Dinnie won 10,000 prizes worth £26,000.

reached six feet seven inches. Up until 1800–10 in Braemar, there were adders of unusually large size, perhaps even a different genus of snake; but this was never scientifically confirmed and they may simply have been very old and large adders. Within the past century in Glen Dye, 'a huge long-legged animal was observed – more like wolf than fox' and though shot several times, it did not fall and was never found.[57]

Two different types of humanoid giants are featured in the Deeside drovers' tales of Big Bill Stewart, another very tall man, who was born in the late 1850s. Though he was himself a debunker of such legends, Stewart's stories demonstrate at least that his fellow drovers – both as listeners, and as peripheral characters within the tales themselves – might have been susceptible to belief in giants in the years around 1900. The oldest Deeside giant legend, however, may be that of Thunderbolt Carline. This powerful witch could chew down mountains and once threatened to eat a new channel for the River Don, bringing it to Morven.

In Birse, tales were told long ago of an evil laird, Billiebentie, a giant who once coughed so hard he broke his horse's back. He has been identified as George Stuart of Inverchat. As such, he may have been, or been related to, the owner of Shannel and Tillenteach in the north of Birse parish along the river. These lands were granted to a Stewart family in 1544 by the papacy and taken away in 1657 by Oliver Cromwell, who gave them to Thomas Spence, presumably an Englishman. The real owners returned in 1678 and sold up to the Protestant Farquharsons in 1711, but a Roman Catholic chapel with attached

Prof. J. Norman Collie in a cartoon of 1939. Ben Macdhui is the second highest peak in Britain, but in contrast to the 'splendid isolation' of the highest, Ben Nevis, Macdhui is surrounded by other mountains almost exactly as tall: its immediate neighbours, Braeriach and Cairntoul, being both less than sixty feet shorter.

priest's house was allowed to remain on Tillenteach, and was in use well into the twentieth century. It is now a private house.

The most disturbing 'giant' legend is also the most recent. It holds that in 1891, Glassel-bred mountaineer J. Norman Collie was climbing on Ben Macdhui when he sensed, and then heard, himself being followed by an enormous creature. It took the form of a grey man, between ten and twenty feet tall. This being was subsequently identified with or as *Fear Liath Mór*, the 'Big Grey Man' of the Cairngorms. He was seen again, fairly regularly, beginning in the 1920s, and was shot at with a revolver in 1943. There is speculation that *Fear Liath Mór* is a genuine mirage, i.e. the observer's own shadow cast upon an otherwise unobserved wall of white mist (similar to a phenomenon described by Big Bill). However, this would not explain tracks which were found in 1952 and 1965. Though always at least ten feet tall, *Fear Liath Mór* can be much, much taller; nor is he always grey – one sighting claimed his fur was brown – or indeed always furred. Sometimes he is a man in his shirtsleeves; sometimes an old-fashioned shepherd with bonnet, plaid and crook; sometimes the Devil himself. Always, however, he fills those present with nameless dread, rising to panic. Collie, who had twenty-one first ascents in the Canadian Rockies, was a professor of Organic Chemistry at University College London for thirty-two years and a Fellow of the Royal Society. A non-fiction book on the phenomenon written by Affleck Gray is highly entertaining but in the end proves nothing, except that being on Ben Macdhui can unnerve quite sensible people in a wide variety of ways.

Braemar Castle with its ugly ground-floor annexe, since demolished. Fenton Wyness was of the opinion that this relatively modern castle marks the site of the ancient fort of Doldencha, built before AD 800 and later utilised by King Malcolm Canmore. Kindrochit Castle, a mile away in Braemar village, was a much later fortalice dating only to 1390 and, as such, possibly not the source of the name Castletown of Braemar.

LOST IN THE RETELLING:
DEESIDE FOLK TALES AND THE TRUTH

Macbeth, Edward Longshanks, William Wallace, Robert the Bruce, Queen Mary Stuart, the marquess of Montrose and Alastair MacColla, 'Bobbing John' and others all came to Deeside in warlike posture, but the commemoration of these visitations has been meagre and often inaccurate. Queen Mary did not watch the battle of Corrichie from the spot called the Queen's Chair, as she was then in Aberdeen, though she may have surveyed the empty battlefield from that point some days afterwards. And, despite Sir William Cunliffe Brooks's bulky memorial in granite in the Fir Mounth to Edward I having crossed by that route in 1296 and 1303, that king almost certainly never used it, preferring what is now the B974 Cairn a' Mount road for his southward journeys in both years, and the Crynes Corse Mounth and Causey Mounth for his northward ones. Montrose is said (on Cunliffe Brooks's same monument) to have used the Fir Mounth, but this too has been seriously questioned. Montrose's victory at Alford was one of the bloodiest engagements ever fought in the Mar region, with as many as 1,600 Covenanters, or three-fifths of General Baillie's force, killed outright on the day, many of them in close combat with daggers. Its memorial stone lies buried now under a municipal rubbish tip.

There is, on top of all this, a marked tendency of Deeside folklore to affiliate every historical event between the fall of Rome and the Industrial Revolution

Kindrochit was a ruin by 1618 when John Taylor the Water-Poet saw it, but was probably still in use a hundred years earlier when this silver-gilt brooch, found on the site, was made. One thing of which we can be fairly sure is that Kindrochit was neither built nor inhabited by Malcolm Canmore (d.1093), as some still insist. While we're at it, neither did he establish the Braemar Games as a continuous tradition; their modern format cannot be traced to before 1817.

with one or the other of just two persons: Col. John Farquharson of Inverey, 'a rough, raging, roaring, roystering, rioting, robustious rascal . . . a second Hotspur',[58] and King Malcolm Canmore. Two examples of this are worth repeating here, one from the north and one from the south of the river. The first was told some time between 1819 and 1852 to William MacGillivray the ornithologist. The illegitimate son of an Aberdeen lass by a university student from the Isle of Harris later killed at the siege of Burgos, MacGillivray clearly favoured the Highland side of his parentage and upbringing. Each year in the school holidays he would walk from Aberdeen to the coast opposite Harris, before taking the boat across to his paternal uncle's estate at Northton. On these prodigious walks, it was on Deeside at the Pass of Tullich that MacGillivray felt he had left behind him 'the Lowlands and all their horny-fisted, hard-hearted, mammon-worshipping inhabitants'. He complained of 'how little local knowledge the people about Ballater possess', blaming this lack on their 'agricultural state'. Highlanders

> are full of local knowledge, and can readily name every hill, rock, knoll, river, rill, and pool; but the people of the Lowlands, even when Celtic, as they generally are, cease to form acquaintance with natural objects, and their descriptive powers are most miserable.[59]

He provided an example of Highland local historical knowledge, wherein a local man regaled him with the story of a battle between Molloch, general of the invading Danes, who took up position on top of a high hill, and King Malcolm Canmore, who lived 'in a castle built on a little island in Loch Ceannor [Kinnord]'. On the appointed day of battle only twelve men came to Canmore's aid. Canmore 'dismissed them in anger' but they 'made a great circuit' and attacked the Danish position from the east, killing Molloch and routing his troops.[60] MacGillivray accepted this information as fact; and it was still in circulation a generation later, when John Grant retold it, again as fact, with significant additional details proving that Grant had not simply lifted the tale from MacGillivray. But you would search the annals of Malcolm Canmore for it in vain, because Grant's and MacGillivray's informants were describing the battle of Culblean, fought nearly two centuries after the last recorded Viking raid on the Scottish mainland (by King Eysteinn on 'Apardion', Aberdeen), and two and a half centuries after Canmore was killed by Morel of Bamburgh. Indeed, as Peter Marren points out, North-east Scotland 'scarcely figures in the recorded history of the Viking Age and archaeology has so far yielded little to fill the vacuum'.[61]

The actual battle of Culblean settled, among other matters, 'a land dispute between the Strathbogie earls of Atholl and the Gordons as tenants of the earls of Mar' – which is to say that the participants on both sides were Scots.[62] David de Strathbogie was titular Steward of Scotland within the English-backed Edward Balliol regime that had been inaugurated by force in 1332. The wife of Sir Andrew Moray was besieged at Kildrummy, the principal fortress of the earldom of Mar, which she was holding with 'stowt and manly resistens' on behalf of King David II. Her husband raised a relief force of at least 800 experienced men (some say as many as 3,300) and led them to Glen Tanar, which they reached via the Fir Mounth on 28 November 1335. De Strathbogie lifted his siege and moved south to Culblean to block the main approach to Kildrummy from a 'strong hilltop position' between Culblean Hill and the west bank of Loch Kinnord, and athwart one of three north–south roads passing through the immediate area.[63] Moray forded the Dee at Mill of Dinnet and the two armies met. As night was falling, they did not fight immediately. Leaving an audio-visual decoy in the form of large campfires attended by just a small number of fellows (could it have been twelve?) who loudly shouted and sang, Moray's main force crept back down to the Dee and circled around behind the pro-English troops in a clockwise direction, reaching the northern slopes of Culblean Hill at dawn.

De Strathbogie valiantly resisted this attack from an unexpected direction (and elevation), and eventually became an inspiration for the brave character Fitz-James in Walter Scott's *Lady of the Lake*:

> He mann'd himself with dauntless air,
> Return'd the chief his haughty stare,
> His back against a rock he bore,
> And firmly placed his foot before.
> 'Come one, come all! This rock shall fly
> From its firm base as soon as I.'

Casualties were light on both sides but de Strathbogie was among the dead, and Moray was completely victorious. There was, furthermore, a peel tower on the larger of the two islands in the loch; it was owned not by David II, however, but by a de Strathbogie supporter, Sir Robert Menzies.

More recent and more cautious writers than MacGillivray and Grant tell us that the famous Deeside ballad 'The Baron of Brackley' describes an actual event in Glen Muick in 1666. The basic story, common to all four surviving versions of this ballad, is that a band of ruffians surrounds Gordon of Brackley's house. Brackley is reluctant to confront them. His wife summons her female servants, whom she orders to fight off the raiders with rocks, because her husband is less than a man. Stung by this, Brackley arms himself, goes out (predicting his own demise), and is killed. At this point, Lady Brackley's real motivation is revealed: to play host to the raiders' handsome leader – in one version, even keeping him 'till morning', though a sexual motive on someone's part is implicit in each retelling. In two of the four versions, the leader of the killers is identified as Inverey, and in one as Invery; and his motive for being so far from home with an armed band is plain robbery:

> Ther's four-and-twenty milk-whit calves, twal o them ky,
> In the woods o Glentanner, it's ther thei a' ly.
> Ther's goat i the Etnach, and sheep o the brae,
> An a' will be plunderd by young Inverey.

So far so good, for as a young man, Capt. John Farquharson of Inverey *was* involved in an armed scrap at Brackley that left Gordon of Brackley dead. The Farquharsons, concluded the Victorian author A.I. McConnochie, 'appear to have outlived their time, clinging with almost fatal persistence to the "divine right" of Highland gentlemen to descend on the richer Lowlanders and "lift" their cattle'.[64] But as we have seen, the Farquharsons were probably Upper Deeside's most modern and modernising family, and it seems that McConnochie's characterisation of them was merely back-formed from their later Jacobite activities and his own anti-Jacobite bias.

In various arguments (legal and otherwise) that were made in the immediate aftermath of the September 1666 incident, the quarrel between Inverey and Brackley was variously described as being over fishing fines, stolen cattle, or stolen horses. Neither man was a habitual criminal; far from it. Both were, in effect, public officials: Brackley's responsibilities being similar in nature to those of a magistrate, while Inverey acted as a rather senior proto-police officer. Inverey was accompanied by armed men on this occasion – as was usual for him when going to keep the peace at Tullich market – but also by a notary, and the minister of Glen Muick kirk. The first really major alarm bell, however, is rung by the fact that in the subsequent investigations, neither side mentioned Lady Brackley: who was not 'Kate Fraser' (as the only ballad version to give her full name would have it) but one of the aristocratic Burnetts of Leys, and a cousin of Gilbert Burnet, the famous historian and Anglican bishop of Salisbury. If the motive for the crime was at best adultery with, and at worst the rape of, this august woman, then the case would have been one of the sensations of the age, not buried in the lesser annals of the fish and game laws.

Secondly, in two versions of the ballad, Brackley either expects to receive, or actually receives, military assistance from Craigievar. But Craigievar Castle was, in 1666, owned by the Forbeses, with whom the Gordons were in a state of permanent feud. If help is coming from Craigievar – and the ballads make clear that this is a person, not merely troops moving from that vicinity – it must be because Craigievar is still a Gordon ally. This suggests that the Craigievar-mentioning ballads date from before 1610 when 'Danzig Willie' Forbes acquired the property. This is confirmed, albeit vaguely, by the fact that three versions of the ballad mention Gordons of Knock being killed on Brackley's side. According to an almost equally questionable but universally repeated legend, the Gordons of Knock had c.1600 been completely liquidated by the Forbeses, in one of Deeside's goriest incidents.

Francis James Child, the great Harvard ballad expert, printed all four versions of the ballad and marshalled most of the evidence for and against a date of 1666. He concluded 'that two occurrences, or even two ballads, have been blended'.[65] And sure enough, *another* Gordon laird of Brackley was also

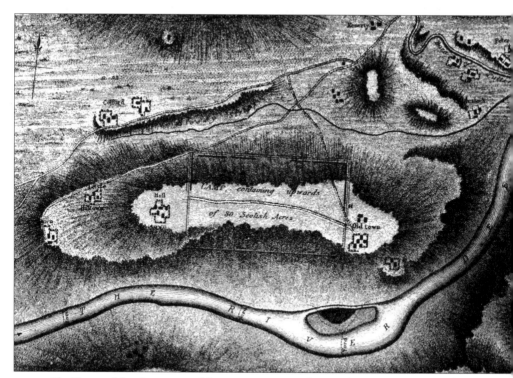

The Normandykes Roman marching camp, as surveyed c.1800 by Capt. Henderson of the 29th Foot.

murdered, in November 1592, in circumstances that fit the ballad tale much more closely – the major difference being that the Farquharsons of Inverey had nothing to do with it. The spelling 'Invery' in one version further muddies the waters as there is a place of this name, so spelled, on Lower Deeside near Banchory-Ternan. However, Child's and Archbishop John Spottiswoode's suggestion that the real killer of 1592 might have been Campbell of Inver*awe* (near Oban on the west coast) strikes me as a very long trip for Mr Campbell, and one coincidence too many.

It perhaps goes without saying that none of the versions of 'The Baron of Brackley' mention John Grant's two favourite elements of the tale: first, that Inverey participated in the famous Reel of Tullich on his way down to Brackley; and second, that after their night of sinful passion, Lady Brackley gave Inverey a magical black mare that could run up vertical cliffs – and which did so, later the same day, carrying the colonel to safety from hotly pursuing Williamite troops. Never mind that there were no Williamite troops (or Williamites) before the late 1680s.

The really striking thing about the oral traditions of both Culblean and Brackley is that they are almost exactly half true – and not half true merely, but half true in *substantially the same way*: with the tale-tellers accurately remembering the pettiest details of military tactics, whilst forgetting the true names of the chief protagonists and the eras in which the fights occurred. This is not an Upper Deeside phenomenon only. Probably between AD 208 and 211, some 12,000 Romans marched over the Elsick Mounth to Tilbouries, forded the Dee, and on the north bank there built a magnificent if not untypical marching camp about 940 yards long by 540 yards wide. By 1794, this structure was known by the name Normandykes and its actual, Roman, origin was unsuspected. It was assumed – largely from its name – to be either of Danish Viking origin, or built by William the Conqueror. About seven years later, it was surveyed by one Col. Shand, the Capt. Henderson of the 29th (Worcestershire) Regiment who drew the map illustrated here, the laird of Drum, and a Professor Stewart. These gentlemen confirmed it to be Roman and of the same pattern as the Raedykes marching camp by Stonehaven. Unfortunately, the remains of Normandykes were 'almost entirely obliterated' by 1840,[66] and as late as the 1890s some still believed Normandykes was actually Norman – or, in a new twist, Ptolemy's Devana, the only *polis* of the Taexali tribe. Rejecting the Shand-Henderson survey by name, John Mackintosh flatly denied that the Romans 'ever advanced twenty miles to the north of the Tay', his only counter-evidence being what he perceived as the strategic impossibility of the Romans operating 'more than a hundred miles from their line of defence, with a hostile country behind them.'[67]

LOST ARTEFACTS

It is disappointing that, for all the great strides made in the nineteenth century in our understanding of the past of Deeside, so little was then done on behalf of historical or archaeological preservation. To speak of things left undone is probably too mild altogether. Iron Age earth-houses, amounting to whole subterranean towns, were once more abundant in Mar than anywhere else in Scotland; they were concentrated in the Howe of Cromar. Agricultural practices in the early twentieth century ruined most of them. In Leochel-Cushnie, eight of the nine cairns mentioned in the *Old Statistical Account* disappeared due to agriculture before the completion of the *New Statistical Account* of fifty years later. The sole survivor, at Mill of Brux, was a 'confused scatter' in 1968, by which time the contents, if any, had long since disappeared.[68]

In the same parish, Lenturk Castle, built in 1514, was the home of the famous lawyer Alexander Irvine, whose *De Juri Regni* was published at Leiden in 1627 and at Helmstadt in 1671, and still read and respected two centuries later. He was also the grandfather of Parson Gordon the mapmaker. Still notable in 1792, its remains were called 'rubbish' by William Campbell in 1842 and 'now disappeared' by Alexander Taylor in 1843.[69] A single, incomplete gunloop survives as part of the steading, and other parts may have been used to build a farmhouse and Seceder church on the site – both of which were themselves later abandoned.

Migvie Castle, capital messuage of the lordship of Cromar in the Middle Ages, stood until the eighteenth century. Archaelogical preservation of its remains cannot have been helped by the erection of a parish hall on them. It too is now gone. At Castle Maud, not far from Torphins, 'thick walls' were seen in 1885, and 'walls . . . six feet in height' in 1898; but shortly after the First World War, it was a 'mere formless pile of rubble'.[70] There are limits to what lightning can do; one suspects that people who needed cut stone had been helping themselves for some time. The minister of Durris dismantled a Stone Age burial cairn to get stones for a flood-control project, in or soon after 1829; and the walls of the Chapel of St Valentine (or St Columba), on the Geldie Burn, were 'removed by neighbouring farmers to build dykes' about 1850.[71] In light of this, it is less surprising that there was a medieval chapel at Balmoral 'of which both site and name have been lost'.[72]

Archaeologist Douglas Simpson supposed that the region's many single standing-stones were 'for the most part survivors of plundered stone circles'.[73] Certainly, local superstition held that it was unlucky to demolish a circle *entirely*, which would explain the phenomenon; but over the course of the nineteenth century, this tradition was also becoming lost, as evidenced by the stone circle at Inchmarlo which was complete in 1800, a single stone about 1840, and gone by 1880. A Pictish symbol stone from Keith's Moor in Drumoak parish was removed by workmen 'who intended to build it into the walls of Park House'; this was prevented, but not before the ancient monument suffered 'serious defacement'.[74]

The embalmed head of the fifth- or sixth-century St Ternan, probable founder of a monastery at Banchory-Ternan, was kept there until an unknown date. The saint's miraculous bell, *Ronecht* ('songster'), found in 1875, was lost again by 1944. 'A still more precious relic, associated with St Ternan, is also lost – a copy of the Gospel of St Matthew cased in silver and gold, which was preserved in Banchory till the Reformation.'[75] Banchory-Devenick's church bell, inscribed 'H.B. ALLEINE GOT IN DER HOGE SEI ERE 1597', was last seen in 1859 and may have been melted down to provide raw material for its own replacement. A hoard of silver coins, probably from the mid sixteenth century, was unearthed on Dalmaik farm in about 1810, but 'they had all disappeared, except one', by the time Adam Corbet came to examine them in the early 1840s. More coins were found during the draining of Loch of Leys in 1850, but before they could be closely examined, one of the workmen grabbed them, ran off, and

Ronecht is not known to have been photographed during the sixty-odd years between its discovery and (re-)loss, but this detailed drawing of it purports to be from life.

Piece of a dormer window from the thirteenth-century chapel of the Knights Templar at Maryculter. Removed 'for safekeeping' in 1954, it had disappeared by 1968.

presumably tried to spend them. When the famous Chain of Nigg – a Pictish relic dating to the eighth century AD – was discovered in 1796, a large part of it was almost immediately destroyed: 'broken in a thousand pieces' or 'drawn out into wire' in a fruitless attempt to determine whether or not it was silver.[76] (Experts disagreed on this as recently as 1914, but the surviving part of the chain is in fact a silver and bronze alloy of 95 per cent silver.)

For such an immense and expensively constructed work, Coull Castle had a very short life of about eighty years (c.1228–1308). Eighteenth-century excavations revealed a structure of stone and lime with a gothic arch in freestone, 'four gates and five turrets, of very extraordinary dimensions':[77] 150 feet on a side and with walls 15 feet thick. It was the seat of the Durward family, who owned land in Skene, Echt, both Banchorys, and Midmar as well as at Kincardine O'Neil where they built a hospital and bridge (*Lost people*, p. 110). Ironically, perhaps, it was the 'folly' of overenthusiastic excavation of the castle complex, ending in 1923, that left the place a 'crumbling ruin' once more.[78]

Allegedly, the lost duck pond of Glen Tanar Home Farm has at the bottom of it an ornate sculpture or mosaic of the Prince of Wales's badge of feathers, but this pond is now filled in and overgrown with grass. Elsewhere in Glen Tanar, on Knockie Hill, 'one of the most extraordinary collections of bronze objects ever found together in Scotland' – at least fifty-five pieces of jewellery, weapons and drinking vessels – was unearthed in 1843.[79] By the 1940s, all were thought to have vanished without trace. In fact they had been acquired within five years of their discovery by the minister of Aboyne, passed down as private property to the minister's son, then to the son's housekeeper, then to *her* son, who (not knowing what they were or where they had been found 130 years before) donated the mere sixteen surviving objects to a museum in the south-west of England.

Also on the Glen Tanar estate but not in the glen itself is Ballaterach Farm, where tourists once flocked to see the box bed in which the future Lord Byron slept as a young lad. Nowadays, people say that the farmer found this attention so irksome that he burned the bed. Having slept in one box bed, studied two others, and designed a fourth, I can assure you that burning a box bed without burning down the house around it would be close to impossible. They are not so much furniture as built-in cabinetry. An older version of the tale is more plausible but almost as disheartening. This holds that the bed in which the poet was *said* to have slept did burn up, in an *accidental* house fire, in 1868. But that bed was a fake: constructed specifically to distract tourists from the fact that the bed Byron *really* slept in had been converted into a cheese-press and sold.

Several canoes were retrieved from Loch Kinnord between 1859 and 1875. An earlier find of a Kinnord dugout was destroyed by herd boys as it lay drying on the shore. Another was said to have been found during the draining of the Loch of Leys, though this may have been the lake's medieval ferry, mentioned in a document of 1324. Both of these lochs have crannogs, and it seems very sensible that the people who lived on these artificial islands would have had a better means of getting to them than swimming. One specimen of Kinnord's impressive Iron Age watercraft was owned in the late nineteenth century by Charles Wilson, of Dinnet House, who ran the 'old chapel' of Meikle Kinnord, which was neither old nor a chapel but a private museum built c.1880. When Wilson decamped to Lincolnshire in 1896 he took the canoe with him – though not before sawing it in half so it could fit into the railway carriage. Amid what sounds like a badly deteriorating marriage, Wilson's other 'relics' were all 'hurled . . . out on to the moor'.[80] Even before this outrage, however, John Mackintosh had rightly complained that 'a considerable number of prehistoric relics and objects have been found in and around Loch Kinnord, of which no accurate description has been preserved'.[81]

Wilson's 'old chapel' was just one of several now-lost private museums in the region, arguably including the Great Observatory of Dunecht House, which will be dealt with in its own section, *The lost observatory*, pp. 224–226. The Jacobite aesthete James Byres, previously alluded to, returned to his native Mar after the outbreak of the French Revolutionary Wars, and appears to have established at Tonley a museum of some kind in which 'many . . . articles of curiosity were brought together', along with a 'singularly attractive' garden.[82] By Easter Micras, William MacGillivray met a peasant naturalist, the 'most intelligent and communicative' Mr Brown, who had 'very carefully read' MacGillivray's *British Birds*, and built a museum in his one-windowed, divot-roofed hut. It contained a very considerable number of expertly stuffed animals and birds including a golden eagle and a sea-eagle.[83] MacGillivray himself had been banned from keeping such a museum in the early 1830s by his then employers, the Edinburgh College of Surgeons, but seems to have done so in secret. The anti-slavery activist Alexander Thomson of Banchory-Devenick was a massive acquirer of taxidermied birds and other specimens whose collection reached museum-like proportions, with the overflow being donated to Aberdeen's Marischal College. The scope of Thomson's activity is suggested by the fact that in 1859 he engaged Capt. van der Held of the *Maria Adriana* of Rotterdam to import three huge crates containing 176 specimens from Batavia (now Jakarta, Indonesia). This area of genuinely proto-scientific activity spilled over into modern-style

Capercaillie are occasionally able to cross-breed with pheasants in the wild. This rare example of the offspring of such a mixed union was shot on the Monymusk estate in the nineteenth century.

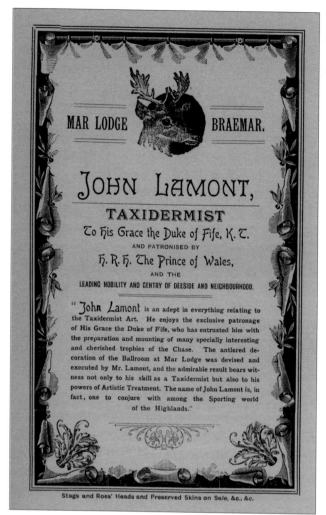

An 1890s advertisement for the services of John Lamont, taxidermist, from the Crathie Kirk bazaar book.

commercial 'trophy' taxidermy, as taxidermists including A.C. Waters, Frederick Waters and James Birch Waters moved to Deeside: in this case, to Aboyne from London and Kent. The dark side of such projects includes the fact that the sea-eagle, once fairly common on Deeside and avidly collected as a taxidermy subject, was hunted to extinction in the UK by 1916. It has recently been reintroduced in Fife.

The Roman camp called Normandykes, despite the recognition of its age and archaeological significance in the first decade of the nineteenth century, was mostly ploughed under within a generation. We could multiply similar examples of nineteenth-century obliteration of what would, nowadays, be conserved as a matter of course. The right to destroy one's own property seems at every turn to have trumped not only the social and moral pressure to preserve it, but even the profit motive. So much has been destroyed, forgotten, misremembered, or mislaid that we are pleased to hear that *anything* – for example, St Ringan's Cross which used to adorn the Cairn a' Mount road – made it into a museum collection rather than simply vanishing from its original site without trace or explanation. In a famous essay of 1966, Professor Gordon Donaldson argued the case for 'Scotland's Conservative North'. The tag has stuck in Aberdeenshire, and in some respects it is true, particularly in the relatively intangible fields of politics and religion. But when it comes to the *material* artefacts of our ancestors, the 'Conservationist North' we are not; and 'ding it doon utterly' remains all too often the attitude toward older structures, however beautiful or rare.

I must also mention one outrageous example of a not-very-old structure that immediately acquired, and has tenaciously retained, a spurious history. This is the octagonal tower at Durris, built by the duke of Gordon in 1825 in commemoration of winning a big lawsuit (or, as a Victorian observer more delicately put it, 'his coming into the possession of Durris as heir of entail to the Earl of Peterborough'[84]). That date was placed over the door. Just seventeen years later, however, the tower was identified in print (not by the duke) as marking an ancient victory of the Irvines over the Keiths. This 'fact' reached the Ordnance Survey people, who duly marked it as 'Keith's Tower' on maps; and it was as 'Keith's Tower' that it was listed, upon becoming an officially listed building in 1972. *Lest we forget: lost histories in the making*, p. 238, is offered as a hedge against any more of this sort of thing happening, in the cases of some convincingly 'early modern' houses that have been built on Deeside since 1980.

LOST LITERATURE

It seems unlikely that the children's classic *Treasure Island*, set principally in Bristol, on board ship, and on an island in the Caribbean, would have been composed at the farthest point from the sea in all of Scotland. Yet, during the book's inception and much of its composition – from early August to late September, 1881 – its author Robert Louis Stevenson lived in Castletown of Braemar, along with various relatives including his American wife's son by a previous marriage, thirteen-year-old Lloyd Osbourne. Seeking indoor amusement during the unseasonably rotten weather that year, young Lloyd drew a map and suggested that Stevenson write a story based on it. The results of this peculiar collaboration were read aloud nightly after dinner, later

Treasure Island *illustration drawn by George Edmund Varian (1865–1923).*

serialised under an assumed name, and finally published under Stevenson's real name, at which point the lawyer-turned-author's reputation was made. Fans of the bestselling book and its numerous film versions can be glad that the sun did not shine on Upper Deeside on that occasion. The invention of the book's characters may not have been an entirely indoor pursuit, however. A detailed theory now exists that at least six of the people in *Treasure Island* were based on Braemar locals – including one of the two John Silvers, father and son, who are known to have lived in the village at the time. On the whole, this seems no less plausible than the persistent 'urban myth' that attempts to map *Treasure Island* onto the landmarks of Heriot Row gardens in Edinburgh.

Somerset Maugham's short story 'Sanatorium' provides us with an eyewitness account (albeit fictionalised) of Banchory's private tuberculosis hospital Nordrach-on-Dee in its heyday. Maugham, who had become a British spy because he was too short to join the army, was a patient at Nordrach-on-Dee from 1918 to 1920, allegedly after having tried and failed to prevent the Russian Revolution from breaking out. If the short story is to be believed, the hospital was a genteel place with a good library (the real one boasted 3,000 volumes), numerous bridge games, and few firm rules. People of all ages and both sexes stayed there, some for a few months, some for half of each year, and some for years on end. Many died there. What they all had in common was tuberculosis, an airborne bacterial disease for which there was no vaccine until 1921 and no cure until 1946; it killed Maugham's mother when he was seven and his long-time lover, Gerald Haxton, half a century later. Poorly understood, the disease was blamed on everything from masturbation to vampires, but even the well educated saw it as closely associated with poverty and sin. For one of Maugham's characters, a thoroughly conventional suburban English business-man, it was 'monstrously unfair':

> He could have understood it if he had led a wild life, if he had drunk too much, played around with women, or kept late hours. He would have deserved it then. But he had done none of these things.

Even with excellent sanatorium care – and Nordrach was the best in Britain – one patient in two died.

Deeside was as cold then as now, but fresh air of any temperature was seen as potentially curative, and the weather didn't seem to stop the innumerable rounds of bridge: though 'there had been heavy snow for several days,' Maugham wrote, 'they played, in a veranda open on three sides to the wintry air, in fur coats and caps, with mittens on their hands.'

The sanatorium's director, in real life called Dr David Lawson, was remembered as

> a good enough doctor, an excellent business man, and an enthusiastic fisherman. When the fishing season began he was inclined to leave

Nordrach-on-Dee when in use as a sanatorium before 1929.

the care of his patients to his assistants; the patients grumbled a little, but were glad enough to eat the young salmon he brought back to vary their meals.

In the story, Dr 'Lennox' allows two patients to marry each other, but draws the line at non-marital 'hanky-panky', as one of the characters put it.

Three or four years ago there was a woman here who was pretty hot stuff. Her husband used to come and see her every other week-end, he was crazy about her, used to fly up from London; but Dr Lennox was pretty sure she was carrying on with somebody here, but he couldn't find out who. So one night when we'd all gone to bed he had a thin coat of paint put down just outside her room and next day he had everyone's slippers examined. Neat, wasn't it? The fellow whose slippers had paint on them got the push. Dr Lennox has to be particular, you know. He doesn't want the place to get a bad name.

The hospital's reputation remained sound; but tuberculosis, which at one time had caused as many as one in four British deaths, ceased to be a public health problem through much of the rest of the twentieth century. Despite having been built as recently as the 1890s at the vertiginous cost of £670 per bed (at a time when coal miners earned £50 a year), Nordrach-on-Dee never functioned as a tuberculosis hospital after 1955, and became derelict in 1990.

William Meston, son of a blacksmith, was born in Midmar about 1680 and graduated from Marischal College in 1698, thereafter working as schoolmaster and private tutor. After participating in the 1715 Jacobite Rebellion, he hid in the hills and there 'composed satirical verses and songs to amuse his companions'. These works were intermittently published beginning in 1723, then printed as a collection in 1767. They have recently been praised as 'witty and energetic Hudibrastic satire'. Meston's wit is aimed mostly against Presbyterians and Whigs, who are portrayed as hypocritical drunkards, lovers of war, enemies to learning (even of grammar), rude, flatulent, superstitious, and at the end of the day, foreigners. Swimming to this country from Geneva, they disdain pedigrees, even their own, 'As if like mushrooms they had sprung / From heaps of rotten earth and dung'. Of his most famous character, 'Sir John Presbyter', Meston writes:

Well could he piece a long oration,
And shape it in the newest fashion,

Which is not valued for the strength
Of argument, but for the length.
Full well he knew the long-ear'd crowd,
Is pleasèd most with long and loud,
Whose judgement is not so profound,
As to dive deeper than the sound . . .
Which serves him in good stead, when he
With ancient church cannot agree:
As when *St Paul* writes to the *Romans*,
That all their peers as well as commons
Should subject be to supreme powers,
That was for their times, not for ours[.]

'Sir John' finds his most enthusiastic disciple in 'MacGregor', a well-known robber. Taking the preacher's logic regarding the aristocracy's right to overthrow the monarchy, and applying it to everyday life, 'MacGregor' argues that he should be allowed to take anyone's inherited lands, goods, or 'whatsoe'er I can command / Either by force or slight of hand'. It almost goes without saying that the purse of 'John Presbyter' is his first acquisition.

Meston survived the aftermath of the '15 and returned to his previous career, establishing at least four private schools in the north of Scotland, one of them in Aberdeenshire. Nevertheless,

Meston's reputation suffered severely during the nineteenth century at the hands of whiggish and unionist critics. He was branded (unjustly) as a mere plagiarist of Samuel Butler, and dismissed as 'a gay, thoughtless, clever, extravagant, restless, indolent, careless, unsteady, witty, dissipated dog' ([J.] Robertson). As standards of morality changed, his 'coarseness' became an unsurmountable barrier to recognition, and in the twentieth century he was virtually forgotten.[85]

Another local poet of a rather different sort was Johnnie Moir, a shopkeeper by the Bridge of Feugh in Banchory-Ternan. In the years around 1900, Moir composed new works daily on blackboards outside his shop. Being totally blind, he kept his chalk within the lines with the aid of pieces of string. His output was eclectic, ranging from commonplace but competent nature poems in standard English, including 'River Thoughts' and 'Phases of Winter', to broad Scots versions of the Lord's Prayer and psalms, to an acrostic about Nordrach-on-Dee which spelled out 'SANATORIUM'. Much of Moir's work, however, was verse news and advertising, with reports on school-board meetings, and lost property ranging from bicycle pedals to sheep:

> A lodger on the farm near
> Has lost her brooch, not far from here;
> The very place is not quite clear;
> If found, confer with Mr. Weir.

Anything but forgotten, George Gordon, Lord Byron, was recently the subject of a multi-part television documentary hosted by film star Rupert Everett. But Everett called Byron, who was born and raised in Aberdeenshire, an 'Englishman' or an 'English gentleman' throughout the programmes, which made no mention of the poet's Scottish, let alone Deeside, connection. Lest such omissions continue, I will conclude this section with the following, from Byron's 'The Adieu, Written Under the Impression the Author Would Soon Die' (1807).

> Adieu, ye mountains of the clime
> Where grew my youthful years;
> Where Loch na Garr in snows sublime
> His giant summit rears.
> Why did my childhood wander forth
> From you, ye regions of the North,
> With sons of Pride to roam?
> Why did I quit my Highland cave,
> Marr's dusky heath, and Dee's clear wave,
> To seek a Sotheron home?

Lochnagar itself is constantly changing, a 'great mass' of the mountain having been 'shattered and sent to the bottom by lightning' in the early nineteenth century.[86]

CHAPTER 3

NATURE

LOST HABITATS

The Deeside tourist industry appears rather sedate and old-fashioned, which is as it should be. Amid such exotic fare as glider rides, water-skiing, kayak lessons, or the opportunity to drive an old army tank, the summer people mostly come to camp, in tents. They put on walking clothes, and walk around, and look. The miles-long traffic jams of caravans that are now the harbingers of the Cornish high season are unknown on the roads of Deeside – in part because the great majority of the ancient road system here has never been made suitable for cars.

Increasingly, if quite erroneously, the Cairngorms are marketed as a 'wilderness'. Certainly, there are worse lies that could be told. Unlike their American cousins, few European people today would knowingly wreck a wilderness, whether on the 'macro' level of clear-cutting and building bungalows, or the 'micro' level of filling up a stream with fast-food wrappers. Yet, because of this new mythology, the Deeside region's lost people are in danger of becoming doubly lost: first driven from the land, and now driven from its history as well, in the name of a bogus natural experience. In fact, humans have been vigorously and intelligently exploiting Deeside since the Stone Age, when a brisk trading network brought flints into the area from Buchan, and sent in return timber, horn, and furs. Even An Sgarsoch, which (being over 3,000 feet high) is supposedly 'unaffected by man' and 'purely natural', was the site of a thriving early modern cattle fair.[1]

The idea that the area is 'pristine' also obscures the turbulent history of Deeside's plant and wild animal life. We congratulate ourselves, for instance, on the presence of red squirrels on Deeside. Further south in Britain, the invasive North American greys have driven them out through a combination of physical bigness and resistance to squirrel pox. Because the reds are a British native species, and now live in the North-east of Scotland, we imagine it to be their ancient homeland, the squirrel redoubt, and the Dee as perhaps its 'last ditch'. Thus it may be surprising to learn that there were no squirrels of either type in Kincardineshire in 1807, or on Deeside as recently as the 1850s, when William MacGillivray predicted they 'would no doubt thrive' if introduced.[2] Likewise, there were reckoned to be fewer than a hundred rabbits in the whole of Aberdeenshire in 1811; they first reached Alford in 1833 and Braemar a few years after that. Hares, however, are native, and particularly noticed in Birse and Logie-Coldstone, but not only there. There were so many on Lochnagar in 1850 that MacGillivray speculated the mountain's name came not from *Lochan-a-gharidh* (the topographically descriptive 'little lake of the wall'), but *Lochan-nan-cear*, 'little lake of hares'.[3] In January 1877, the entire keeping staff of the Glen Tanar estate shot hares for four days in a row. Across Britain, the number of brown hares fell from over 6 million in 1880, to 1 million in 1980, to 750,000 in 2004. However, they are on the uptick again in Grampian, thanks to more sensitive farming practices and a police crackdown on coursing. The mountain hare, a distinct species, numbered nearly 350,000 in 1996.

The Victorian inhabitants of Glen Tanar also considered hedgehogs and marten to be vermin, and apparently caught them in leg-hold traps, which must have been quite small. Their descendants are now proud of the occasional sighting of the elusive pine marten, which actually became extinct locally for a time, but returned – and, moreover, seems to leave red squirrels alone, while driving invasive grey squirrels away. On the negative side, the pine marten is a ruthless killer of another threatened (but stabilising) local species, the capercaillie. These massive grouse, weighing up to sixteen pounds, became extinct in Scotland in 1785. After an unsuccessful attempt to reintroduce them on Upper Deeside's Mar Lodge estate in 1827, they were brought to Tayside from Sweden, and had returned to Deeside overland by 1879. Fatally, they are fearful of people on foot, but not of cars; and they remain vulnerable to fox snares and other man-made features. Deer fences alone kill one-fourth of the juvenile birds. François Fouin, who grew up in Glen Tanar in the interwar years, recently wrote that capercaillie had left the glen; but the estate is making strides in the creation and maintenance of their habitat and won an award for this work in 2006. It perhaps goes without saying that a lifestyle of shooting capercaillie whilst wearing a marten-fur coat has been lost for good.

Many parts of Deeside today give an impression of a dense forest stretching endlessly in every direction, but gauging the overall amount and type of tree cover in earlier ages can be quite challenging. Joseph Smith wrote of Birse in the 1790s that 'No trees . . . grow in what is called the Forest'. Absurd as this may seem to modern ears, the oldest *Oxford English Dictionary* definition of 'forest' is any place 'set apart for hunting wild beasts and game'. Glen Ey was cleared of humans to make room for more deer in 1840. By 1855, 10,000 red deer – incredible survivors from the distant era of the mammoth and the cave-hyena – inhabited the contiguous estates of the duke of Atholl, the duke of Richmond, the earl of Fife, and Farquharson of Invercauld. The explosion of the deer population was not at the expense of people merely: the silver birch, the visually arresting tree that has always grown on Deeside and remains symbolic of the region, used to extend as 'almost a continuous forest from Inver Ey to Banchory-Ternan', a distance of forty-five miles.[4] More than any other factor, grazing by super-abundant red deer is responsible for its now much-reduced dimensions.

The use of birch-bark for tanning had ceased on Deeside by the 1850s, but the sap was still being fermented into 'an agreeable drink'.[5] It is not clear that this was the same beverage as 'birch wine' – so 'tedious' to make that it was largely 'discontinued' by 1831, but still available for a shilling a bottle at Birkhall in 1845.[6] I live in hope that the latest owner of Birkhall will soon cause birch wine to reappear in supermarkets throughout the land.

As with the red squirrel and the pine marten, Deesiders congratulate themselves on the survival – in both Glen Tanar and Ballochbuie – of untrammelled portions of the Great Caledonian Forest of prehistoric times, which grew up to cover more than 5,000 square miles across Scotland in the wake of the last Ice Age. It is now thought to have consisted chiefly of pine, birch, rowan, aspen (staple food of the beaver before its local extinction in the medieval period), juniper and oak – the 'Scots' pine having immigrated from England, where the climate had become too warm for it. The birch generally dies by age 70, the oak by 600. While self-cloned communities of alder can be several thousand years old, no tree in the world has yet lived beyond 10,000 years; therefore, those hoping to find primordial giants in this ancient woodland can be thwarted in their quest. MacGillivray confessed himself 'disappointed on finding hundreds of stems not a foot in diameter, intermixed with others varying from that to three feet . . . [T]he finest trees are scarcely ever more than eleven or twelve feet in circumference.'[7] Edwin Lankester likewise complained that 'the greater and by far the finest part of the Braemar Pines were sold and cut down' in the forty years after 1811.[8]

Arson was also an occasional problem: in 1748, it was reported that 'three miles' of Glen Tanar were 'consumed', and 'The two fellows that set it on fire are fled'.[9] Not all destruction of tree cover has been man's fault. Severe June forest fires destroyed extensive tracts of woodland in Glen Tanar in 1688, 1719, 1726, 1820 and 1920, the last-named killing 77,000 trees over 2,000 acres. The Hill of Fare was also struck in 1921. And on 'Black Saturday', 31 January 1953, a severe gale killed 5 million trees worth nearly £1 million. Nevertheless, the

Deeside woods remain extensive and diverse – considerably more so, on both counts, than in medieval and early modern times. At the time of the battle of Culblean, which took place between Culblean Hill and the west bank of Loch Kinnord in 1335, only pine, birch, oak and juniper were seen there.

Adam Corbet correctly perceived in 1842 that there was, on Lower Deeside, little connection – or at least no direct relationship of descent – between the larch, fir and birch extensively planted '[w]ithin the last thirty years', on the one hand, and on the other, peat-bog evidence of 'the wreck of the noble forests which once adorned this part of the country', including fir and birch but also oak.[10] A few years later, MacGillivray claimed that Deeside's 'trees of natural growth' were the birch, hazel, oak, aspen, rowan, bird-cherry and willow; and that the pine, spruce, ash, larch, beech and elm had all been introduced by man.[11] Despite his strong feelings on the matter – he once complained that 'mixtures' of foreign and native trees should not be admired aesthetically[12] – MacGillivray cannot have been correct about the pine. When it came to trees, the great ornithologist may have been confused in other respects. The assessments of modern experts tend rather to the support of Joseph Smith's 1792 comment that Deeside's pine, birch and common ash occurred naturally *and* in 'plantations'.[13] To MacGillivray's list of the naturally occurring trees, Smith would add the holly and alder, and from it, subtract the willow. Ash and beech trees near Craigievar were considered very old in the 1840s; and the debate over the ash tree's nativeness, ongoing in 1880, may yet be unresolved. Certainly, however, the planting of alien tree species, whether for commercial, religious, or merely decorative purposes, has been taking place for a very long time. In Birse, an ash tree called the 'Maiden of Midstrath', older than the Union of the Crowns, was twenty-one feet around by the time it was knocked down by a gale in 1833. The Farquharsons of Invercauld alone were said to have planted 15 million fir and larch trees by the end of the eighteenth century; and the Burnetts of Leys 356,000 oaks and larches between 1839 and 1842. At Muir of Inver, trees first planted at the end of the 1820s wrecked the 'extended prospect' two generations later.[14] Rightly or wrongly, the people of Pannanich recollected in 1833 that the woods there had been 'sown' by the laird of Monaltrie.[15] Of Echt in 1842, William Ingram remarked that '[w]ood is scarce, but will be plentiful in thirty or forty years.'[16] The systematic planting of trees at Balmoral was begun by Prince Albert in 1850 and continued for the rest of his life. In 1878, his widow purchased Ballochbuie Forest, saving that remnant of the Great Caledonian Forest from destruction.

The now heavily wooded hill on the north side of the Dee at Potarch Bridge was described as 'bare' in early Victorian times.[17] Half a century later, McConnochie reported that the rock formation above Invercauld House known as the Lion's Face 'is now so overgrown with trees that the lion-contour is lost'.[18] Tree-cover in the parish of Midmar increased sevenfold in thirty-five years. In 1902, King Lewanika of Barotseland (north-western Zambia) visited Deeside and reportedly said of Dinnet Moor, 'It is Africa!'[19] – a comment that would hardly have been inspired by today's neat stands of young conifers. The process continues. The wooded area of Glen Tanar has nearly doubled since 1935, despite intensive logging during the Second World War (*Forgotten heroes*, pp. 142–150). Since 1919, new types of heavy equipment and chemical fertilisers 'have made possible the successful afforestation of sites previously considered unplantable', especially 'high, exposed heathlands'.[20] Indeed, one of the most complained-about 'losses' on Deeside since 1850 is the loss of former views – of great houses, bridges and so forth – due to the ever-increasing number of trees.

The 'Wild Laird' Archibald Farquharson of Finzean (d.1841) became so indebted and preoccupied with social matters that he felled his woodlands and did not replant them; but the horror with which this is still remembered – not least by his successors as lairds of Finzean – is a good indication of how unusual such actions would soon become. The Mactiers, who had succeeded the Frasers and the Gordons in turn as lairds of Durris in the mid nineteenth century, planted 'vast numbers of rare trees and shrubs' there.[21] The sudden appearance of a royal court on Deeside in the 1840s might well have led to 'gentrification', and in some ways it has. But substantial reafforestation (among other factors) has very much mitigated the negative effects that this might have had on the landscape.

The late eighteenth-century minister of Braemar and Crathie reported enthusiastically the success of a livestock protection programme that led to the killing of 2,590 birds of prey, including 70 eagles, over a ten-year period. His figure did not include those killed by poison. '[S]till greater advantages must be derived from a scheme of this kind,' he wrote, 'if it was extended over the whole Highlands of Scotland.'[22] Half a century later, in Strachan, at least seven different species of falcons were being shot; and in Banchory-Ternan, it was reported that eagles, which came to the area hunting for lambs, were sometimes trapped alive. Surprisingly, 'when their legs are bound, they make no resistance with their beak, but are carried like a turkey under the arm.'[23] Over the second half of the nineteenth century, a measure of protection was extended to golden eagles in parts of Deeside, and by 1903 there were nests by the Old Bridge of Invercauld, on Socach Mor in Glen Ey, and in Glen Tanar. The Glen Tanar birds were still there in the interwar years, at the quartz cliffs near the headwaters of the Tanar, but no longer. There were just twenty-five pairs in the whole of the north-eastern counties in 1963; and the 2008 *North-East Scotland Bird Report*

Around 90 per cent of Glen Tanar House was demolished in the 1970s; of the structure shown here, only the ballroom remains.

found that golden eagle persecution on Deeside was ongoing.

Swifts used to nest in the eaves of Glen Tanar House, which was largely demolished in the 1970s. They have moved to outbuildings, but truly lost bird species of the glen include the kite and – for the most part – grouse. Like partridges, grouse were seen 'in profuse abundance' in the wider region in 1807; but Deeside experienced a local collapse in the red grouse population c.1825–1850, while black grouse were considered extinct in Drumoak by 1839. Quail, called 'so much decayed of late' in an act of the Scots Parliament in 1685, were still breeding around Craigmyle, Tarland, Banchory-Ternan and Kintore in the 1860s and '70s. Though sighted at Coull and the marsh still called Loch of Leys in 2008, they no longer breed locally. Fortunately, the widgeon population around Loch Kinnord and Loch Davan grew sharply from the 1950s to the 1980s and remains strong. They do not inhabit the river itself, which is 'too shallow, fast flowing and nutrient-poor to allow the growth of aquatic plants on which they depend'.[24] 'Thriving breeding populations' of waterfowl on the Loch of Aboyne disappeared soon after 1981,[25] but part of the loch was declared a Site of Special Scientific Interest three years later and many of the birds have returned. Like the rabbit, the now-numerous pheasant was introduced to the area only after 1800.

Forty-four wildcats were killed in Deeside's five westernmost parishes between 1776 and 1786. Fifty years later they were reported only around Birse

Some relatively familiar styles of game-bird shooting would have been recent additions to the routine at Aboyne Castle when these fellows were observed there in the mid nineteenth century.

and Cushnie; but the wildcat is a very intelligent and secretive creature, and in the late nineteenth century they were seen again in Glen Dye, on the Mar Lodge estate, at Invercauld, in Glen Tanar and in Glen Muick.

A too-often-quoted traditional rhyme, called 'old' in 1797, suggests that 'A foot of Don's worth two of Dee / Except it be for fish and tree'. However tired they may be of hearing it, no one doubts its veracity. Deeside has some of the worst agricultural land, and some of the best fishing, in the surrounding area. In the 1780s, farm servants protested at being fed salmon for dinner more than three times a week. A generation later, it was said that a practised angler could catch six to ten salmon a day on the Dee at Banchory-Ternan; but by 1842 the 'rare limit of his success' was three fish.[26] Due to extensive, round-the-clock use of stake nets at the mouths of both rivers, 'the noxious refuse of so many manufactories that run into the river', and 'the annoyance given by the harbour improvements',[27] salmon in the latter year were thought to be threatened with extinction on the Dee and the Don. Even one of the Dee's North-Sea-adjacent commercial salmon stations, known as Mid Chingle, had closed by 1838. Conflicts over fishing were nothing new, of course: and a 'fishing war' between the Irvines of Kingcausie

Fishing on the Feugh, 1850s.

and Andrew Harvey of Blairs erupted as early as the sixteenth century.

None of this is to suggest that either line or net fishing had always been the norm. As elsewhere throughout the Gaelic world, salmon fishing was often conducted with spears or tridents, two-pronged and four-pronged instruments being known as well. All were called leisters, and the sport as leistering or pouting. Deeside people also trained otters to catch salmon on their behalf. Visitors to the west of Ireland were already bridling at the spear-fishing of salmon as 'barbaric' in the early seventeenth century, but amazingly, this practice continued on Upper Deeside right up until it was prohibited under penalty of £5 by the Fishing Act 1868 – Queen Victoria herself having previously participated. Seals were also netted and killed by the commercial salmon fishers of Nigg. Even though the heyday of sport fishing, the 'industrial' form of game-bird shooting, and motorised transport were all still in the future, one gets an impression that 1840s Deeside experienced an environmental crisis that is only now being healed. With undue pessimism and probably unintentional pathos, a twentieth-century scientific study remarked that the only 'unusual or important' vertebrates remaining on the banks of the Dee were the otter and the long-eared bat.[28]

Leister-heads.

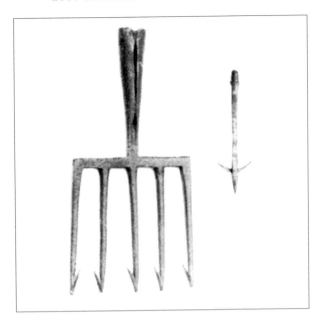

LOST LOCHS AND THE LIKE

A substantial part of Dinnet Moor was drained as recently as the early 1980s, the culmination of a long and environmentally dubious process of land reclamation. Before the (westernmost) Loch of Park was substantially drained, it was home to white and yellow water lilies, water lobelias, Merlin's grass, Baltic rushes, 'and many other interesting plants'.[29] Loch Auchlossan by Lumphanan, drained in 1860 by James W. Barclay, was a mile long and, in places, half a mile broad on the eve of its destruction. It had been even larger prior to a partial drainage of the late seventeenth century, and 'once it was much more extensive than any historical record shows'.[30] It formed a habitat for eels, ducks, geese, swans, widgeon, redshank, and pike up to six feet long weighing twenty-five pounds, not to mention horsetails, bogbean, purple marshlocks, kingcup, brooklime, speedwell, blinks, soft-rushes, bur-reed, and water-milfoil. It was an obstacle to travel only in spring and autumn. In winter, it froze solid enough to walk across, and in summer, it dried up to a point that a natural causeway appeared. Though its plentiful waterfowl made it one of the best spots for shooting in the north of Scotland, these birds were also considered very destructive to agriculture. For this and other reasons, including local air quality and especially the potential value of the land beneath, a plan to drain it a second time was already afoot in the 1790s. As Auchlossan and Auchinhove are only two miles apart, Loch Auchlossan is almost certainly the same as the large 'Lake of Auchinhove' which historians of the Clan Farquharson inevitably and confusingly claim was drained in 1859. In any case, despite deep-cutting and tunnelling work that cost £6,000, Loch Auchlossan was drained only to the extent that it now dries up in summer time – which perhaps explains a 1944 plan to re-drain it to plant crops for the war effort.

An editor's note in William MacGillivray's posthumous *Natural History of Dee Side and Braemar* states that 'the greater part of the parishes of Tarland, Coldstone and Coul . . . at some remote period, has formed an immense lake, the remains of which has only of late years been drained by the Earl of Aberdeen'.[31] This 'immense lake' is not seemingly a reference to Auchinhove. It may however have been Bog More, which was drained in or after 1830. On South Donside, 'a large marsh, called the Strath of Tough, or Kincraigie' was drained at the end of the seventeenth century.[32]

The Burnett family built their first castle in the Loch of Leys, on a prehistoric crannog, or man-made island – in this case, made of alternating rows of oak and birch trunks with the bark left on, earth, and stones. It is said that they lived there until the later sixteenth century. The loch was imperfectly drained in July 1850; many references to it being drained in 1746 also exist, in the context

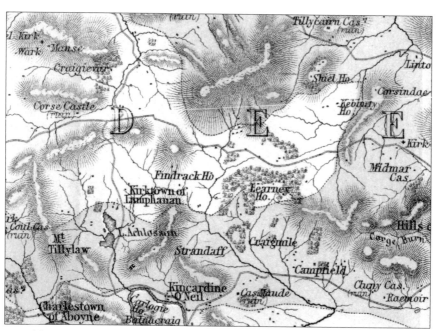

Detail from A.K. Johnston's map of the Dee basin, published in 1855, showing Loch Auchlossan's shape and position relative to the towns of Aboyne, Lumphanan, and Kincardine O'Neil, and the castles of Craigievar, Corse, Midmar, Cluny and Tillycairn.

of an explosives accident that took the life of the young heir-apparent to the Leys estate, but this earlier drainage project must be regarded as never completed. The site remains a weedy marsh of about 120 acres. As a lake, it was 140 acres on the eve of being drained the second time, and an estimated three to five times that size in earlier periods. It is conceivable that the Bog Loch of Kincardine O'Neil (which still exists, in a small way, approximately halfway between Bridge of Canny and Tillydrine), the Loch of Leys, and the Loch of Park were part of a single very large lake in the very distant past. Fortunately for future archaeologists, the position of the Leys crannog is still obvious and marked on Ordnance Survey maps.

The nearby Loch Drum was described as being nearly of a size with Loch of Leys in 1800. The former was 300 acres in 1811 but by 1842 had diminished to 84 acres; between the same dates, the depth had also been reduced (by the design of Sir Robert Burnett) from eight feet to four inches, and though still 'beautiful' it was in danger of becoming 'an unsightly morass'.[33] A much smaller lake on the opposite side of Drum Castle, now indiscriminately (and in either case erroneously) referred to as Loch Drum and Loch of Park, would have suffered the same fate, but it was saved by being lined with clay in the mid 1880s. After that,

> [t]he water in the loch could be controlled by a sluice for the purpose of cleaning to prevent over silting. An elderly estate worker back in 1951 . . . remembered the sluice being opened before the second world war, the silt collected in the first hundred yards of the ditch; 'far thir wis nae muckle run, sine thrown oot bi shovel.' He spoke of the next time, which was to be the last time the sluice was opened. On the 31st December 1949, one of the estate keepers that 'wis affa fond o the whisky bottle; it bein hogmanay efterneen he decided tae try tae open the sluice jist tae see if it ey workit, it opened but widdna close.' Resulting in the loch being drained, the culvert under the North Deeside road blocked with hibernating frogs and silt, a considerable area of the road was a foot deep with the same mixture.[34]

Despite this disaster, the small lake was still eight acres of open water in 1989, but only a two-acre portion of it still survives, probably because of the ongoing removal of water for irrigation. Even the current small area is continuing to shrink, and Diana Robertson, head gardener of the Drum estate (to which the small lake ceased to belong many years ago) anticipates that it will dry up completely by 2020.

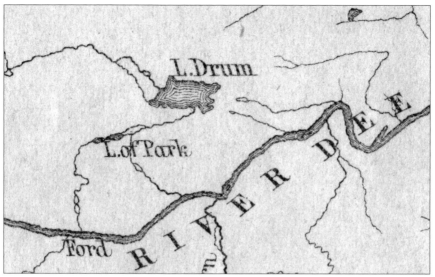

Detail from A.K. Johnston's 1855 map, showing the actual relationship between Loch of Park, Loch Drum, and (at upper right) the as-yet-unnamed Robbie Rossie's Loch.

Loch of Park or Loch Drum; it was identified as both in a popular book of the early 1900s.

A.I. McConnochie mentioned seeing *only* Loch Drum in 1898, and Alexander Bremner, *only* Loch of Park, which he described as 'slowly draining' by a natural process, in 1912.[35] Less than ten years later, G.M. Fraser plausibly conceived that Loch Drum had been renamed Loch of Park due to a boundary change between the two estates; and perhaps due to Fraser's well-deserved influence, officialdom nowadays regards Loch Drum as a mere alias of the Loch of Park.[36] However, two lochs are shown distinctly, Drum much larger than Park, on a map made by A. Keith Johnston, geographer to Queen Victoria, in or before 1855.

The surviving two acres of open water, which is located in woodland two field-widths east by north-east of Drum Castle's formal gardens, has acquired a third name: Robbie Rossie's Loch, after the labourer from Belskavie who saved it by lining it with clay. I would urge the Royal Commission on the Ancient and Historic Monuments of Scotland (RCAHMS) and other such bodies to begin referring to it as Robbie Rossie's Loch. Having two places both called 'Loch of Park' within two and a half miles of each other is a disservice to both history and cartography.

In an era that too often saw agriculture as a cure-all for the nation's social as well as economic problems, the creation of little scraps of agricultural land – however small or marginal – was hailed as a victory for humankind. In its own echo of the bitter conflicts on Upper Deeside that had led to the elimination of the Dalmores by the Auchendrynes (*Lost people*, p. 112), Banchory-Ternan witnessed a conflict over a new island in the Dee that had been created by the great flood of 17 September 1768.

> Mr. Douglas of Tilquhillie erected a stone jetty on the south side of the river below the junction of Feugh and Dee. The Laird of Leys, however, interdicted him ... The Lord Ordinary refused the interdict craved, and by his decision, the jetty complained of will, as an aid to the Feugh, force the Dee to the north, and in due time turn the Dee from the old channel on the south of the island into the new channel on the north side. Thus, if it continues unchallenged, the Laird of Tilquhillie may become Lord of the Island.[37]

The Dee has changed its course in various places since c.1600, and the farm called Insch in the parish of Peterculter commemorates this, having been (for a time) an island with the main part of the Dee flowing to the south of it. Likewise, it is thought that the Dee used to run not north of, but south of, Balmoral and Abergeldie – at a period after the castles on those estates were first constructed. The period of transition must have been rather nerve-wracking for the inhabitants. Whether or not Tilquhillie succeeded in claiming it, actually using Banchory's new island was unwise: a schoolmaster, the Rev. Mr Ogg, lost an entire flock of sheep who were grazing there when the great flood of 1829 hit. Ten years later, extensive (and expensive) flood-control preparations had been made on the Water of Feugh, but it burst through these in two successive years, covering the crops 'with mud and gravel, in some instances to the depth of . . . two to three feet'.[38] Eight acres were still in a state of ruin three years later.

People sometimes seemed more concerned with saving arable land than with saving their own necks. In 1846, when once again 'Great mounds of mountain debris were hurled together on fruitful fields, and the Dee flowed black with soil', a group of people became so engrossed in trying to retain their dirt that they did nothing to save a nearby house, with tragic results.[39] Though mass death has not been caused by the river, the death of individuals was so commonplace that it led to a traditional rhyme: 'Bloodthirsty Dee / Each year needs three.'

Adam Corbet suggested in 1842 that the unprecedented fury of the Dee, in his time, could be blamed on the removal of lochs and other similar operations.

The increased exertions which, of late years, have been made throughout the country generally, to effect a more perfect drainage of wet land, have rendered the Dee subject to more frequent and much higher floods than formerly, so that embanking is now absolutely necessary for the protection of its haughs.[40]

Corbet added that in the autumn of 1841 the river had risen 'to within a few inches' of its height during the great flood of 1829. This would happen again in October 1847. On the other hand, the Georgian clergyman Francis Douney blamed the area's lakes for the general ill-health of his parishioners in Banchory-Ternan, where even young people suffered from frequent sore throats and consumption. He may have been right. Half a century after the drainage was completed, Banchory was thought one of the healthiest places in Britain for people with respiratory disease, and was specially chosen as the site of the Nordrach-on-Dee tuberculosis hospital. This air-quality benefit – if it in fact occurred – would seem to be the only positive outcome of the Victorian lake-drainage projects, which destroyed wildlife habitat, places of sport and recreation, and much-admired scenery, in whose place we now find squelching bog land not seemingly suited to, or used for, any purpose at all. Even Loch Davan, one of the region's healthiest, 'has diminished very considerably even within living memory.'[41] Lakes can also appear suddenly where none were before: as for example at Allanaquoich, which during the 1829 flood acquired surface water of sixty continuous acres. Floods having now occurred once every generation since 1738, some degree of aquatic chaos seems set to continue as long as people and the River Dee coexist. At least the wild geese have returned to Auchlossan.

A photo of the Nordrach-on-Dee hospital in the early stages of landscaping, taken shortly after it opened. Later a hotel, then a barracks, then abandoned, Nordrach-on-Dee was immortalised in prose by its most famous resident, Somerset Maugham.

The three-mile-long and (in places) fifty-foot-deep gorge known at its northern end as the Leuchar Burn and at its southern as the Culter Burn connects the Dee to the Loch of Skene. Rob Roy MacGregor supposedly leapt over the burn, an impossible task for a normal man, and this is commemorated by a rather depressing 1991 statue of the famous outlaw, the fourth such on the site since 1850, which can be seen from the so-called 'Rob Roy Bridge' on the North Deeside road.[42] In 1794, George Mark described a spectacular annual migration of perhaps 3 million eels, lasting three or four days between mid-May and mid-June. The eels would swim up the Dee, then up the Culter Burn and so into the loch, then return to the Dee at harvest time, by which point some of them had quadrupled in body length. The local people found them tasty and pickled them in earthenware jars or wooden casks. A hundred years later, George Sim observed an eel migration in the Muick and stated that the *anguilla vulgaris* is 'not now used as food';[43] however, close observation reveals that the river's otters and herons still find them delicious. Mark hoped that the Culter and Leuchar burns could be made into a canal, continuing to the River Don between Castle Fraser and Kemnay. But his canal scheme, the eel migration, and other aquatic migrations along the same route (including those of salmon and sea trout) were stopped by the erection of a twenty-foot-high dam a few years later. The River Dee Trust now proposes to make the dam passable to fish once again, or remove it altogether. However, either of these options will be 'a challenging task, requiring money and engineering expertise'.[44]

The first 'Rob Roy' statue on the Culter Burn was taken from a ship, Highlanders being a common theme of the figureheads of Aberdeen-built wooden ships of the time; a 'Highland Chieftain', for instance, adorned the 980-tonne tea clipper Cairngorm, *launched in 1853. This is the second incarnation, c.1865–1926. The headgear, facial hair and general aspect of the current, fourth, statue are more redolent of the Royal Tank Regiment of c.1940 than of any famous outlaw, fictional or otherwise; and were clearly painted in ignorance of the fact that 'Roy' (ruaidh) means 'red-haired'.*

LOST CONNECTION:
DEESIDE AND THE SEA

It is not necessary here to re-state G.H. Martin's thoughtful and well-documented attack on the commonplace idea that in medieval Britain, 'journeys were ordinarily made by water' or 'could only be so made', amounting to 'an unwillingness to suppose that the roads were used for anything at all'.[45] *Some* waterways connected the people along their shores to one another, but the Dee has not been conspicuous in this regard. Other than sport fishermen, few today would perceive any particularly strong link between the Dee and the North Sea beyond. Douglas Simpson, alone, seems to have thought that the few pockets of ancient Roman trade goods found along the Dee valley – for instance, at Cushnie and Crathes – were brought there in Roman ships as part of a 'sea-borne commerce penetrating up the river valleys'.[46] The Vikings, renowned for their riverborne inland raiding and trading from the Shannon to Russia, did not come here. And among all the Deeside parishes whose male population declined steeply over the course of the eighteenth century, in only one – easternmost Nigg, home to a significant sea-fishing fleet – was this blamed on naval impressment. This is not to suggest, however, that the native inhabitants of other parts of Deeside did not have watercraft of their own devising. The region's many ferries will be discussed in *Lost bridges, ferries and fords*, pp. 175–185. Loch Kinnord's dugout canoes, fashioned of oak, were up to thirty feet long and more than three feet wide: much larger than most oaks growing in the area today. If Roman items did travel up the valley by boat, it may have been in craft such as these, almost certainly not piloted by Romans.

In 1792, the Rev. George Morison of Banchory-Devenick – the Deeside-to-seaside parish south-west of Aberdeen that includes the town of Portlethen – reported the Dee 'not navigable here', and called flooding 'very sudden and very high'.[47] The farther up the Dee you go, the more true this becomes. In nearby Peterculter two years later, it was noted that due to the silting up of the Dee, tidal changes were not visible, though they had been in the past. Rightly or wrongly, the floating of log rafts was said to be only possible from seven or eight miles upstream of this point; '[f]arther up, single trees only can be floated . . . because of the rocks, shallows, cataracts, &c'.[48]

Maryculter and most other Deeside parishes suffered in the particularly bad floods of September 1768 and August 1829. The latter, caused by the unusual convergence of storms from Iceland and the Bay of Biscay, is still remembered as the Muckle Spate o' Twenty-Nine. It is commemorated in a hilarious and frequently reprinted 1851 poem of that name by an eyewitness, David Grant, as

Old Mar Lodge and surroundings, by Gibb. Its replacement, New Mar Lodge (formerly known as Corriemulzie Cottage), was covered in deer heads and featured black creosoted 'rustic' logs. Perhaps unsurprisingly, it burned down in 1895. The current, third, house has resumed the position of the first; as to the wisdom of this, time will tell.

This mill on the Clunie in Auchendryne was one of the most photographed sights of Aberdeenshire in the nineteenth century, but is now a mill-wheel-less private dwelling.

well as in Sir Edwin Landseer's painting *Flood in the Highlands*. Old Mar Lodge
was so severely damaged in the 1829 floods that when it was rebuilt, a different
site was used. Two years later, during an 'ice speat', the 'best' part of the glebe
of Durris 'was entirely carried off, and nothing left but bare gravel'; nearby,
'about three acres of the best land entirely disappeared, and now make part of
the bed of the river.'[49]

So dangerous and unpredictable has the Dee been in all periods that water-
mills were never successfully built on it, only on its tributaries such as the Feugh
by Banchory-Ternan and the Culter Burn. The sole exception proving this rule,
dating from the first third of the nineteenth century, was the small cutler's wheel
and turning lathe at Cairn-na-Cuimhne. This had become a dwelling house a
hundred years later. The number of bridges that the Dee has swept away,
whether of wood, stone or iron, would make a small book in itself. But in this
context in particular, it is worth noting that Potarch Bridge – which links the
Aboyne–Kincardine O'Neil stretch of the A93 with Birse on the other side of
the river – was nearly destroyed while under construction in 1812 by a mass of
cut logs, which had been placed in the water upstream, one by one, but which
arrived all at once. A successful lawsuit against the timber's owners, combined
with a public appeal, raised £1,483 for remediation of the disaster, and the bridge
was completed two years later. As a direct result of this episode, a law was
passed (53 George III c. 117) making it easier to collect damages in such cases.
The first bridge to be built on the site, Potarch is still in daily use by myself and
quite a few others – *pace* G.M. Fraser, who called its interest 'almost entirely
historical'.[50] A raging confusion of rocks and ice can very often be seen below.
At the end of a century-long agitation for this bridge to be built, in 1810, the
lairds of Learney, Craigmyle, Balnacraig and Tilquhillie stated that on the 'large
and rapid' Dee,

> when in flood in the summer and autumn months from heavy falls of
> rain, or in spring from melting of the snow in the upper district, or in
> winter, when gorged with ice, the passage of Kincardine O'Neil is
> rendered extremely precarious, and often impracticable altogether for
> days.[51]

Sharp-eyed readers will have noted that no season of the year was *not*
mentioned in the lairds' lament.

As far back as the reign of James VI, John Taylor – who was not just a poet
but also a professional waterman – declared the entire River Dee to be 'not
portable'.[52] He remarked wistfully that his friend the earl of Mar owned as many

The Inch of Culter ferry and ferry-station. Like ministers, public ferry operators were given small parcels of land on which to grow their own food. This practice is commemorated by the part of Banchory-Ternan called Cobleheugh, from coble, *thirteenth-century Scots word for a flat-bottomed ferry propelled by oars, and* haugh: *flat and usually fertile land by a riverbank.*

growing trees 'as would serve for mastes (from this time to the end of the world) for all the Shippes, Carackes, Hoyes, Galleyes, Boates, Drumlers, Barkes, and Watercraftes, that are now, or can bee'. Unfortunately, he could see no possible method of getting them out.[53] Fifty miles nearer the sea, a different attitude was struck in the same period: oak from Drum was used in 1609 to build the *Bon-Accord*, inaugural effort of the shipbuilding industry that would thereafter thrive in Aberdeen.

Abergeldie Castle, showing the rope and winding apparatus of the notorious 'Cradle'. This device was replaced by a suspension bridge, itself now derelict and badly warped, in 1885.

The 'Cradle' in action, c.1850.

I have found one reference to a coracle being used on the Dee; it sank. Boats of larger size than coracles and kayaks did ply the Dee until recent times, however – not up and down it, but across. Twenty-four public ferries on rural Deeside were enumerated by Fraser, who found three – Blairs, Inch of Culter, and Kincardine O'Neil – still in use in 1921, having been there from time immemorial. By the late 1960s, Inch of Culter's ferry had succumbed but the other two soldiered on. There were at least seven private ones also, one of which, operating somewhere between Braemar village and Braemar Castle since 1564, was still going in 1968.[54] Though he was aware of its existence, Fraser did not list the Boat of Bonty at Aboyne, for reasons that are not now clear; including it would raise the region's total of public ferries to twenty-five.

So unlikely was traffic up- or downriver in about 1810 that the ferry at Inchmarlo was 'managed . . . by a wire rope stretched across the river and fixed to a tree on either side.'[55] At Abergeldie there was an extreme version of this, which was not even a boat but 'a big box, balanced between two lines of rope' in which people were hauled across the river suspended in the air. This thing, known as the Cradle, passed out of use after it caused the death of a newly married couple.

In 1797, an anonymous writer proposed 'raising a canal from Aberdeen at once to the level of Hazlehead' and continuing it to Kincardine O'Neil via Hirn, Raemoir, and Glassel, perhaps with a second branch toward Alford via Skene, Cluny and Monymusk. This, it was thought, would be worth £1,500 a year to the Glen Tanar forestry industry, that is, quadrupling its value of £500 a year. No such canal was ever built – Fraser remarked that its proponent was 'no engineer'[56] – but by the early nineteenth century, this difficulty was being overcome through sheer hard work.

The fifty-hut hamlet called the Black Ship, a glorified lumber camp (in which nevertheless 150 children were born), existed from 1809 to 1845 about one and a half miles beyond Glen Tanar House. A clipper ship, built in Aberdeen using timber from this area in 1842, was called the *Glentanar*. She joined the *Countess of Aboyne*, a 99-tonne brig 'entirely of oak taken from Lord Aboyne's woods', built in 1795.[57] An earlier Aberdonian *Glentanner*, of 161 tonnes, carried emigrants to Quebec and Nova Scotia in 1820. In all, at least seventeen wooden ships constructed in Aberdeen between 1795 and 1869, with a combined tonnage in excess of 6,400, were named for Deeside locations: five for lairds' houses, four for towns, three each for hills and glens, and two for the river itself. This was a strikingly high percentage of all the Aberdeen ships named after places. In some instances, it can be confirmed that the wood used to build the ship came from Deeside: as with the 1,000-tonne *Invercauld* (1863; wrecked in the South Pacific, 1864), which was made of timber from Ballochbuie Forest. This naming practice took on a life of its own, and persisted long after wood had largely ceased to be used in shipbuilding. Among iron-hulled Aberdeen ships built from 1870 to the outbreak of the First World War, we find 10 per cent so named, including the *Deeside*, a 600-tonne schooner-rigged screw steamer of 1883. Among steel hulls of the same period, the *Crathie*, *Aboyne*, *Morven*, *Culblean* and *Drumoak* were converted to minesweepers in 1914; two of them were sunk. It would not be amiss here to mention that in spite of the landlocked nature of his patrimony, Thomas Coats, Lord Glentanar became one of the great yachtsmen of the interwar years. His 1930s pleasure yacht, *Elk*, had internal panelling made from Glen Tanar trees, a telephone and a radio in every room, and a granite fireplace.

Collections for the release of Scottish sailors taken captive by the Turks or Algerians were commonplace in Deeside churches about the year 1700, but most of these men did not hail from the immediate vicinity. Neither, originally, did Admiral Robert Duff, sometime governor of Newfoundland, successful defender of Gibraltar in 1779, and latterly the proprietor of Culter. By and large, Deeside, where uncountable numbers of soldiers have chosen to retire since the advent of professional armies, has been home to few sailors. One who caught the public imagination, however, was John Fordyce, gunner's mate of the *Centurion*, Admiral George Anson's sixty-gun flagship. During their gruelling four-year circumnavigation of the world (1740–44), fighting the Spanish all the way, they faced typhus, malaria, dysentery and scurvy as well as both extremes of weather – but captured enemy ships, bullion and cash worth an estimated £240,000. This was ten to twenty years' wages for every man who lived through the experience, on top of the four years' back pay they had earned in the usual fashion. Given the expedition's survival rate of 11 per cent, Fordyce was lucky indeed. Luckier still, perhaps, in that heyday of highwaymen, he travelled all the way from London 'on horseback . . . with his prize-money in specie in his saddlebags' to buy the Ardoe estate in Banchory-Devenick, for a reported £1,783 6s 8d.[58] Fordyce's family became extinct by 1839, however, and the estate was sold again, this time to a soap manufacturer.

LOST WOLVES

In medieval leases of 'shepherd lands' on Deeside, the tenants were 'bounden to keep dogs' specifically to defend against wolf attack. John Taylor saw wolves in Braemar in 1618, but these majestic predators were not solely a phenomenon of the high hills. In the Garioch, there was a Wolf Cairn 'but it is now entirely removed' and has 'no local tradition connected with it'. Similarly, there was a place called Wolf-Holm in the western part of Birse in the 1790s, reflecting the presence of wolves there, though it (like the wolves) has vanished. Other

The arms of Alexander Skene, sixteenth laird of Skene, and his wife Giles Adie, 1692, showing the three skewered wolf-heads, as well as a rare pre-eighteenth-century depiction of Deeside Highland clothing.

suggestive place names within Aberdeenshire include Wolf Stone in Cluny, Wolfholls near Turriff, and Wolf Holes in Strathbogie – to which should be added any number of Gaelic place-names with the element *mhadaidh*.[59] These include the *Allt a' Mhadaidh Allaidh* or 'Wolf's Burn' in Glen Lui, thought by some to commemorate the death of the Forest of Mar's last wolf. A probably apocryphal tale holds that the family and lands of Skene are so named because a local Robertson was rewarded with them, for saving the life of King Malcolm Canmore from a wolf attack – killing the animal with his *sgian* (knife). True or not, no one would have been expected to believe the story had wolves not been a common sight almost on the outskirts of Aberdeen at one time.

The most extraordinary local legend involving wolves is that of the Wolf MacDonalds. This family was said to have been descended from a boy child who was stolen from his mother's cottage by a she-wolf, and raised as one of the animal's own cubs. He 'came on well with his companions, grew up a hairy monster, [and] joined in all their plundering expeditions'.[60] His own human mother would set the dogs on him when he came round, for which he never completely forgave her when eventually he returned to society and married a human girl. The descendants of this unusual marriage were declared to be still living in Glen Clunie, Ardearg and Altchlar in Victorian times. The probably unrelated Macdonald lairds of Rineton, in Glengairn, were declared extinct as of 1876, but many other MacDonalds of long-standing Deeside stock remain; the oldest branch claims to have arrived in the early fifteenth century. Werewolf lore is decidedly thin on the ground, but the ability of the local wizards, witches and warlocks to transform themselves into cats, hares, mice, greyhounds and weasels is widely repeated.

LOST CONNECTION: DEESIDE'S DOMESTIC ANIMALS

The title of this section is on the face of it surprising. Surely, Deeside remains one of the doggy/horsey-est places in Britain if not in the whole Atlantic world; a place where people in riding boots and breeches can be seen on any day in any supermarket, and no estate car is complete without its 'dog guard'. Yet, Deeside has seen a dramatic decline in the connectedness between human and animal life just since the 1950s.

Though the first practical motor car was invented by Karl Benz as early as 1885, and steam-powered tractors were banned from the area's bridges as early as 1897, motor vehicles were actually quite slow to catch on. Ballater had a post

Top. Deeside's first car, a Benz given by Lord Granville Gordon to Robert Milne (right).
Bottom. A rough-and-ready family sledge of the early twentieth century.

horse within living memory. Andrew Lawson's steam-tricycle of his own invention, with iron tyres provided by the Lumphanan blacksmith, was used for postal deliveries on the roads between Whitehouse Railway Station and Craigievar (illustrated p. 137); but this was such an extraordinary novelty in the 1890s that it has been the subject of several books. In the 1930s, even those local families lucky enough to have cars still used horse-drawn sleighs in the winter. Some were purpose-built, and others were wheeled vehicles with their wheels replaced by skids on a seasonal basis. A beautiful sleigh, imported from Canada

Deeside before and after the coming of internal combustion: c.1900 and c.1925.

but of otherwise unknown provenance, is currently on display at Balmoral. Aberdeen is thought to be the only city in Britain to have used sleighs as public transport; seating twenty, they were pulled by four horses, and first ran in 1878.

Horse ownership both facilitated and necessitated lengthy journeys. Chrissie Gibson recalls, as a little girl in the 1920s and '30s, having one horse looked after by smiths and farriers as far apart as Strachan, Finzean and Torphins, and her family shopping – the horse pulling a cart – in Banchory-Ternan and Aboyne. Deeside farm horses were not renowned for tractability in general, but she remembers one group of Clydesdale colts as particularly huge, vicious and terrifying. During a scarlet fever epidemic, the Aboyne hospital filled up, and additional cases (including Gibson and two of her fourteen siblings) were sent to Inverurie in one of the first non-horse-drawn ambulances in the region – though Gibson remembers that this was 'just an ordinary van' with 'no special equipment', and that its driver 'was just a driver, with no first-aid training'.[61] Among the lost creatures of Deeside we should probably include the true Garron, as opposed to Norwegian, Hebridean, and other cross-breeds.

The Rev. George Mark wrote of Peterculter in 1794, 'we are still so Gothic in some places, that a horse and an ox are matched together' at the plough.[62] Whether he meant 'Gothic' as actually medieval, or actually German, or simply as disparagement is not now clear. But in Mark's day, similar practices were very widespread on Deeside and South Donside. His colleague Thomas Birnie reported from Alford that more than a third of all the cattle in that parish were oxen for the plough, though the smallest farmers 'yoke oxen, horses, and even bulls, cows, and young cattle, promiscuously'.[63] A different source specified that

A mixed team, driven by sixteen-year-old Charlie Gordon in 1944: a horse ('Star') and a young bull ('Jack').

two horses and two oxen were most commonly used there. Robert Farquharson stated that the mixed plough teams around Logie-Coldstone consisted usually of two horses and two cows; or, one horse, two cows and two small oxen. In Echt, it was two horses plus four oxen.

In the late Middle Ages, however, ploughing in the region was associated with oxen only. The medieval equivalent of our modern acreage was not an abstraction based on linear measurement, but animal-driven. As we shall see in *Lost people*, p. 101, the ancient local land measure, the davoch, was used as the basis of military recruitment. To say it is exactly 416 acres is an oversimplification: usually, it was four 'ploughgates' of about 104 acres each, each in turn consisting of four 'husbandlands'. This was the real basis of the system: each of the four husbandmen who cooperated in farming a ploughgate contributed three healthy oxen for the communally-owned 'twal-owsen-pleugh' (twelve-oxen plough), 'whose whole force was often necessary to tear up the wild and matted surface' of the land.[64] Around Banchory, the ox-positions were called (from fore to aft) the 'steer-draught', 'on steer-draught', 'fore-throck in fur', 'fore-throck on land', 'mid-throck in fur', 'mid-throck on land', 'hind-throck in fur', 'hind-throck on land', 'fit in fur' and 'fit on land' (with 'fur' indicating the furrow side). The number of ploughgates reckoned to be in a given parish could be remarkably consistent between the twelfth century and the eighteenth. Each husbandland, finally, was reckoned to be two 'oxgates' or 'oxgangs': the *actual* amount of land, locally, that one ox could plough in one day. The size of the davoch might therefore vary dramatically with the size of the oxen, the hardness of the ground, and difficulties of access to the land being ploughed. The 'twal-owsen-pleugh' was last seen in use on Deeside in 1816.

CHAPTER 4

MEN AND WOMEN

LOST PEOPLE

In the wake of the 1715 Rebellion, a large number of Deeside men were 'transported' – exiled – to British colonies. The authorities did this even, or perhaps *especially*, to men whose commitment to the Jacobite cause was wavering or uncertain. From among the tenants of David Lumsden of Cushnie alone, Francis Ferguson was sent to Antigua; Jerome Dunbar, John Finnie, William Moir and James Rae to Virginia; and Robert Henderson, Thomas Forbes, Alexander Gordon and Robert Grant to Maryland. All had protested that they were, in effect, drafted by the earl of Mar and not really Jacobites at all. Of the men here named, only Dunbar is known to have made it home again.

During and prior to the Jacobite wars, the goal of many Highland proprietors was to accumulate as large a population as the land (through subsistence agriculture and small-scale cattle-rearing) could support. Selling the produce of the land was not generally contemplated; well into the nineteenth century, rent in Glengairn was paid in hens and anyone who used money there was thought 'rich'. Traditionally, the larger the population, the larger would be the chief's military retinue and the greater his glory in war. In 1715, the feudal underlings of the earl of Mar were required to provide him with twenty armed men from every davoch (416-acre parcel) that they possessed. Assuming that males fit to fight made up one-third of the total population, this implies a very precarious food supply based on less than seven acres of land per person – quite apart from losses due to war, floods, hail, and landlords' unreasonable consumption routines. Indeed, unlike in the Middle Ages, cottars in more recent times often had no land other than a kailyard, and J.G. Michie thought that on the whole, people in Micras in the 1830s lived on the produce of an acre apiece, almost all of it oats and potatoes, supplemented by one pig per house per year. Unsurprisingly, famine frequently threatened Scotland as a whole, with 'King William's ill years' being the worst on record. One-fifth of the human population of

Aberdeenshire died or left between 1695 and 1699. The county's sheep population was halved between 1690 and 1780 because so many sheep that would have been used for breeding purposes were instead eaten; and in Nigg over the same period, the number of sheep was said to have fallen from 2,000 to nil. Some communities were hit harder than others. Milltown of Crathie was still a large and bustling place in 1696, but its mill and ferry were both gone a century later; the former ferry-house lingered on as a disreputable inn only until 1824.

With peace imposed from without, in the second half of the eighteenth century, the structure of society changed rapidly. As the earl of Selkirk put it in his lengthy pro-emigration tract of 1805:

[M]any of the people, who were thought necessary in the feudal times, and have since been suffered to remain on the land, will, under any system of cultivation, be found superfluous as workmen, and dismissed. All of these have been hitherto enabled to live by possessing land at a rent below its value: directly or indirectly they are a burthen on the proprietors; and unless some new and profitable employment can be devised for them, they must continue to be a burthen as long as they remain in the country.[1]

Though Selkirk would probably not have approved of it, the first 'new and profitable employment' for many people was illicit whisky distillation (see *The lost policemen*, pp. 153–156).

The family of Farquharson of Invercauld was lauded as remarkable, in the nineteenth century, in that their policy was 'never to dismiss a dependant or remove an old tenant, except for some flagrant offence, or the most hopeless incapacity'.[2] It speaks volumes that such an ordinarily humane policy, which is nowadays largely enshrined in law, would have been singled out for high praise at that, or any time. The loss of so many of the region's people immediately became, and remains, an emotive issue:

How mightily are the cowards exalted, and how desolate are the glens that once teemed with a brave people! They tell me to rejoice because I am a civilised man in a civilised country; but when I look to Glendee, Gleney, Glenlui, Glencuaich, Glencluny, Braemar, Strathdee, Glen-gairn, Glenfinzie, Morven, and Glentanner, I cannot but exclaim, oh! desolate! oh! dreary! oh desert civilisation! At the same time, I laugh at their fictions of barbarism, their fictions of disloyalty, their fictions of sorning and cattle-lifting, their fictions of sturt and strife. If countries or districts are to be laid waste for these very wise reasons, I ask myself, why do the Saxon and Lowland inhabitants of glass-houses begin to throw stones at us? For scattered and harassed as we are, in case of a French invasion, the Celts would defend themselves and their country as gallantly as the lowlanders or Saxons. Perhaps –

By 1908, this was all that remained of the twin clachans of Torgalter and Greystone: 'a place of considerable note in the olden time', containing 'all that was deemed necessary for the social and physical comfort of the inhabitants' (J.G. Michie).

The Micras, a characteristic clachan which was radically transformed after 1850.

who can say – were they as numerous as when they went forth to Kilsyth, Killiecrankie, and Culloden, the country might be saved as much in coast defences now, as the surplus balance of gain made by turning our fields into deer-forests.[3]

As the above passage suggests, it was generally speaking not commercial sheep-farming but quasi-commercial deerstalking for which the glens here were 'cleared'. Most notably, this occurred in the case of nine clachans in Glen Ey in 1840. The elimination of families and entire communities is hardly exclusive to the upper part of Deeside, however. In the later Middle Ages, there was a fairly substantial village called Gardin in the north-east part of the parish of Peter-culter, but all physical traces of it had been lost by 1892. The site was later called Gairn but should not be confused with Glengairn (formerly also known as 'Glengarden'), forty miles to the west. So many (very degraded) remains of former small villages occur on Upper Deeside and Upper Donside that they form the subject of an entire excellent book, *Land of the Lost* by Robert Smith, to which readers are referred for more specific information.

Prior to the parliamentary union of England and Scotland in 1707, Scots were denied the right to reside in the English colonies, but over the eighteenth century this changed. Colonies of Jacobite Highlanders were formed in rural New York, North Carolina, Georgia, Nova Scotia and Prince Edward Island. Many Scottish officers and soldiers of the British Army, meanwhile, took up land grants in North America when the Seven Years' War ended in 1763. Prominent in both these movements were the tacksmen – the old Highland military middle class, officers of the clan regiments – who were being squeezed out in Scotland as the chiefs took direct control of land management, and the central government took direct control of the military. Many tacksmen 'hoped that in America they would be able to reconstitute the clan system, with themselves as chiefs'.[4]

Similarly, the majority of emigrants from the North-east Lowlands in 1774–75 might nowadays be described as *petit bourgeois*: clerks and skilled workers with fairly sizeable personal savings. At most times before about 1815, it was a fear of becoming poor rather than 'existing destitution' that led northern Scots to emigrate, and in the North-east this pattern persisted even after the Clear-ances caused severe and widespread destitution elsewhere in the country.[5] The 1803 Passenger Act was intended to stop emigration altogether by making it too expensive, but this legislation largely failed: Scottish emigrants had then, and had *always* had, much more money than the government supposed. Even after 1830, the North-east Scot's permanent departure 'was not usually an inevitable or spontaneous flight from sheer poverty or even from outright victimisation, but the result of careful consideration and planning'.[6]

Many Scottish ports, even very small ones, were involved in timber importation from Canada in the earlier nineteenth century, a trade fomented initially by embargoes on Baltic timber during the Napoleonic Wars, and which reached its height between 1815 and 1842. Thus empty ships arriving twice-yearly from Canada were always available to be filled up with persons on the return journey. One ship, the *Albion*, carried timber to, and emigrants from, Aberdeen during twenty-four consecutive years, 1829–53. Vessels did not leave empty for the US in this 'automatic' fashion, and emigration to the new republic was therefore commensurately more expensive. This did not, of course, prevent it. Five families in Banchory-Devenick ruined by the floods of 1829 were sent £10 the following year by an American who may have been a relative. James Thompson, a baker's apprentice from Aboyne, became a farmer in Ontario after a period spent working in California and Chicago. Four other members of his family joined him in 1856.

Another factor we should not ignore, especially in the 1840s, was eviction of tenants for religious reasons. At a time when landlords 'could still deprive a tenant of his home and living without explanation', this was apparently a common practice, especially when the tenants in question were Free Church and the landlord Church of Scotland.[7]

Between 1840 and 1844, emigrants from Peterculter went exclusively to Australia; by 1852–80, Australasia was preferred by Scots over Canada and the USA in three years out of four. One fairly prominent Deesider to take this route was Alexander Reid, wood merchant from Midmar, in 1854; the previous year, a group of Aberdeenshire families hatched a scheme to buy their own ship, and sell it upon reaching Australia. Birse and Kintore reported no emigration between 1840 and 1844 but significant emigration in an unspecified prior period. Also in the 1840s, the people of Midmar were described as too poor and ignorant to be able to emigrate, though they might want to, given more money and more information!

This pattern, or rather lack of a pattern, would change dramatically in the half-century between Canadian Confederation and the outbreak of the First World War. Canada waged a not-always-scrupulous but entirely successful campaign to corner the market in emigrants from the North-east of Scotland, and from Aberdeenshire in particular. Farming in Canada was promoted as a cure-all at repeated public lectures to audiences of several hundred, many but not all of whom had any experience of agriculture. On Deeside in particular, these lectures – or less formal but equally vigorous promotion – took place at

Tarland (1888, 1911 and 1914), Kincardine O'Neil (1893), Aboyne (1908), Banchory (1908 and 1909), and Ballater (1908 and 1911), as well as several times at the Braemar Games. The majority of nineteenth-century British emigrants went to the USA, and many North-east Scots to the West Indies, Australia and Ceylon up to 1880. After that date, however, 'the history of emigration from the North-East region [of Scotland] became virtually the history of emigration to the Dominion of Canada alone'.[8]

The emigrants themselves – if they were agriculturists rather than fisherfolk – were largely happy with their new lot: smallholding at home was 'onerous and often unrewarding' by this time, not least because of the immense difficulties in finding any suitable housing for the newly married.[9] However, the Scottish press and churches wondered aloud what the net effect on the mother country would be. And well they might: 1.15 million Scots left the country between 1880 and 1913. Some individual Aberdeenshire villages sent out more people than the whole of Inverness-shire. Aberdeenshire lost 1 per cent of its population to Canada in 1907, and another 1 per cent between 1910 and 1913, this time including seven members of the excellent county constabulary.[10] According to legend, only the Aberdeenshire-born would be hired by the police department of Vancouver, British Columbia, in the 1920s. One such officer was Robert Gordon MacBeath, who survived the battle of Cambrai – where he won the Victoria Cross, Britain's highest award for bravery – only to be shot and killed, aged twenty-three, by a suspected drunk driver.

Oddly, Deeside was largely spared the colonies' campaigning. From the north banks of the Don to the sea, and west as far as Inverness, the agricultural population was bombarded with pro-Canadian and pro-emigration propaganda; but south of the Don, only Alford and perhaps Tarland can be said to have shared equally in the phenomenon. Queensland, Australia – Canada's closest competitor for North-east Scots' bodies and savings – likewise sent a settler-recruiting agent to Aberdeenshire in 1881. Yet, even though he was coming up from Angus, the agent's itinerary did not include any place south of Kintore, on the Don. One gets the impression that a very particular type of farmer was sought and that Deeside, unlike the rest of Aberdeenshire (and indeed, the rest of Kincardineshire), was not thought likely to provide him, either by the Canadians or the Australians. In the event, the Deesiders who did emigrate between 1880 and the Great War – in contrast to their north-of-Don neighbours – seem to have been either quite well-to-do or very marginal. One gentleman was serving in the British Columbia legislature before the turn of the century. Two 'prominent' Deeside farmers left in 1910, one of them buying nearly 1,000 acres in Alberta. A blacksmith from Banchory-Devenick was able to pay more than C$8,000 – surely his life's savings? – for a 640-acre farm in Saskatchewan in 1904; fortunately for him, it more than doubled in value in three years.[11] At the other end of the spectrum, two Echt farm labourers were only able to scrape together £1 each toward their passage to Ontario in 1912 – and they were swindled out of it by an agent. A family of seven, also from Echt, took a year after arriving to acquire a parcel of just forty acres on Lord Aberdeen's ranch in British Columbia. And at least three illegitimate orphan boys from Aboyne, aged twelve to fourteen, were packed off to Canada, as part of a programme organised by the Orphan Homes of Scotland at Bridge of Weir.[12] (In Prince Edward Island, such orphans – adopted as farm labourers – were known as 'home boys', as distinct from local, usually Francophone boy farmworkers of the same age.) Deeside was also commemorated in the name of British Columbia's Midmar Ranch, which was settled by Lumphanan people about 1904.

In the twentieth century as in the seventeenth, the numbers of people killed

Members of the Cairngorm Club, possibly including author A.I. McConnochie, in 1899.

in wars had significant demographic effects. In the First World War, 7th (Deeside Highland) Volunteer Battalion, Gordon Highlanders, lost 708 men killed, a number approaching its entire peacetime strength. In all, 29,000 or 58 per cent of the Gordons who enlisted were killed or wounded. The Cairngorm Club alone lost nine members, seven of them officers of the Gordons. In the Second World War, the regiment fielded a 7th (Mar and Mearns) and a 9th (Donside) battalion, the former serving at El Alamein and in Normandy and the latter, converted to a tank regiment, in Burma. There was also a significant loss of female Deesiders to Canada, occasioned specifically by the war. The Canadian Forestry Corps (*Forgotten heroes*, pp. 142–150) stationed some 1,400 men all along the river between Banchory-Ternan and Inverey; when they paraded together on Charleston Green in Aboyne, they effectively doubled the town's population. Everywhere on Deeside they mixed very freely with the locals at pubs and dances, and when they brawled in the streets, it was almost always among themselves. Though the soldier-lumberjacks hailed mostly from Quebec, there was no significant language barrier, with fewer than one man in ten speaking French only. An incredible one in four of the CFC men who were single on enlistment took Scottish wives, and only a handful of these couples remained in Scotland when the war ended.

Fortunately, Deeside was spared German bombing, with the exception of

Wreck of Imperial German Navy Zeppelin L20, the only German aircraft to have bombed rural Deeside.

Shown here in Canadian colours, the Fairey Battle was one of the RAF's least successful designs, and was destroyed in vast numbers during the Battle of France. The one that crashed by Braeloine Bridge, Glen Tanar in 1940 had experienced non-combat-related engine failure.

a single flare, dropped harmlessly on the slopes of Sgór Dubh by the Imperial Navy Zeppelin *L20* on the night of 2 May 1916. Apparently having lost its way, the Zeppelin turned around and dropped its bombs on three locations on North Donside before heading out to sea again. The next day near Stavanger its luck ran out. Crash landing in the sea within yards of shore, three of its crew died and the other sixteen were interned by the Norwegians. Early in the Second World War, a British light bomber – a three-seat Fairey Battle – crashed in Glen Tanar. The crew had first attempted to land on the estate's no-longer-extant nine-hole golf course, but noticed in time that the fairways were covered with anti-glider traps. They came to rest instead in a beech tree by Braeloine Bridge. 'The sight of an aeroplane blocking our route home from school was . . . never to be forgotten', a resident remembers.[13] The plane lost a wing, and the tree was killed, but amazingly, both the pilot and the tail-gunner were unharmed – as were the five-man crew of another British bomber that was struck by lightning, crashed and exploded near Marywell of Birse later in the war.

The MacRobert Building and MacRobert Memorial Garden are well-known sights in Old Aberdeen, the latter commemorating the loss of Rachel Workman MacRobert's three sons, one in a flying accident immediately before the Second World War, and the other two whilst flying in the war. A lesser-known memorial to them was built at Tarland, taking the form of a 300-seat village hall. With these boys' lives ended the baronetcy of Cawnpore and Cromar, created just twenty years earlier for their father, who having been born poor in Stoneywood became a fabulously wealthy industrialist in British India. The family home was at Douneside near Tarland, but the MacRoberts also acquired the nearby Alastrean House (originally called House of Cromar), with 9,000 acres, in the interwar years. More than 6,000 acres are still owned by the MacRobert Trust, a diverse charity which among other things makes Douneside available to officers of the armed forces as an inexpensive but luxurious guest house from Easter to mid-October each year. Alastrean House became a nursing home in 2005, but its links to the RAF have been maintained.

Deeside is notable for the persistence, over time and in space, of its most eminent families, particularly the Farquharsons, Gordons, Burnetts and Irvines; but some families have been utterly removed. The great strongmen of the area in the early thirteenth century were the Durwards, relatives (and rivals) of the old Celtic mormaers of Mar. As with 'Stuart', Durward was not a true surname so much as a reflection of the family's status or function as hereditary door-wards to the Kings of Scots; their original surname was De Lundin (as that of the royal Stuarts had been FitzAlan). The 'door' in question was Deeside itself, through which marauding Norsemen and Highlanders alike would need to pass to attack the south-eastern heartlands of the kingdom. The Durwards' main sphere of influence on Deeside extended from Coull in the west to Skene in the east, and south from Alford to Invercannie. Thomas Durward built the first bridge across the Dee about which anything is known: a wooden structure of *c.*1220 at Kincardine O'Neil. About fifteen years later, his son Alan built the Hospital of Kincardine O'Neil, directly adjoining the church, which remains Deeside's largest and most impressive ecclesiastical ruin (discussed further in *The Church as landlord and neighbour*, pp. 121–123). Alan Durward's star was still on the rise: he claimed the earldom of Atholl from *c.*1233–37, and was *de facto* ruler of Scotland for several years during the minority of King Alexander III. But his bids for both the earldom of Mar and the Scottish Crown were unsuccessful; he fled to England in 1258 and vanishes from history a decade later. The Durwards' principal seat was at Coull, the Province of Mar's most impressive castle, second only to the earl of Mar's own residence at Kildrummy ('broken but majestic specimen . . . of the English baronial style in its best developed shape'[14]). Coull was garrisoned against Bruce by pro-Comyn forces

Kildrummy Castle before the collapse of the Snow Tower.

led by a sergeant of the sheriff of Aberdeen; it was sacked in 1308 and never rebuilt. North of the Tay, only Banff Castle survived Bruce's onslaught that year. Both Coull and Kildrummy were, however, built of stone where earlier castles were largely of wood, and as such they set the tone for those castles of Mar that still remain, including the original tower of Drum.

Of the same era as the Durwards were the Bissets of Aboyne and Glen Muick. Normans planted in the area as recently as the reign of William the Lion (1165–1214); they fell from favour in the 1240s, and in 1251 the head of the house, Walter Bisset, was exiled to the Isle of Arran, then belonging to Norway. Several decades earlier, Walter had established the Knights Templar in Aboyne (they had been in Maryculter since 1174). After the Bissets' departure, Aboyne was held by Frasers and Keiths before passing to the Gordons, who are still in possession, in 1441. Glen Muick likewise passed through the same series of owners and most of it eventually was purchased by the Crown, whose property it remains. It is not known whether Aboyne and Glen Muick's Bissets were related to the Baldred Bisset who argued the case for Scottish Independence to Pope Boniface VIII in 1301. It is certain, however, that they helped to spawn one of Northern Ireland's most powerful families, the MacDonnell earls of Antrim, when Margery Bisset of the Seven Glens of Antrim (and of the exiled Deeside Bissets) married Ian *mór* Maconnill of Dunyveg, chief of Clan Donald South, in or about 1400.

Despite their herculean multi-generational effort to reclaim the earldom of Mar, a struggle which lasted from 1435 to 1635, the Erskine family did not enjoy their victory for long. The role of the 22nd earl as leader of the 1715 Jacobite Rebellion led to the confiscation of his lands and titles. The Erskines to whom he was directly related have owned no land on Deeside since 1739.

Other lost families of Upper Deeside include the Forbeses of Strathgirnock, the Mackenzies of Dalmore (later named Mar Lodge), the Stewarts of Auchendryne, and the Lamonts of Inverey. The Dalmore Mackenzies were never particularly popular in the region, and eventually were ruined in a legal dispute with the Farquharsons of Auchendryne over a flood-control project.

> The Duffs bought the estate, and the [Dalmore] family removed in the first place to Lary on Gairnside, where they rented the surrounding country from Lord Aboyne, and sub-let it to a great number of small farmers or crofters. They tormented the life out of these, and at the same time spent the remains of their money; and at length departed to some other country to the great joy of the men of Glengairn.[15]

So wicked were these Mackenzies, the same author goes on to state, that after the '45 one of them tried to sell out 'Balmoral the Brave' – the Black Colonel's youngest son and fire-breathing Jacobite in his own right – whom Mackenzie discovered living behind a false wall in a barn at Auchlossan. Even the British Army found Mackenzie's behaviour so despicable on this occasion that they intentionally allowed Balmoral to escape.

Clan Farquharson is much reduced, in the sense that the lands of the Farquharson lairds of Balmoral, Tullochcoy, Monaltrie, Inverey and Auchendryne all eventually fell to their principal chiefs, the Farquharsons of Invercauld. The Invercaulds' ostentatious non-Jacobitism (though only after 1715) was eventually expressed in the 168-room monster mansion of Invercauld. This entombs the tasteful old house, where the 1715 Rebellion was plotted, within a style one might call Scottish baronial via Newport, Rhode Island, in the 'Gilded Age'. Non-participation in the '45 (in contrast to the '15) also helps serve to explain the continued local prominence of the Gordon earls of Aboyne; though it is frequently said that the nineteen-year-old 4th earl *wished* to participate, and that rather than encouraging this, his friends 'wisely conveyed him to Paris under colour of completing his education'.[16]

On Lower Deeside, the Cumins of Culter House are now extinct in Scotland – in part because of the bizarre life and career of the second-to-last laird, Alexander Cumin. After working briefly as a lawyer in Edinburgh, Cumin

A NEW HUMOROUS SONG,

ON THE

CHEROKEE CHIEFS.

Infcribed to the LADIES of GREAT BRITAIN.

By H. HOWARD.

To the Tune of, *Cæfar and Pompey were both of them Horned.*

I.

WHAT a Piece of Work's here, and a d—d Botheration !
Of Three famous Chiefs from the *Cherokee* Nation ;
Who the Duce wou'd ha' thought, that a People polite, Sir,
Wou'd ha' ftir'd out o' Doors to ha' feen fuch a Sight, Sir ?
Are M——rs fo rare in the *Britifh* Dominions,
That we thus fhou'd run crazy for *Canada Indians*.
Are M——rs fo rare, &c.

II.

How eager the Folks at *Vauxhall*, or elfewhere, Sir,
With high Expectation and Rapture repair, Sir ;
Tho' not one of them all can produce the leaft Reafon,
Save that M——rs of all Sorts are always in Seafon.
If fo, let the Chiefs here awhile have their Station,
And fend for the whole of the *Cherokee* Nation.
If fo, let the Chiefs, &c.

III.

The Ladies, dear Creatures, fo fqueamifh and dainty,
Surround the great *Canada* Warriors in plenty ;
Wives, Widows and *Matrons*, and pert little *Miffes*,
Are preffing and fqueezing for *Cherokee* Kiffes.
Each grave looking Prude, and each fmart looking Belle, Sir,
Declaring, no *Englifhman* e'er kifs'd fo well, Sir.
Each grave looking Prude, &c.

IV.

That *Cherokee* Lips are much fofter and fweeter,
Their Touch more refin'd, and their Kiffes repleter;
The fair ones agree——nay, I mean not to flatter,
For who like the Ladies can judge of the Matter ?
Ye Nymphs then, who like 'm, indulge your odd Paffion,
Be fw——d by the Chiefs of the *Cherokee* Nation.
Ye Nymphs then, &c.

V.

Ye Females of *Britain*, fo wanton and witty,
Who love even Monkies, and fwear they are pretty ;
The *Cherokee Indians*, and ftranger *Shimpanzeys*,
By Turns, pretty Creatures, have tick'd your Fancies ;
Which proves, that the Ladies fo fond are of Billing,
They'd kifs even M——rs, were M——rs as willing.
Which proves, that, &c.

VI.

No more then thefe Chiefs, with their fcalping Knives dread, Sir,
Shall ftrip down the Skin from the *Englifhman's* Head, Sir ;
Let the Cafe be revers'd, and the Ladies prevail, Sir,
And inftead of the Head, fkin the *Cherokee* T—l, Sir.
Ye bold Female *Scalpers*, courageous and hearty,
Collect all your Force for a *grand Scalping Party*.
Ye bold Female Scalpers, &c.

VII.

For Weapons, ye Fair, you've no need to petition,
No Weapons you'll want for this odd Expedition ;
A foft Female Hand, the beft Weapon I wean is,
To ftrip down the Bark of a *Cherokee P—s*.
Courageous advance then, each fair *Englifh* Tartar,
Scalp the *Chiefs* of the *Scalpers*, and give them no Quarter.
Courageous advance then, &c.

Sold by the AUTHOR, oppofite the Union Coffee-Houfe, in the Strand, near Temple-Bar, and by all the Print and Pamphlet-fellers;
[PRICE SIX-PENCE.]

N. B. In a few Days will be publifhed the *Political Bagpiper.* A new Song, with a Head-piece.

The good relations between Britain and the Cherokee long outlived Alexander Cumin of Culter. A later Cherokee embassy to London provided the inspiration for this frankly pornographic contemporary song, price sixpence, written by H. Howard in 1762.

in consequence of a dream of his wife . . . undertook a voyage to America, with the object of visiting the Cherokee Indians. On 3rd April, 1730, in a general meeting of chiefs [at Nequassee, modern-day Franklin, North Carolina] he was crowned their commander and chief ruler. Returning to England with six Indian chiefs, he presented them to George the Second at Windsor, when he laid his crown at his Majesty's feet, the chiefs at the same time also doing homage. He propounded certain schemes for the establishment of banks in America and other places, connecting them with the restoration of the

Culter House was built c.1630–50 and retained much of its original form when this drawing was made two centuries later. It was severely damaged by fire in 1910. Since then, with large side-wings added, it served as a boarding house for St Margaret's School for Girls, and as a nursing home, before returning to private ownership.

Jews, for which, he argued, the appointed time had arrived, he himself being alluded to in several passages of scripture as their deliverer. Finding that the Government officials would not listen to his wild projects, he proposed, on his own account, to open a subscription for Five hundred thousand pounds for the purpose of establishing these banks, and settling three hundred thousand Jewish families among the Cherokee mountains. All his schemes proving futile, he turned his attention to the study of alchemy, and began to try experiments on the transmutation of metals.[17]

Alexander Cumin died penniless, and his son, though he had attained the rank of captain in the army, also went insane; and with the son's death ended the line of Cumins of Culter: 'unquestionably, a small remain of the Cummins, Earles of Buchan, who were once the powerfullest ever Scotland saw'.[18] Ironically, the elder Cumin of Culter's strange diplomatic efforts are now thought to have helped keep the Cherokee Nation on the British side during the American Revolutionary War.

LOST AND FOUND: 'INDIAN PETER'

Perhaps the most astonishing lost Deesider of the eighteenth century was Peter Williamson, born in the early 1730s at Hirnley in Aboyne parish. Aged between eight and eleven, he was sent to Aberdeen to live with an aunt, and while playing on the street near the harbour, was tricked by two men into going on board a ship called the *Planter*, and kept in captivity with other children. Among the men involved in the kidnapping scheme were John Burnet and Alexander McDonald, merchants, and procurator-fiscal Alexander Cushnie.

About one month later, when the hold became full of children (nearly seventy of them), it sailed for Virginia. After a passage lasting eleven weeks, it ran aground a mile off Cape May, New Jersey. The crew initially left the children to die, and returned for them only after it became clear the ship would not sink. Taken to Philadelphia, Williamson was sold for £16 for a term of seven years to a fellow 'North-Briton' from Perth, Hugh Wilson, who had himself reached America in the same way, through kidnapping. This master proved kind, and in spite of or because of this, Williamson stayed with him until he died nine years later. Wilson being childless, Williamson inherited his clothes, £200 Pennsylvanian (about £120 sterling), and a horse. After working for seven more years as a free man, he married and acquired 200 acres of land, '30 of which were well cleared and fit for immediate Use', on the frontier. In 1754, on a day when his wife was not at home, Williamson was captured by a band of French-allied Native Americans and his farm and animals burned. For reasons not now entirely clear, he was allowed by them to live as a kind of slave, carrying their baggage and being the butt of rough practical jokes, amounting in some cases to actual torture, for several months, though his treatment got better as time passed. While with these warriors he witnessed the massacres of five settler families and four unattached Irish men. At last he effected his escape by hiding in a hollow tree. He reached his father-in-law's house in Chester County in early 1755, only to find that his wife had died a short time earlier.

Not wishing to repeat his experience of frontier farming, Williamson joined Capt. Shirley's company of colonial infantry in Boston. Though he had deplored 'scalping' and the burning down of enemy civilians' houses by the Indians when he was their prisoner, he now set his men to it, and practised it himself, 'with the utmost Chearfulness and Activity'. Joining the garrison of Oswego, he was sent by mistake in an expedition against Niagara: being one of about thirty-five men detailed to guard the boats containing officers' baggage – which alone were sent to confront the enemy, the main attack having been called off due to lack of food. His own boat was wrecked in river rapids and he nearly froze to death. Williamson's sense of the mismanagement and waste of the entire campaign is palpable, and he clearly considered the French failure to capture Oswego, on this occasion, a sort of miracle. Promoted to lieutenant after the death of Capt. Shirley, he was involved in a church siege in Pennsylvania which only five of his twenty-seven men survived. In a subsequent action he was shot in the left hand, losing the use of two fingers. He was captured in August 1756, when Oswego at last fell to the French with the loss (by Williamson's reckoning) of 116 artillery pieces, 23,000 pounds of gunpowder, 2,800 barrels of food, several small warships, and 18,000 livres in cash. After a month's imprisonment in Quebec, he and 500 others were sent to Plymouth. Deemed unfit because of the wound in his hand (despite having fought in several battles since receiving it), he was discharged and given six shillings: a pitifully small sum even in those days when contemplating a journey from one end of Britain to the other.[19]

Williamson, who had learned to read and write while in Hugh Wilson's 'employment', wrote a book about his experiences which sold 1,000 copies in three weeks and continued to sell well for decades. At first, however, a positive outcome was far from assured:

Arriving in Aberdeen in 1758, he was prosecuted for libel by merchants for his account of the kidnapping in which he exposed the role played by local magistrates and businessmen. He was at once convicted, fined, and banished from the city, while his tract . . . was ordered to be burnt by the public hangman at the market cross. In response Williamson brought legal action against the magistrates in Aberdeen, and in 1762 was awarded £100 damages by the court of session. He was also successful in a second suit brought in 1765 against the parties engaged in the trade of kidnapping.[20]

These parties included William Fordyce & Co. and the Aberdeen town clerk, Walter Cochran. Perhaps unsurprisingly, Williamson left Aberdeen for good. He moved to Edinburgh, where he opened a coffee house, established a penny post office, and remarried, fathering nine children before his 'bitter' divorce in 1789. Long after returning to Britain he wore the costume of the Lenape (Delaware) tribe, and was apparently buried in this garb.

Williamson's 'tract', *French and Indian Cruelty; Exemplified In the Life And various Vicissitudes of Fortune, of Peter Williamson, A Disbanded Soldier*, was printed in nine editions in Scotland, England and Ireland by 1792, and his legal battles with Fordyce and others were also printed, forming one of the eighteenth century's characteristic 'pamphlet wars'.

THE CHURCH AS
LANDLORD AND NEIGHBOUR

The River Dee was worshipped as a goddess in the pre-Christian period, but Christianity of the Celtic type was fairly well established on Deeside by AD 600. St Ternan's monastic establishment near modern Banchory-Ternan trained, among others, St Erchard – born near Learney – who is said to have founded and run the first church at Kincardine O'Neil. It is also claimed that St Machar (of Aberdeen cathedral fame) had a church on Balnagowan Hill near modern-day Aboyne. St Colm allegedly worked in Birse, St Comgall in Durris, and St Kentigern at the mouth of the Gairn. Their work continued over the following century with the establishment of the first churches at Inchmarnoch and Formaston (both near Aboyne), Lumphanan, Midmar, Migvie, Dinnet, Coull, and Tullich, all before 733. The Formaston foundation was by St Adamnan, known locally as Skeulan, and the tying of rags to 'Skeulan's Tree' by the church there on Skeulan's Day, 23 September, was supposed to bring prosperity. Broadly speaking, the process of Christianisation completed by 900 was peaceful but slow, and spread up and down the valley from the middle: the last two churches founded in the pre-feudal period were Banchory-Devenick, nearly at the seaside, and Crathie, next to the present Balmoral Castle, high in the hills. No church buildings from this early period survive, even as ruins.

The parishes of Deeside date to a much later period, after reformist monarchs including in particular David I and his mother, Queen Margaret (canonised as St Margaret of Scotland in 1251), introduced Roman Catholic holy orders and rites. Alongside parishes came the first planned royal burghs, and feudalism *per se*, with its systematic exchange of land for military service, and the orderly descent of the Crown in the direct male line. Previously Scottish kings were, like many clan chiefs, elected from among – or asserted themselves within – a well-defined but fairly large group of brothers, cousins, uncles, and male descendants of the previous leader. This process, known as *tanistry*, was not always peaceful; but it eliminated the two great evils of modern- or continental-style kingship, inheritance of the Crown by infants and the mentally incapable. In any case, by the early 1100s, following a decade of wars between rival tanists, the introduction of formal feudalism was seen in Scotland as a progressive step. These changes were concentrated in the twelfth century, and can be said to have ended on Deeside in 1388, the last year in which serfdom is mentioned in a local charter. Deeside's oldest church buildings date from this period. All are now ruins, but interestingly, none of them was destroyed during the initial fury of the Reformation. The possible exception, known as Abbot's Walls (parish of Nigg), is believed to have been the Abbot of Arbroath's summer house and not a church as such.

The old kirk of Tullich was about the same size as that of Maryculter, and like it, a centre of Templar activity. Its ruins boast a fourteenth-century doorway and sixteen Celtic cross-slabs, though traces of a thirteenth-century defensive

The seal of the Knights Templar as used in Scotland.

The parish kirk of Crathie, with seating for 1,400 people, which stood from 1804 to 1893. Derided as 'heritors' gothic' by some, its stylistic marriage of gothic and more modern elements could have been far worse – as the current building amply proves.

wall (identified by A.I. McConnochie in 1898) are now disputed and may have been a drainage project. Another Templar-connected church, Formaston, is ruined to a point that exact dating would be difficult without archaeological investigation; it is still in use as a burial ground.

Used for burial into the nineteenth century, the grassy mounds located to the south of later churches at Skene and Migvie may hide the remains of their respective medieval churches. Douglas Simpson believed part of the ruins of St Fittick's, Nigg, to be thirteenth century; later observers have been unable to confirm or deny this. The oldest extant church in Crathie, St Manir's (not to be confused with the old parish church illustrated here), is also probably medieval, and by the standards of Deeside ruins, better preserved than most.

The pre-Reformation but not necessarily medieval church of St Triduana, Kinnellar, was obliterated by the new church, now a private residence, in 1801. The 1520s bridge chapel of St Mary at the north end of the Aberdeen Brig o' Dee was also destroyed without trace, though the bridge itself has been the subject of repeated preservationist interventions. Nothing at all can now be seen of the old parish kirks of Echt, Tough, Lumphanan, Coull, Coldstone, Logie-Mar, Strachan, or Glen Muick. How much of their medieval fabric remained, as of the dates they were destroyed, remains a matter of pure speculation. At

Right. Kintore sacrament house.

*Below. The 1632 church of St Anne, Kemnay –
dark, dank, smelly and small-windowed – was
completely rebuilt between 1844 and 1845,
thrice remodelled between 1870 and 1928, and
finally removed to a former UFC church
(heavily renovated in a modernistic style) in
December 2000. The bellcote of the original
church, shown here, was built into the north
walled garden of Kemnay House. Of St Anne's
sister church in the same parish, St Bride's, all
that remains is a rumour that the font is now
in use as a garden pot.*

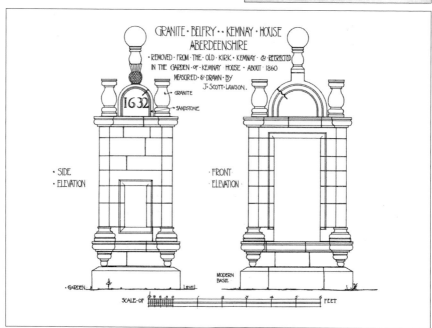

GRANITE · BELFRY · · KEMNAY · HOUSE
ABERDEENSHIRE
· REMOVED · FROM · THE · OLD · KIRK · KEMNAY · & · RE-ERECTED
IN THE GARDEN · OF · KEMNAY · HOUSE · ABOUT · 1860
MEASURED · & · DRAWN · BY
J · SCOTT · LAWSON ·

GRANITE
1632
SANDSTONE

· SIDE
· ELEVATION

· FRONT ·
· ELEVATION ·

MODERN
BASE

· GARDEN   LEVEL

SCALE · OF   FEET

Birse kirk, only a single fifteenth-century sculptured slab depicting a sword and two crosses (or a sword, a cross and an axe) made it through the 1779 rebuilding. South Donside has generally been luckier than Deeside in these matters: a sixteenth-century sacrament house was preserved within the Archibald Simpson-designed Kintore kirk of 1819; and many seventeenth-century details survived the late-Georgian reconstruction of the 1603 church of St Andrew, Alford.

Deeside's largest medieval parish church to begin with, and its most intact today, is located in Kincardine O'Neil. Practically touching the southern edge of the A93, it is still the dominant feature of the village. As part of the changeover from Celtic Christianity to Roman Catholicism in the area, the dedication to St Erchard was reassigned to St Mary; across the road from the church, the

Monymusk Priory in its 'steeple period', 1822–91.

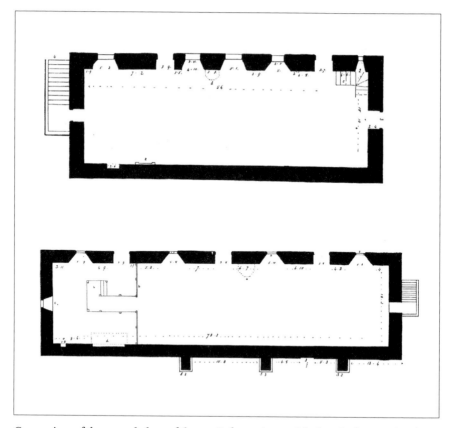

Comparison of the ground plans of the pre-Reformation parish church of Durris (1537)
against post-Reformation Dalmaik: built in the seventeenth century using earlier
materials, remodelled in 1737, and abandoned in 1836. The Aberdeen District Council's
1940s plaque on Dalmaik confuses the issue by stating the church is from 'ante 1062 A.D.'
but this refers to the site, not any identifiable stonework. The also essentially similar
ruins of St Nidan's, Midmar, date back only to 1677.

village well-head covers up the old holy well of the earlier saint. The outward-
facing side of the church's east gable seems suspiciously like an *interior* wall,
and it was this that first suggested to modern researchers that the building might
at one time have been longer. Further study revealed that it had been more than
twice the size it is now, extending eastward an additional 81 feet (or 148 feet in
all). It is now thought that the vanished eastern end was the Hospital founded
by Alan the Durward in the second quarter of the thirteenth century – and
which had been sought in vain elsewhere by antiquarians and archaeologists
for many years. The demise of this institution, more properly 'a bede-house or
asylum for the support of eight old men',[21] occurred within the period 1625–1725.

A perhaps equally elaborate, possibly medieval church at Cluny, South Donside, was demolished in or about 1789. South Donside is again lucky, however, to have the Province of Mar's most impressive church outside Aberdeen: the *c.*1180 Augustinian priory of St Mary, Monymusk. Anything but a ruin – it is still in use – Monymusk Priory did lose fourteen feet of its tower in 1822, receiving a steeple instead. The same tower was 'Anglicised' in 1891 by the addition of crenellations; the steeple was also removed at that time. A variety of new windows and doors were added between 1685 and 1822, and a late medieval window rediscovered in 1940. The priory's extensive restoration work of 1929 has been both praised, as 'sensitive' reclamation of a still authentically Romanesque building (Ian Shepherd), and condemned, for creating a structure that is 'mainly modern' (RCAHMS).

Monymusk and Kincardine O'Neil aside, tremendous continuity born of simplicity marks the churches of the region. Though it looks superficially similar to the medieval churches of Tullich and Kincardine O'Neil in its current ruinous state, the old kirk of Glen Tanar first appears in the written record after 1600

Dalmaik in 1941.

and is probably post-Reformation. Newhills's church was first built in the Restoration period (there was no parish of Newhills until 1666). There is no strong reason to suppose that the old kirk of Banchory-Devenick, which had vanished by 1961, was much older than its bell (1597) and kirkyard wall (1608). St Bride's, Cushnie, of which some pieces remain above ground, was built in 1637. The 'dangerously leaning' ruins of St Marnoch's, Leochel, appeared to the Ordnance Survey in 1968 to be 'considerably older than eighteenth century, but no definite date could be established' and no definitely pre-1700 artefacts were found. Similarly, the surveyors found that the ruined parish kirk of Glengairn, abandoned c.1800, was 'probably eighteenth century'. The remains of St Mothulach's, Tarland, are definitely from the period 1762–1870. There is no indication of the age of the Peterculter parish church that collapsed in October 1673.

As great as the influence of the Church was, its role in medieval society can be overstated. Local publications sometimes claim, for instance, that the region's many open-air markets and fairs were started by monks (hence their being named after saints); and that market crosses were used to preach from in the Middle Ages. The latter idea is disproved by the work of the great historian of medieval preaching, Gerald Owst. Sermons were only delivered on hallowed ground, which market crosses were not – being symbolic of royal, not ecclesiastical, authority. Market crosses have probably been confused with purpose-built preaching crosses (none of which survive here), located not in 'profane' market squares but mostly in churchyards. As to the naming of fairs, the use of a saint's name was a simple and straightforward way of advertising the date on which a fair took place. Because neighbouring villages were unlikely to share the same favourite saint, the practice also helped to prevent rival fairs occurring on the same day in the same locality.

The relative insignificance of Deeside's fairs by the Restoration period is suggested by their total absence from James Paterson's *Geographical Description of Scotland* (1685). Paterson named scores of fairs both north and south of the area, but not one on Deeside; his 'Dinet' is in fact Dunnet, in Caithness. This is something of a mirage, however; Tarland alone had seven annual markets as late as 1842: Breag Fair (Martinmas), Yule Fair (January), Horse Market (March), Rood-Fair (Whitsunday), 'a market for cows the week following' the previous, Luag Fair (July), and Lammas Fair (August). Its weekly market ceased as late as 1820. Banchory-Ternan had about the same number of fairs, also until the mid nineteenth century, held in February, March, June, July, August and September. Up to 600 vendors came to St Ternan's Fair each June, and 100 to 400 attended each of the others. Highland Deeside also participated:

The 'Feill Macha', or Mungo's Fair, once a considerable market, was
. . . yearly held on the longest day in summer, in that hollow, pass, or
cut of the ridge of the hill behind the farmstead of Abergairn.
Numberless ruins of houses, walls, and enclosures remain yet to show
that a considerable village must have once existed there.[22]

It was not the Reformation, but the modern style of shopkeeping (underpinned
by motorised transport) that dealt these colourful markets their death blow.

Though no break with Rome was contemplated, the Scottish Crown kept
the Scottish clergy on a pretty short leash by the end of the fifteenth century.
And, though it was not formally confiscated, a large amount of clergy-owned
Deeside land passed into secular private hands between 1528 and 1542. This
transfer included, but was not limited to, the estates of Auchlunies, Heathcot,
Westertown, Shannaburn, Blairs, Maryculter, Ashentilly, Altries, and Kingcausie. Milton of Murtle, Kirklands of Banchory, Pittenkerrie, Invery and
Brathens followed by 1557. If transfers on such a scale occurred simultaneously
in other parts of the country, it might tend to support the controversial argument
that James IV and James V between them achieved something like a Gallican
church settlement, or even a Henry VIII-style Reformation *avant la lettre*. Be
that as it may, the Catholic Church throughout northern Europe was by that
time in serious trouble.

*Blairs in the 1850s. Now, most of what can be seen there dates from 1898–1911. Closed as a
seminary in 1986, it is now a museum.*

Blairs, once again in Catholic Church hands, has been so only since 1827, when the last of the Menzies owners donated it for use as an educational establishment for priests. John Menzies came from the same Menzies of Pitfodels family who controlled politics in the city of Aberdeen for over three centuries. Pitfodels, their principal residence/fortification during those turbulent years is now forgotten, and its remains lie hidden and archaeologically unexamined somewhere beneath the lawns of the Norwood Hall Hotel. The family were also closely associated with two former properties of the Knights Hospitallers: Arnlea and Middleton of Pitfodels.

The college now housed at Blairs was previously located north of the Don at Aquhorties near Inverurie, in a building remodelled by James Byres of Tonley in 1797, and before that, secretly, at Scalan in Glenlivet since 1716. Catholicism was in effect de-criminalised via a series of laws enacted under George III between 1778 and 1791 (despite violent initial opposition in some other parts of Scotland, and London). It was made fully legal, other than for the royal family, during the prime ministership of the duke of Wellington in 1829. As part of the general hatchet-burying in this era, the last Stuart pretender, Henry IX, left the Scottish coronation ring to George III in his will; while Deesider Peter Grant, the last Jacobite veteran of Culloden, was awarded a pension of £52 per annum by George IV.

At the risk of appearing trendy, I fear I must mention that one of the great landowners on Lower Deeside in the thirteenth century had been the Knights Templar. The regional headquarters of this wealthy, powerful and numerous order was at Maryculter, and unsurprisingly, the medieval parish church of Maryculter was one of Deeside's most magnificent. Eighty-three feet long and twenty-eight wide, it had walls more than three feet thick and neatly executed gothic arches. It was, as John A. Henderson put it, 'altogether . . . unusually refined and beautiful'.[23] Abandoned in the 1780s, it quickly fell into ruin; '[t]he holy water stone, which was beautifully ornamented with Gothic figures, long stood "in Petfoedels cloess" as a poultry drinking trough, but it has since disappeared.'[24] It is now unclear whether the oldest (1618) part of the Maryculter House Hotel is built over the original vaulted basement of the thirteenth-century preceptor's lodging, or if its own basement was made using recycled thirteenth-century materials. Likewise, a remarkable black oak door, said to have been the door of the Grand Master's room, was built into the farm of Tilbouries but gone by 1892.

The Church in Maryculter was apparently a decent landlord, by the standards of the time and place, its cottars receiving up to nine acres of land in exchange for six shillings and nine days' labour per year. This was not the case in all areas, however, and when the Church wanted to eject John Crab from the lands of Murtle in 1383, the bishop of Aberdeen acted as judge, even though he was a party in the case. Trial law was in its infancy, but this was already considered questionable practice and Crab appealed to the sheriff; the bishop got what he wanted in the end.

About the chief story attaching to the Templars on Deeside, Henderson wrote that the 'small substratum of fact that may be in it is almost entirely buried under the weight of purely legendary matter'.[25] The legend holds that a Deeside-born Templar named Godfrey Wedderburn, a fierce fighter, was wounded and left for dead in a battle against the Saracens, but slowly nursed back to health in a cave by a beautiful daughter of the Saracen nobility. She gave Wedderburn a magical jewel that would protect the wearer from illness, provided he was pure at heart. They loved each other deeply, but the knight-monk did not violate his vow of chastity. One day, being alone in the cave and mostly recovered, he saw some Templars passing and went home to Deeside with them. A few years later, who should show up at Maryculter but Wedderburn's mystery woman. The Grand Master, convinced that some hanky panky had gone on, openly accused Wedderburn of breaking his vows. In the ensuing argument, the knight struck his superior in the face, knocking him down, a crime punishable by death. In lieu of execution, he was allowed to die by stabbing himself in the heart. The Saracen lady, seeing Wedderburn's death, explained to the assembled Templars that the fact that he, and she, could both wear the charm proved that they had been chaste. She dared the Grand Master to put it on. He did so, and was immediately incinerated by a vertical streak of blue lightning. The resulting 'Thunder Hole' was, at one time, eighty yards across and ten deep, but was 'gradually being filled up'[26] through the late Victorian period. It is now uniformly described as a 'depression' rather than a hole, and geologists debate whether or not it is a 'kettle hole' caused by glacial calving during the last Ice Age; it still rates as a local tourist attraction. The phantoms of Wedderburn, the lady, and their amulet (together or separately) are said to stalk the area around the Maryculter House Hotel and the Corbie Linn. When the Templars were suppressed in the early fourteenth century, their Lower Deeside property mostly passed to the Knights Hospitallers.

North of the river, an important Church property was Bieldside. This was retained by the Church through the reign of James V and until 1557, when William Gordon, the last pre-Reformation Catholic bishop of Aberdeen, gave it to Gilbert Knollis and his wife Margaret Petcarne. A previous Knollis family member, who died in 1508, had been prior of the Knights Hospitallers, which perhaps serves to explain the bishop's bequest. The Knollises' descendants sold

Above and opposite. Presbyterian communion tokens. These metal 'admission tickets' were given only to those who answered the minister's doctrinal questions to his satisfaction, and could be withheld for other reasons, so that the 'unworthy' could be denied the sacrament. Most were made of pure lead or a lead/tin alloy. Though often thought unique to Scotland, they were adopted by Calvinist churches in France by 1560, Amsterdam by 1586 and Geneva in 1605. About half of these examples are from Deeside.

the land in 1635 to the Irvines of Finnersie (a cadet branch of the Catholic Irvines of Drum) who five years later built the first house on the property about which anything is known. It was this house that the marquess of Montrose used as his military headquarters in late 1645. In spite of, or perhaps because of, this historical connection, Bieldside was razed to the ground and rebuilt in a different style in 1811 by its new owner, a senior Excise officer. By 1840, the existence of the original house seems to have been forgotten: John Stirling reporting only that the present owner had built it. Later authors concurred.

Of course, Protestantism became established after 1560, and the Protestant Church was land-poor relative to its predecessor, but this is not to suggest that the Established Kirk ceased to play a profound economic as well as spiritual role. So many traditional activities were now prohibited that the aggregate value of fines could be quite large. One man was fined £5 in 1574 for opening his door to Christmas carollers; actors and playgoers were routinely fined £1 apiece (as well as being forced to sit on the 'seat of repentance'); so was anyone who skipped church. Gossiping in sermon time cost at least one man £10. And that was for first offences by people of average means; repeat offenders and the well-to-do were charged more. And three infractions of the same type could, in theory, result in the forfeiture of all the offender's goods to the state. That being said, the Kirk was never all-powerful, and at least one Deeside man freely admitted that he had only gone to church to hear the news of the week – a function that he considered fully superseded by local delivery of the *Aberdeen Journal*. Kirk membership also acted as a sort of primitive insurance policy, whereby the loss of a house to fire, or a cow to illness, could be made good almost immediately, through a special collection of money in one or more parishes.

The Collection *by Aberdeen-born John Phillip RA (1817–67), showing money being gathered in a long wooden-handled scoop by a kirk official wearing a tartan plaid.*

LOST HEROES OF
THE SCIENTIFIC REVOLUTION

Alexander Garden was born in 1730, son of the minister of Birse. At the age of sixteen, having previously attended Marischal College in Aberdeen, Garden passed the Royal Navy's surgeon's mate exams and was posted successively to the twenty-four-gun HMS *Tryton*, the sixty-gun *Eagle*, and the sloop *Porcupine*. He left the navy in 1750 with the aim of completing his medical studies, but lacking sufficient funds he emigrated to the British colony of South Carolina in 1752. There he was befriended by William Bull (1710–91), sometimes called the first American-born medical doctor, who introduced him to the work of the eighteenth century's greatest naturalist, Carl Linnaeus (1707–78). Over the course of the 1750s, Garden married a local woman, Elizabeth, in the Anglican church of St Philip, Charleston, and began corresponding directly with Linnaeus, who lived at Uppsala in Sweden, sending him specimens of North American animals 'preserved in rum'.[27] Linnaeus duly published Garden's findings in the twelfth edition of his *Systema Naturae*, and the Gardenia flower was named for Garden in 1760. Garden met and liked Benjamin Franklin and by 1765 was calling himself an American and pro-'independency'. Yet, when war

Carl Linnaeus in Lapland costume.

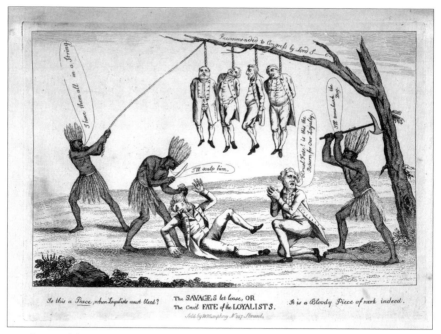

Cruel Fate of the Loyalists, *a political cartoon likening the Anglo-American rebels to 'barbarous' Native Americans.*

came ten years later, Garden and Bull were both notably loyal to the Crown. The plantation of Otranto in Berkeley County, South Carolina, which Garden had purchased in 1771, was confiscated and never returned. Formally banished by the revolutionary republic, Garden himself arrived in London in 1782 and was back in Birse in 1789. Despite being a 'principal figure' in the spread of Linnaeus's ideas, a member of the Royal Society and a major naturalist in his own right, Alexander Garden is '[s]eldom heard of today', and no likeness of him is known to exist.[28]

One particularly fecund Deeside family was practically a scientific revolution and enlightenment in its own right. The Gregories were originally MacGregors, but like so many others before and after them, moved to Deeside under a 'modified' name. Their exceptional genius must have come in from the mother's side, however, for it is noticeable only after Janet Anderson (a niece or sister of Prof. Alexander Anderson of the University of Paris) married the Rev. John Gregorie, minister of Drumoak, in 1621. Within three generations of their marriage, John and Janet's descendants included sixteen British university professors, mostly in the sciences, mathematics and medicine, as well as the Strachan-born Enlightenment philosopher Thomas Reid, author of the *Essays on the Active Powers of Man* (1788). Like the great majority of British scientists of this period, the Gregories' family history was one of active, even virulent royalism. the Rev. John Gregorie was fined 1,000 merks and imprisoned for 'outstanding against the Covenant'. He escaped, found a boat, and was heading out to sea when re-apprehended. One of his sons, James Gregory (so spelled), is credited with the invention of the first useful reflecting telescope. Another son, the meteorologist David Gregorie, was prosecuted for witchcraft for being able to predict the weather using a barometer. He beat the charge and lived to the age of 95, fathering twenty-nine children of whom twenty lived to adulthood. Like his father, this David Gregorie was a committed Episcopalian and anti-Covenanter. He was in turn the father of David Gregory (so spelled), who became professor of mathematics at Edinburgh, succeeding his uncle at the age of 24. There, Gregory taught the works of Isaac Newton – years before they were taught in Newton's own university, Cambridge. Forced out of this post at the Williamite Revolution due to the strength of his Episcopalian views, he decamped to Anglican Oxford in 1691. His much younger brother, Charles, did not seek work in Scotland at all, going directly to Oxford in 1699. Given that Episcopalians from Aberdeenshire alone were instrumental in founding the College of William and Mary in Virginia and the University of Pennsylvania,

This rather dowdy photograph of Florence Nightingale (left) sits oddly alongside her image in the popular press (right).

one wonders whether the 'brain drain' of Episcopalians out of Scotland was as important to the development of the economy, society and intellectual life of the Atlantic world as the later Scottish Enlightenment. Many members of the family remained, however; and during the 1715 rising, it is claimed that Prof. James Gregory (II) was visited in his rooms at King's College, Aberdeen by his even more famous cousin, the cattle rustler and arms dealer Rob Roy MacGregor, who was then on a recruiting drive for the Jacobite army.

Florence Nightingale, fearless campaigner for improved diet, sanitation and medical care, stayed at Birkhall from 19 September to 12 October 1856, immediately after returning, understandably worn out, from the battlefields of the Crimean War. While there, she had saved many lives and laid the foundation of British professional nursing, and had also contracted what she believed to be typhus, but which was probably brucellosis. In daily conversations with Queen Victoria, she sketched her ideas for the reform of the Army Medical Service. By the time the gouty and 'very pompous' Lord Panmure, Secretary of State for War, showed up to attend the sovereign on 5 October, the queen had been convinced. Despite having previously told the Cabinet that Nightingale 'knew nothing of the British soldier', Panmure was also impressed, and Nightingale was given a royal commission to investigate and reform army medical provision. Thus it can be said that in the gardens of Birkhall the modern Royal Army Medical Corps was born. Panmure knew the area well, having in his youth kept low company and 'led the riots' at a certain Invercannie inn.[29] Despite relapses in 1860 and 1861, Nightingale survived her Crimean fever and lived to the age of 90.

LOST REPUTATION:
THE CONSUMMATE 'STEAM PUNK'

George L.O. Davidson was the fourth son of the laird of the Inchmarlo estate, located just west of Banchory-Ternan (illustrated p. 204). An early believer in the potential of heavier-than-air flight, he once criticised proponents of the lighter-than-air variety as 'balloonatics'.[30] He set up an aviation workshop at Inchmarlo Cottage in 1897, and the following year addressed the Aeronautical Society, predicting the use of aerial bombing in war, and that it would one day be possible to fly from London to Manchester in less than three hours. He later upgraded this to a prediction of passenger flights between Chicago and New York, lasting three hours, at $10 per head.

In 1898 – five years before the Wright brothers' experiment succeeded at

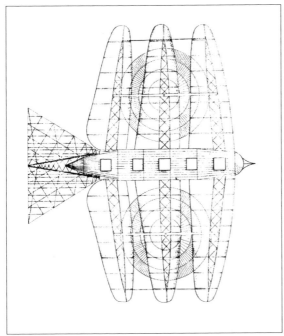

Three versions of the hundred-seat VTOL commercial airliner first proposed by George Davidson in 1907. The model dates from 1911.

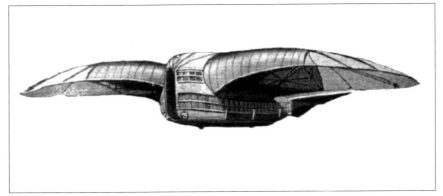

Kitty Hawk, North Carolina – Davidson built a 'flapping wing' aircraft at Inchmarlo, the maiden flight of which attracted large crowds to Burnett Park. Less a flight than a hop, the unnamed craft did not survive, though fortunately the pilot did. Obviously this incident has not been credited as the first heavier-than-air powered flight, but it at least spurred development by showing Davidson and his rival aeronauts that the 'flapping wing' principle was a dead end. (Undaunted, the inventor continued to refer to each new machine's cockpit as the 'beak'.) Davidson himself became sufficiently interesting to the investing public that he almost immediately attracted capital of £20,000 to his Air-Car Construction Syndicate. The Air-Car in question was a wholly new design, a high-wing monoplane with a fully enclosed cabin seating twenty passengers: prefiguring the famous Ford Tri-Motor airliner by nearly thirty years, and several years before the feasibility of heavier-than-air flight (for even one person) was assured.

A.V. Roe, later the founder of the Avro company which built the iconic Lancaster bomber (and ultimately became British Aerospace), was also interested in other possibilities to fixed-wing flight at this early period. It was probably Roe's January 1906 letter to *The Times* defending the possibility of flapping-wing aircraft that first brought him to Davidson's attention. Davidson hired the twenty-something Roe as a draughtsman, the latter's first job in the aviation sector, three months later. They moved to the USA and set about designing a primitive but very large helicopter, 'weighing 6,000 pounds, with a lifting power of 10,000 pounds per foot per second', which was expected to 'specially interest all those who hope for practical results of cargo carrying from an aeroplane'.[31] It was sixty feet long by sixty-seven feet wide and thirteen feet high, and powered by two fifty-horsepower Stanley steam engines. This did fly

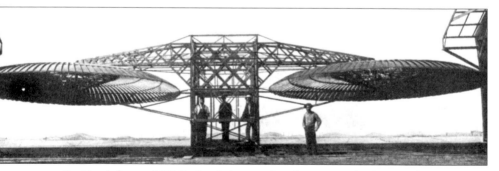

Davidson's first and A.V. Roe's only 'gyropter', under construction in Montclair, Colorado, in 1907. It was awarded British patent no. 1,960 the following year and floated at $1 million. Half the shares went to Armstrong, Whitworth & Company, who many years later created the Whitley bomber – and an experimental VTOL 'flying wing' aircraft.

properly, if briefly. 'The experiments', concluded the London correspondent for *Scientific American*, 'served to demonstrate that a machine could be constructed capable of lifting itself bodily from the ground in a vertical direction.'[32] However, this machine was also wrecked on its maiden flight, when one of the boilers exploded.

At this point, Davidson and Roe seem to have parted ways, but both were back in London by 1908. Davidson now rebuilt the machine, with Californian sequoia wood largely replacing the original's steel tubing. Nevertheless, this one weighed up to 14,000 pounds. *Flight* thought it might succeed, however, and commented that its launch was eagerly awaited by

> a very large number of people dissatisfied with the prospects of the modern aeroplane, who consider that a flying machine is no flying machine at all unless it possesses the capacity of direct vertical ascent.[33]

Davidson was not the only local 'steam punk'. Despite an income of less than £2 per week, Craigievar postman Andrew Lawson designed and built this primitive but functional motor car, in collaboration with a Lumphanan blacksmith, between 1895 and 1897. The car outlived its inventor by many years, and in 1971 became the oldest coal-fired vehicle ever to complete the London to Brighton rally.

Despite these respectable journals' clear assessment that only Davidson had achieved flight on 'the helicopter principle' as of November 1910, credit for it is now, absurdly, assigned to the French Breguet brothers and to the year 1907.

The sequoia version of the gyropter ran into financial difficulties which proved insurmountable, in or about March 1911, and so was never completed. *Aeroplane Monthly* dismissed Davidson as a kook in 1973. Almost utterly forgotten, he lacks an entry in the *Dictionary of National Biography*, or even a mention within A.V. Roe's entry, which in turn fails to mention Roe's first job in aviation, or his time in Colorado. For the early encouragement of Roe alone, George Davidson should be remembered as one of British aviation's pivotal figures, and one whose revolutionary ideas were vindicated by the later emergence of both helicopters and commercial air passenger services.

LOST OCCUPATIONS (I):
THE FLOATERS

In the centuries after 1618, when John Taylor held that the lumber of Upper Deeside would be forever beyond the reach of mankind, sawmilling became serious business in the region – and in some places, the only business. 'The saw-miller and the household of Allanaquoich . . . are now the only inhabitants of a glen once so populous as to require a corn-mill for its own use', A.I. McConn-ochie reported in 1898.[34] This timber mill had by then been operating for 203 years; measured by longevity alone, it must rate as one of Deeside's most successful businesses. Likewise, in 1732, Peter Coutts was hired to build a sawmill on the Tanar near the Haughs of Allachy which apparently still existed there in 1820.

During the Napoleonic Wars, there was a marked transition: from mills 'erected wherever there was sufficient water power, near the part of the forest where the felling was going on', as had been the case since the seventeenth century, to larger, more powerful mills 'within a more convenient distance from the banks of the river where the rafts were made'.[35] In the early 1840s, one circular sawmill was reported in Logie-Coldstone and three, of unspecified type, in Drumoak. One of the latter was under construction 'on the outlet from the Loch of Drum' (see *Lost lochs*, pp. 80–87).[36] Not all such enterprises were long-lived. A sawmill on the Culter Burn, fed mostly by firs from Braemar, was established by Duff of Culter in the mid eighteenth century, but lasted for just ten years. The Rosowsky & Blumstein sawmill at Banchory-Ternan, though considered successful, operated only during the 1940s. Kirkton Mill, a dual purpose meal- and sawmill powered by two waterwheels, was in use into the 1960s in Durris but is now a ruin. Exceptionally, two 1850s mills in Finzean – one for sawmilling proper and one for making wood products including buckets and flooring – were restored to operability in the 1980s.

Milling on the spot, however, was a modification rather than a replacement of the former injurious practice of floating whole logs down the Dee. In the days when 'entire trees . . . were heaped up in great piles' right on the riverbank, and hurled in whole (often with loss of life) at the spring thaw, the floaters would

> take to their boats and follow them down the river. Conceive it in full flood – and the Dee in this condition is a wild cataract throughout the whole stretch between Abergeldie and Aboyne – hurrying along on its foaming billows its burden of logs, mingled with masses of floe ice, impinging now on one bank and again on another, sometimes getting stranded, but often wheeling around and taking to the stream again, and you will have some idea of the excitement and danger incurred by the men in the boats, four or five in each, whose business it is to refloat the stranded logs, often on rocks where they cannot land, but must strike the log with a long clip as they sweep past, and haul it after them . . . This is an exceedingly dangerous operation, and one that requires great care and expertness, for, should the log remain fixed, the clip will either be lost or the boat swamped.[37]

The writer of this account never fully recovered from the work, which on each occasion left him soaked to the skin and having to walk home a distance of up to eight miles. Boys as young as ten regularly participated in this, and other forestry operations of every sort.

The damage that log-jams could do to even the strongest bridges was graphically described, in the context of the collapse of the Thomas Telford bridge at Ballater:

> It stood till the great flood of August, 1829, and had it not been that a great quantity of trees and brushwood and other *debris* brought down by the flood blocked up the arches the bridge would have stood; but the arches became so jammed with wood and other things, including cattle, sheep, pigs, and poultry, that the water was dammed up to such a height that nothing could withstand it . . . and with a crash like thunder the material burst into pieces, and was hurled into the river.[38]

It was

> exciting, and often perilous, work to guide the floating trees down the
> stream, especially when, meeting some obstruction, they jammed in
> huge 'cairns', as the floaters called a big jam. In venturing on this cairn
> and freeing the trees with crowbars, a too daring floater occasionally
> lost his life when the whole mass would break loose beneath his feet,
> and crush him as he sank mid the tumbling trees in the seething
> waters.[39]

With the advent of the mills, logs first had their bark removed and then were
quarter-sawn. The tree-length quarters were then further subdivided into
thinner pieces called 'scantlings'. It was these scantlings that were loaded onto
carts and taken down to the Dee – at the estimated rate of *ten hours a mile*.
Moreover, '[t]he men leading the horses were always in danger of being crushed
when the weight . . . propelled the carts too precipitously down slopes'.[40] At the
river, the scantlings were bound together as rafts, the ropes passing through
rings fitted to iron spikes, not unlike old-fashioned mountaineering pitons. These
were known as 'dogs'. Each raft carried three men, who used long poles (and at
times, ropes) to steer their gigantic, unwieldy 'craft', the goal generally being to
keep it as near the centre of the river as possible.

The 'squeel' or 'eldritch cry' of the Inchbare kelpie, like that of the Irish
banshee, was thought to predict floaters' approaching doom – 'And mony an
awesome shape he took / And raired until the forests shook'. In a world filled

'Log dog' used in the building of rafts.

with constant danger and death, the floaters cultivated a devil-may-care attitude. Earning a guinea a man for each completed journey to Aberdeen, they were among the best customers for smuggled whisky (see *The lost policemen*, pp. 153–156), and were renowned for their loud singing, which carried well from their rafts into the ears of people living all along the river. On some estates, when making rafts, they expected to be served a dram of whisky three times per shift. Floating was not always profitable, of course. Sandy Davidson, a beloved local character of the early nineteenth century, spent many years as a smuggler and poacher, but never lost money on a venture – or spent a night in gaol – until he tried his hand as a floating-timber merchant. 'Notwithstanding all the precautions used . . . the wonder is that so few fatal accidents occurred, considering the foolhardy risks run by these reckless men.'[41]

Opinions differ widely as to when the era of the floaters began and ended. Like so many other things, 'floating' is said to have passed away when, and because, the railway came. The floating-bank at Crathes, for example, did close due to railway competition about 1860. Indeed, as early as 1845, the directors of the railway clearly *intended* to kill off 'floating and logging wood down the river' and to gather 100 per cent of its business (then estimated at £2,000 a year) to themselves.[42] But as with droving – *Lost occupations (II)*, pp. 166–172 – this happened slowly and the linkage is not inescapable. Even in 1870, the amount of wood carried on the railway was one-fourth of the 14,000 tonnes per annum that had been projected. The frequently inaccurate and self-contradictory *Book of Banchory* seems to suggest 'floating' was a phenomenon mostly or entirely of the period 1845–53; but certainly it had begun by 1841, when three men giving their occupation as wood-floaters were noted as residing in Banchory-Ternan; and floaters' well-attested association with whisky smugglers, in the latter's heyday, may by itself push this back before 1830 or earlier. In the neighbouring region of Strathspey, at any rate, these men were termed 'Floaters' as far back as the winter of 1812–13, by Elizabeth Grant of Rothiemurchus who observed their activities and customs minutely. At that time, felling and bark removal were done before the first snows of winter; lopping off of branches and removal to the waterside, immediately winter had ended; and actual floating after that, at 'the proper time', probably as dictated by commerce. As to when the phenomenon came to an end, historian Susan Wilkinson claims only that it 'did not cease until some years after 1884' – which is to say, more than thirty years after the railway was put in.[43] John Mackintosh stated that the trade slowed only with the extension of the railway beyond Aboyne (i.e. after 1866) and that it ended 'about twenty years ago' (i.e. in 1875).[44] However, his evidence for this was that there were no longer any log rafts *in Aberdeen harbour*, which by itself would not prove they were no longer floated to some intermediate point on the river, for example, Silverbank Sawmills or the Culter Paper Mills.

The last wagons of the last train ever to run on the Deeside line carried timber bound for Inverurie and Derby.

FORGOTTEN HEROES: THE CANADIAN FORESTRY CORPS ON DEESIDE IN WORLD WAR TWO

The era of the floaters was gone, but lumberjacking on Deeside was soon to take on new blood. In 1913, Britain was dependent on other countries for 93 per cent of its timber, importing close to 12 million tonnes a year from Scandinavia, North America and Imperial Russia. Even with cuts in consumption, this was unsustainable during the German U-boat campaign – quite apart from the fact that the twentieth-century style of warfare required five trees' worth of wood per fighting man, used for everything from temporary buildings and packing cases to ingredients for explosives. So, in February 1916, Britain called upon thousands of experienced Canadian lumberjacks to join the imperial war effort.

They were assigned initially to two non-combatant battalions. The first was raised and shipped to England within two months; by the last day of the war, there were 31,000 men in the Canadian Forestry Corps, headquartered in Windsor Great Park but with companies serving from Scotland to the Pyrenees. Some underage boys who joined Canadian fighting units under false pretences were also transferred to these non-combatant units if their subterfuge was found out (or strongly suspected). This first generation of 'Sawdust Fusiliers' provided all necessary wood not just for the British Empire forces, but also for those of Belgium, France and the USA, and built about a hundred airfields for the Royal Flying Corps. They also met the majority of British civilian requirements, and timber imports to the UK fell by five-sixths – representing freed-up cargo space 'sufficient to carry food supplies for some 15 million people'.[45] The CFC was disbanded at the end of the war, and around the same time the UK Forestry Commission was set up, in great measure to repair wartime deforestation caused by the CFC's home-front logging activities.

Despite the Forestry Commission's best efforts, however, the British 'timber gap' was even worse in 1939 than it had been in 1913, with 96 per cent of wood being imported. Most of this now came from the USSR, the Baltic states and Finland, and thus was even more severely disrupted by the Nazi conquest of the Baltic region than the Great War supply had been by U-boat attacks. Every economy was tried: newspaper page-lengths were drastically cut, and the British

Above and overleaf. Rarely seen recruitment posters for the two units that would merge to become the Canadian Forestry Corps.

W.R. SMYTH, LT. COL.
OFFICER COMMANDING

HEADQUARTERS
43 BANK ST. OTTAWA

BUSHMEN AND SAWMILL HANDS
WANTED
JOIN THE *Now Recruiting Yale Hotel Room*
238TH CANADIAN FORESTRY
BATTALION *Calgary*

Army was even issued with square tent-poles and square broom-handles to save milling time and costs. Native birch replaced Canadian birch in bobbins; ash replaced US hickory in tool handles; matches were made from local aspen. This was not nearly enough, of course, and in the crisis summer after the Dunkirk evacuation, students, teachers, and school pupils as young as fourteen were paid 15s a week to fell Scottish trees. However, their unprofessional efforts were often more trouble than they were worth. The Women's Timber Corps or 'Lumber Jills', many of whom trained at Park House on Deeside, fared much better, but their numbers were always small.

Accordingly, the British government again called for loggers from throughout the Empire to aid the war effort. The call was answered by Australians, New Zealanders, Newfoundlanders, and British Hondurans, but especially by Canadians. As in the Great War, Canada would pay, clothe and transport its men, and the UK would provide their housing, food and medical care. With fewer trees available to cut, fewer men were sent, and the second generation CFC never numbered more than 7,000. However, they were now

A CFC arm-wrestling match. 'Most bush-cooks in those days were accustomed to going on periodic drunks and it was hard to cure them of that habit by just putting them in uniform', one soldier recalled. Poaching game was commonplace; one member of CFC's Deeside District murdered another; and there was a huge inter-company brawl in Kincardine O'Neil on the night of 31 May 1941. But relations between the Canadians and local people remained almost absurdly cordial.

provided with uniforms and a military rank structure. The enlisted men's ranks were apparently determined by the hierarchy of peacetime industry – mill foremen became sergeants, millwrights were corporals, and so forth – while at least some of the officers were academic experts on forest ecology. After a five-day week of nine-hour days of logging operations (uniforms optional), they would drill as infantry on Saturdays. This was purely tactical drill, as keep-fit exercises were deemed totally unnecessary. A two-man team using axes could fell a tree in seventy seconds and their efficiency was highly lauded locally and by the UK government.

Steam and diesel engines were both used to power two types of mills: the rotary mills brought over from Canada and the local 'Scotch' mills. The Canadians held the latter to be unsafe and extensively modified them to rectify this. The Mar Lodge camp also had a water-powered generator of the troops' own devising. Floating was not used at all, due largely to objections from owners of the valuable salmon-fishings, and so virtually all transport of logs and timber was by lorry, or a combination of lorry and rail. When roads were washed out, as occurred most notably in November 1941, the corps rebuilt them itself.

All Canadian provinces contributed men to the CFC, but in the event, the men sent to CFC District 2 (Deeside and Southesk) were recruited from the eastern provinces of Quebec, New Brunswick, and Nova Scotia. They were deployed as follows:

Camp	Dates there	Thereafter	Company No./origin
Ballogie No. 1	Apr. 1941–Sep. 1943	Canada	III, Quebec City
Ballogie No. 2	Mar. 1941–Oct. 1943	Canada	II, Westmount, Quebec
Glen Tanar	Apr. 1941–Nov. 1944	elsewhere in Scotland	IV, Newcastle, NB
Southesk	Jul. 1941–Nov. 1943	various	XIII, Halifax, NS
Blackhall	Jul. 1941–Apr. 1944	Normandy	XVI, Quebec City
Abergeldie	Jan. 1942–Jun. 1944	Normandy	XXII, n/a
Blackhall	Jun. 1944–May 1945	Canada	XXII, n/a
Abergeldie	Mar. 1942–Jun. 1944	Normandy	XXIV, n/a
Mar Lodge	Mar. 1942–Jun. 1944	Normandy	XXV, Fredericton, NB

For the most part, the camps were completed and ready to receive men by October 1940, and III Company were pleased to find a hot dinner waiting for them at Ballogie on day one. Being used to a continuous snow season and longer winter days, they hated Deeside's rapid alternation of snow with rain, and its winter daylight hours comparable to those of the Yukon. The District was commanded by a lieutenant-colonel based first at Ballogie, then at Guisachan House, Aboyne (April–August 1941), and thereafter at Struan Lodge, Aboyne. Each company consisted of 200 men led by a major. The Huntly Arms Hotel in Aboyne was a favoured haunt of the officers.

In addition to military applications, CFC-cut timber was provided to civilian timber merchants in Ballater, Banchory-Ternan and Peterculter as well as elsewhere in Scotland; scrap wood was also sneaked to poverty-stricken local families to use as firewood. Particular CFC companies were also associated with particular railway stations: II Company with Aboyne Station, III with

CFC men at work in 1943. They were issued with lorries, International TD9 tracked tractors, and a bewildering array of other motorised vehicles, in contrast to local forestry practice up to 1939 which was almost exclusively horse-powered. However, a great deal of the work was done by hand. This photo also punctures the myth that the corps only wore their uniforms on Saturdays. Special events laid on for the Deeside CFC included a concert at Dunecht House; Ballater sheepdog trials; performances by the Feughside Dance Band; and a dance at Crathie attended (though not organised) by Princess Elizabeth and Princess Margaret. Hockey was attempted on Aboyne Loch, but the ice was too thin.

Torphins, IV with Dinnet and XVI with Banchory. At Torphins alone, CFC timber was loaded at an average rate of eight wagons per day. Indeed, there was far too much wood for the railway to cope with; the CFC's historian simply calling it 'inadequate' despite extensive station improvements for just these purposes (especially at Aboyne), and a sextupling of the peacetime number of freight trains running.[46] Minor disappointment cut both ways, as Scottish landlords criticised the unsightly stump-fields which normal Canadian working practices produced, though this was soon rectified.

Blackhall camp.

The Canadian Bridge, Mar Forest.

The best-documented camp was Blackhall, whose sawmill and mill-pond were located about 1,000 feet south-east of Blackhall Castle. The men's quarters, kitchens, workshops and so forth were built in a roughly circular scatter, 700 feet in diameter, beginning a further 500 feet to the south-east. The layout may have been partially in response to a fear of air raids. (These never occurred, but one of the Ballogie camps was nearly destroyed by the crash and explosion of a friendly aircraft that had been struck by lightning.) Blackhall Camp's kitchen and mess hall had vertical siding made from 'slabs' – the semi-round pieces of waste timber produced when a log was squared – and two-pane-wide by four-pane-high windows with external shutters.

Locals recollect that the Glen Tanar camp was called 'Burnroot'. Canadian sources do not confirm or deny this, but the name is still used by the James Jones & Sons sawmill on the B976 between Birsemore and Dinnet Bridge. Canadian soldiers frequented the now dilapidated Norwegian-style timber house on the lawn above Glen Tanar stableyard, which housed a billiard room and library. This building long predated the CFC, however, and was opened by Lord Glentanar as a recreation hall for his estate workers on New Year's Eve 1926. The Glen Tanar-based CFC men cut trees as far away as Blair Atholl in Perthshire.

The 'Canadian Bridge' in Mar Forest was built out of logs and to facilitate CFC logging operations there. Not necessarily meant to outlast the war, it was demolished in or about 1961, after the Cairngorm floods of August 1956 undermined its foundations, making it unsuitable for motor vehicles. Of the camps themselves, 'only partly overgrown sawdust piles remain'.[47] The enduring tangible legacy of the CFC on Deeside is, rather, the minor roads. Early on, an officer referred to road maintenance as the 'main problem to contend with in this operation'.[48] Some roads were built anew by the corps and others improved from dirt to gravel. Some, previously gravel-surfaced, were hard-surfaced by local government, specifically to aid Canadian logging operations. Though 'the private woodlands of the region were . . . almost completely denuded of merchantable timber',[49] it was due chiefly to the monumental efforts of the CFC that Scotland outperformed Nazi Germany in sawn lumber production by twenty to one. It is all the more surprising, therefore, that the corps was the subject of just a handful of obscure publications. 'Even the existence of such a unit is unknown to most Canadians.'[50]

As one might expect, in a district where trees vastly outnumber human beings and seem to be more numerous by the hour, felling and sawmilling remain important sources of employment. The Silverbank mills in Banchory-Ternan have changed hands, but have remained in continuous operation since 1854.

THE LOST POLICEMEN

As I write this, a plan has been mooted to merge Grampian Police, the force which since 1975 has been responsible for the whole of the North-eastern Scottish counties plus the city of Aberdeen, into a new single force covering the whole of Scotland.[51] This would be the logical, if not necessarily desirable, culmination of a series of mergers whereby various, ever-larger police forces have been created and destroyed during the 180 years since modern British policing was first conceived by Home Secretary (later Prime Minister) Sir Robert Peel.

In the earlier Middle Ages, before the founding of the first burghs, Deeside's agricultural settlements would elect, from among their husbandmen, a 'birleyman' to keep the peace in the hamlet. From the later Middle Ages until the early 1840s, most policing in Aberdeenshire and Kincardineshire was handled by the parish constables or 'Toun Guards', or by gentry/clergy vigilantism, or in extreme cases by military action. This last had never been popular with the soldiers, who were

> pretty much between the devil and the deep sea; for if they failed in protecting those entrusted to their charge, they were liable to be tried by court-martial for neglect of duty; while, if in the performance of that duty life was lost, they were tried by the civil power for murder[.][52]

Though often acquitted, it was a stressful, wasteful, and unpredictable process. The Aberdeenshire Constabulary instituted in 1840 was initially made up of an odd combination of the old parish constables and retired officers of the British and Indian armies, with the parish men being weeded out as time went by. They must have targeted door-to-door beggars from the beginning, since they were praised for dramatically reducing this activity as early as May 1842.

Meanwhile, however, a new sort of Toun Guards proliferated under Victorian legislation, especially the Police of Towns (Scotland) Act of 1850, which allowed any self-defined 'populous place' to transform itself into a 'Police Burgh' by majority vote of the inhabitants, whether or not it was already a burgh of some other type. Prior to the 1660s, at least, the right to hold a market was virtually inseparable from burghal status; such right could only be bestowed by the Crown – even when the burgh itself was owned by a noble family or the Church – so the idea of burghs creating *themselves*, and for reasons unrelated to commerce, was a double novelty. Under this new system, Kintore (a royal burgh since the reign of James IV), Banchory-Ternan (a burgh of barony since 1488) and Ballater (never previously a burgh) became Police Burghs in 1873, 1885, and 1891, respectively. Even while this was going on, however, town police forces were systematically being absorbed into the county forces, a process completed by 1893. Finzean storyteller Chrissie Gibson recalls gently tormenting a lone constable at Banchory-Ternan in the 1930s, but he would have been a Kincard-ineshire officer, not a burgh one, by that date. At that time, a veteran recalled, 'there were so few motor vehicles about that policemen on patrol walked along the centre of the street'.[53]

The Aberdeenshire force consisted of six divisions, each led by an inspector, of about twelve men apiece. One of these was headquartered at Aboyne. In the early 1890s, constables' uniform jackets were essentially similar to the five-button 'serge frock' issued to army rifle troops from 1881, and their headgear, the army officers' 'pill box' forage cap; the cap badge appears essentially similar to the regimental badge of the Black Watch. The shire force never entirely lost its original military flavour, though to describe it as paramilitary would be quite incorrect: one officer in the 1890s was severely reprimanded for carrying a pistol which went off accidentally on his patrol, even though it did not cause harm. Always frowned upon, the carrying of firearms was thereafter categorically forbidden. The high quality of ordinary recruits to this force is suggested by the fact that the two Aberdeenshire constables who died in the Second World War were both serving as pilot officers, one in the RAF and the other in the Royal Navy's Fleet Air Arm.

Not long after the war, Aberdeenshire Constabulary was merged with the

Canberra jet bomber crash site on Carn an t'Sagart Mor, November 1956.

Kincardineshire Constabulary, July 1888. Both photos on this page appear by kind permission of the Grampian Police Force Museum.

*Aberdeenshire PC9, Alexander
Auchinachie, in 1891, courtesy
of John C. Green at
scottishpoliceinsignia.com.*

rather sleepier and not particularly martial Kincardineshire force – which only handled one murder investigation, not on Deeside, in the 107 years of its existence. The merger also included the county forces of Moray and Nairn (previously merged with each other), Elgin, and Banff, and all towns within these counties with the exception of Aberdeen. This new six-county force was called the Scottish North East Counties Constabulary, or SNECC. All of Donside was placed in the new force's Inverurie sub-division, and much of Deeside in its own eponymous sub-division, headquartered at Aboyne and including the stations at Braemar, Ballater, Tarland and Banchory-Ternan. Greater Deeside, including the Aberdeen sub-division's stations at Echt, Culter, Cults and Skene, had a high proportion (one-third) of the forty-three stations operated by SNECC as a whole. There must have been a very significant reduction in the overall number of stations operating: Aberdeenshire Constabulary alone had had forty. Nor, in some respects, was the new super-force as kind to its members as the old ones had been: 'an officer's furniture, on transfer, was often conveyed in a lorry normally used for transporting fish.'[54]

Long before the advent of county police forces, Deeside and other parts of Britain were policed, for certain purposes, by the Excise men. Their chief concern was tax evasion, especially the distribution and sale of illicitly brewed

PCs Doug Low (right) and Frank Laurie at the Braemar Games, 1955, with a radio set borrowed from the RAF. (Grampian Police Force Museum)

alcohol. As we have seen (*Lost people*, pp. 101–102), this became an economic necessity for the rural poor after Culloden; around Coirevrach, for instance, many farms 'were only viable . . . because barley could be grown for illicit whisky distillation'.[55] Mostly, though not exclusively, distilled in the upper reaches of the valley and surrounding glens, Deeside moonshine had to be physically transported to the regional trading centre, Aberdeen. Unable effectively to police large, remote, and heavily forested areas such as Glen Tanar (which alone had fourteen stills in 1800) and Strathgirnock (which had eleven), the officers concentrated their efforts on the city's western suburban fringe,

SNECC's mountain rescue team practising in the middle 1960s. (Grampian Police Force Museum)

through which the shipments would have to pass. The smugglers were aware of this problem and employed people from all along their routes as scouts. Generally speaking, the gathering of barley was done by the men, 'often going to the low country for it, and fetching it home in currachs and crook saddles on the backs of a whole herd of Highland ponies'.[56] The actual distilling was performed by the women, and the transportation of the finished product to market by the men. However, one old woman in Drumoak in the 1890s remembered smuggling whisky in 'kegs or bladders' and once, fearing that the visiting Excise men would have their suspicions roused by a large quantity of malt lying about the place, disguised a bag of malt as someone's baby.[57] What she did with the actual baby has gone unrecorded. Other smugglers in the vicinity of Banchory-Ternan once disguised themselves as a funeral procession, inside whose coffin was no body, only whisky.

Neverthless, the Excise men were often successful, and their total extirpation of illicit distilling in Birse was credited with a 19 per cent decline in the population of that parish between 1827 and 1841. More than once, sanguinary battles were fought between these opposing forces, the Excise men being armed with a variety of firearms and not afraid to use them, even against smugglers armed only with clubs. One of the most widely recollected fights occurred about 1800 in Peterculter between the Excise men led by the notorious Malcolm Gillespie, and a Braemar gang with ten cart-loads of whisky. The use of carts was fairly rare, however, the usual method of transport being pony-trains, with each animal tied to the next in single file and carrying several twenty-pint kegs called ankers. It was reckoned in 1821 that the illicit distillers of the Highlands were producing 2 million gallons annually, and I would be very surprised if the Braes of Mar were producing less than a fifth of that. Even Invercauld, the mighty chief of Clan Farquharson, was reputed to have his own still.

In the seaside parish of Nigg, the Excise men had additional help – though in practice, often more of a rivalry – with the 'preventivemen'. These were the officers of the Customs service, then a separate department, its curious bureaucracy including collectors, comptrollers, landwaiters (sometimes just called 'waiters') and tidesmen. Originally, Excise dealt with items moving *out* of the country, and Customs with items moving *into* it, but these distinctions became increasingly blurry. Both groups were empowered to call on the assistance of the army, though the direct involvement of Customs officials in violent conflicts with smugglers diminished sharply after the establishment of the Coast Guard in 1821. The penalties for smuggling increased over the course of the eighteenth century: in the case of non-violent activity, from imprisonment initially, to transportation, to execution. Smugglers who harmed officers would be executed and their bodies suspended in chains. The apprehension of a smuggler by a civilian carried an automatic reward of £20.

While the received wisdom about the illicit whisky trade is that it died out rapidly upon the introduction of licensing in 1824, this was not the case on Deeside. Braemar Castle's 58-man British Army garrison remained on anti-whisky duty for another seven years – and were also, apparently, some of the smugglers' best customers. Certainly, the Excise men were still on patrol during the adulthood of Mary Robertson (the 'sweet Mary' of Lord Byron's *Hours of Idleness*): she married one who was stationed at Crathie. The builders of the present Balmoral Castle were great customers in the 1850s, and in Castletown of Braemar, the trade is thought to have continued even up to and beyond Robert Louis Stevenson's period of residence there, in 1881 (*Lost literature*, pp. 66–67). A Catholic priest remarked that the people of Gairnside in the 1890s were 'proheebited fae naething'.[58] Perhaps the illicit stills continue to this day.

Other experiments in policing the region also took place: most notably, the independent Highland companies or Old Black Watch, formed (with extensive Deeside participation) in the 1730s. According to J.G. Michie, the first six of the thirteen companies raised were staffed overwhelmingly by gentlemen's sons, even in the lower ranks. After being combined into a regiment, initially designated the 43rd Foot, the companies retained a sense that they were for internal security duties only. Led by a Deesider named Farquhar Shaw, four companies mutinied on hearing they were to be sent to Flanders; Shaw and two other ringleaders were executed. The eleventh, twelfth and thirteenth companies, raised on Deeside in early 1745 and commanded by James Farquharson the younger of Invercauld, were also intended as police; but like their fellows, they would soon enough be involved in major warfare. Whether or not one agrees with Michie that locally recruited members of the Black Watch fought the Jacobites 'with a bad grace' and served as a humanitarian check on the baser impulses of the rest of the victorious Hanoverian army in 1746,[59] it is hard to escape the fact that formal policing – of any kind – was probably superior to James VI's Machiavellian policy of pitting every clan against another, in hopes that continuous low-intensity warfare would make them, collectively, harmless.

LOST CORPSES

Another category of 'lost crime' entirely predating the police *per se* was body snatching. The use of genuine human corpses for anatomy dissections was illegal until 1832, but as Aberdeen was a world centre of medical education, bodies still needed to be found. Because of its proximity to the city, the 'resurrectionists' particularly targeted the kirkyard of Banchory-Devenick. In response, the parish built a watch-house, where the deceased's loved ones could wait, with firearms at the ready, taking this duty in turns until the body was presumed so decayed as to be of no use for medical purposes. Another fine example of such a watch-house can be seen at the old Kirkton of Leys site in Banchory-Ternan. The parishes of Peterculter, Maryculter, Drumoak, Durris, Skene, Lumphanan and Coull also witnessed this grisly cat-and-mouse game. Nor did legalisation immediately end it: huge cast-iron coffin-shaped coffin covers called 'mort safes' were bought by several Deeside parishes, and used until the mid 1850s.

The most spectacular case of body snatching in the history of Scotland, however, occurred at Dunecht House, half a century after most tomb-raiding had come to an end. On 3 December 1881, Alexander, 25th earl of Crawford and father of the astronomer Lord Lindsay (*The lost observatory*, pp. 224–226) had been dead for ten days short of a year. It was then discovered that his remains had been stolen from the family vault. This caused an immediate press sensation. The earl had died in Italy, and after being embalmed, he

> was placed within three coffins, the inner one being of soft Italian wood, the middle one of lead, and the outer one of polished oak, elaborately carved and mounted with fittings of chased silver. These three coffins were deposited within a huge walnut shell, on the top of which was a cross carved in high relief, the weight of the whole amounting to nearly half a ton.[60]

The crypt, itself of granite, was sealed with four immense slabs of Caithness granite, each six feet by four feet and weighing nearly 1,700 pounds, mortared into place. These were then thickly covered with earth and planted over with shrubs, grass and flowers. Some months later, the Dunecht estate's solicitor received a bizarre note:

> Sir,
> The remains of the late Earl of Crawford are not beneath the chaple [sic] at Dunecht as you believe, but were removed hence last spring, and the smell of decayed flowers ascending from the vault since that time will, on investigation, be found to proceed from another cause than flowers.
> [signed] Nabob.

Peterculter's mortcloth had not been used within living memory when this photo was taken in 1937.

Though this was ignored initially, it was later found to be correct: one of the giant Caithness slabs had been shifted, and all three coffins opened. Despite their rich ornament, nothing was stolen but the earl himself.

In the absence of any genuine clues – bloodhound searches failed – the press and public opinion soon blamed Italians, who among other things were said to have taken the body back to Italy for reasons unknown. 'Nabob' now wrote again, assuring the estate that, while he had not been party to the crime himself, he knew the body had not left Aberdeenshire. A reward of £600 was offered. Two men from the Echt area were arrested in February 1882, but released after a week. Five months passed before 'Nabob' himself was identified as Charles Soutar, a former Dunecht rat-catcher, who had been dismissed by the deceased earl for poaching. Soutar claimed that, whilst poaching, he had observed the body being stolen by two men with commonplace Aberdeenshire accents and two gentlemen wearing masks. His information led to the recovery of the body – in a shallow grave 500 yards from the house, near a gravel pit – but he was tried as a perpetrator of the crime nonetheless. After a complex trial, Soutar was sentenced to five years' penal servitude, but his accomplices (who in the court's opinion must have numbered at least two) were never identified. The motive was also thought by the court to have been ransom, though this too was never firmly established, no ransom demand having been issued.

THE LOST REGIMENTS

The 'Royal Regiment of Scotland' was devised in 2004 by a now-fallen government who seemed bent on pursuing Americanisation at any cost, irrespective of utility or even ideology. To a greater degree than with the police services, an unimaginative and ill-informed approach driven by generic notions of efficiency and rationality has run headlong into regimental tribalism and specific local ties, the twin guarantors of military morale. Renaming the Black Watch '3 Scots' is not likely to win you many friends among the Black Watch or anyone else: Annabelle Ewing MP called Geoff Hoon MP a 'backstabbing coward' for his role in the fiasco; Michael Ancram MP called it 'appalling' and 'a dark day'; and even the Labour Party's then First Minister said he was 'disappointed'. The public, meanwhile, muttered darkly about the destruction of Scotland's heritage – and in some cases, took to the streets in protest. Perhaps even more importantly, the 'super-regiment' scheme simply hasn't worked: at a parade of '4 Scots' in Old Aberdeen in late spring 2010, they were not only spoken of as 'the Gordons' by the assembled crowd, but in some degree uniformed as such. Their band's page on the social networking website Bebo takes obvious pride in the unit's continued use of 'forbidden' badges.[61]

Amalgamations have always gone on, of course, and the Gordons' identity was, with the Queen's Own Highlanders, submerged into 'The Highlanders' in 1994 by a previous government's 'Options for Change' policy. The Queen's Own, in turn, was a 1961 amalgamation of the Seaforths and Camerons, while the Argyll and Sutherland Highlanders (now 5 Scots) was two regiments until 1881. In all, therefore, sixteen different Scottish regiments that were founded between 1633 and 1900 are 'represented' – some much better than others – in the new Royal Regiment. Others are not represented at all.

For Deeside, these wholly lost units include several infantry regiments raised between 1756 and 1759, including the 77th (Montgomerie's Highlanders), raised in the first instance mostly on Deeside and counting Charles Farquharson the younger of Balmoral among the officers; the 81st (Aberdeenshire Highlanders), largely from Glen Muick and Aboyne; and the 87th (Keith's Highlanders), raised partly in Braemar. The fate of many of these men was emigration to North America under the military's land-grant schemes (*Lost people*, pp. 101–106). For some, this would also include re-enlistment in American loyalist corps such as the Royal Highland Emigrants, who successfully defended the city of Quebec against an American revolutionary siege in the bitterly cold winter of 1775–76. The Emigrants later merged with Montgomerie's and rejoined the British line as the 84th Foot. The 81st mutinied in 1783 on being asked to serve in Asia, and were disbanded, though no one was punished.

None of this is meant to suggest that Lowland regiments did not also recruit in the area in the later eighteenth century. One such, apparently, was the 1st Foot, which had existed since 1633. Neither the recruiters nor those they recruited were any more popular in Lowland Mar than they were in England; and several Deeside contributors to the *Old Statistical Account* highlighted that their parishioners did not often join up, or that they did not make very good soldiers when they did. One lazy and sport-obsessed Peterculter schoolmaster, who had to flee the area after getting a servant girl pregnant, became the unlikely subject of an extremely popular ballad that was reprinted and sold *ad nauseam* in the eighteenth century:

> When he committed all these tricks
> For which he well deserv'd his licks
> With red-coats he did intermix,
> When he foresaw
> The punishment the kirk inflicts

On fouks that fa'.
Then to his thrift he bid adieu
When with his tail he stap'd his mou',
He chang'd his coat to red and blue
And, like a sot,
Did the poor clerk convert into
A *Royal Scot.*

According to some, the initial raising of the Gordon Highlanders at the time of the French Revolution met with a lukewarm response on Upper Deeside and in the Highlands generally, even though the recruiting officers were generally believed to have a power of compulsory enlistment. (They had not been given such a power, but 'certainly availed themselves of the general belief' that they had.[62]) The unit's initial unpopularity was short-lived, however, and it performed brilliantly in the Peninsular War and the Waterloo campaign. To join the eighteenth-century British Army, even in a Scottish regiment, was in a sense to convert to Anglicanism for the duration, as there were no non-Anglican chaplains allowed before 1827; in practice, it took a further generation for either Presbyterian or Catholic chaplains actually to appear, and the first Jewish chaplain was appointed in 1892. The Canadian troops stationed on Deeside in World War Two, who were mostly Catholics, celebrated Christmas enthusiastically, and their famously good relationship with the local Protestants no doubt helped to tip the balance further in favour of the holiday locally.

The 1st Kincardine Royal Volunteers, formed during the Napoleonic Wars, included some companies recruited exclusively in Banchory-Ternan and Durris. This unit still existed in 1876, when, on being transferred to Banchory, it added companies recruited in Echt, Tarland, Torphins, Aboyne and Ballater. As none of these latter places were in Kincardineshire, it was renamed the Deeside Highland Battalion. Four years later it was redesignated rifle volunteers, and four years after that, the (Deeside Highland) Volunteer Battalion, Gordon Highlanders. Known as the Terriers, they saw action in the Boer War and both world wars, as previously mentioned.

It is worth noting briefly the relationship among the Clearances, army recruitment on Deeside, and the modern (i.e. mid-Victorian) army as these were perceived by J.G. Michie, one of the region's earliest and best historians.

Some have contended that, however cruel or oppressive these clear-ances . . . it was for the advantage of the poor people that they should be removed, as in the altered condition of the nation they could have remained only to be a burden on the country [e.g. the earl of Selkirk, quoted p. 102], or to be once every three or four years subjected to the pinch of famine; and that, as a nursery for soldiers, the time had passed away when Britain required such a nursery, the surplus population of our large towns being more than sufficient to supply our military wants. On the other hand, it has been maintained that the cruelty was great at the time, and the injury to the nation irreparable, inasmuch as the loss of so many hands has been the cause of the great rise in the wages of agricultural labourers and farm servants, and consequently, in order to sustain this rise, a corresponding increase in the price of provisions has taken place, so that the labouring classes are now, not better, but worse off than they were in the olden time. As to the army, being composed as it is now of the scum of our city back slums, it has

Hands across time: a cartoon celebrating the Gordon Highlanders' 111th anniversary. In fact, the Duke of Gordon first raised his regiment in 1794; but the date is correct, in that Gordon's regiment later merged with the 75th Foot (Abercromby's Highlanders), which on the basis of seniority then became the 1st Battalion, Gordon Highlanders.

degenerated so far that no respectable person is to be found in its ranks; and that it will be an evil day for this country when it has to rely for its safety on its army as at present constituted.[63]

THE LOST LEAGUE

Cricket has been played in Banchory-Ternan since at least 1858, and the town had no fewer than four clubs by 1873. Kincardine O'Neil's club was thriving by 1878; Echt, Culter, Aboyne and Torphins all joined in the fun by 1891. Banchory CC also faced a heavily aristocratic Aboyne Castle XI in 1882. At first, the leading Banchory club's home ground was the market stance, a 'dreadful' expedient, with much of the 'fielding' performed by an uncomfortably close row of wooden sheds. It was moved to Burnett Park (created 1887) in 1889, but matches were also held at Potarch and Blackhall Castle, and perhaps elsewhere in the immediate vicinity. One of Banchory's better players in the early days was Dr Lawson, director of the Nordrach-on-Dee sanatorium (*Lost literature*, pp. 67–71). Lawson played for just five years, but with Lower Deeside increasingly becoming commuter territory, many of the best players changed clubs after a year or two.

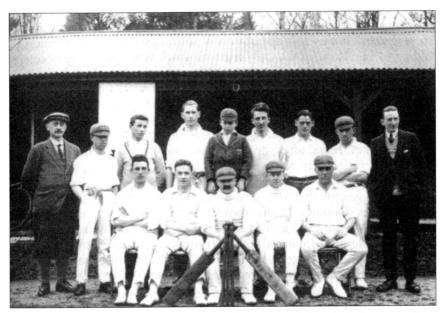

Banchory Cricket Club in 1926. With the possible exception of the titled aristocracy, all socio-economic groups were represented, as were a range of nationalities.

For reasons not now known, Banchory CC did not play between 1906 and 1923, and during this time, their commodious *c.*1894 pavilion in Burnett Park was burned down, along with all of the club's records, by 'drunken tramps'.[64] When the side was reconstituted in 1923–24, it was as part of the Deeside and District Cricket League, which also included Alford and Aboyne, but not apparently any of the other pre-war clubs. Ballater joined later, and corporate opponents included the Royal Mental Hospital, the Balmoral estate, and Aberdeen Bankers. The league itself proved a highly successful arrangement in which the teams competed for the Rhu-Na-Haven Challenge Cup, 'all trace of which has now disappeared'.[65] Banchory won it in 1931, 1932, and 1935, and again in 1939, largely due to the efforts of Billy Douglas, who 'broke all previous records by scoring 409 runs in 13 innings'.[66] Banchory also annihilated Aberdeen University's 2nd XI that year, the last of the Deeside League's existence.

'WOMEN'S WORK'?

Colonel Anne Farquharson has already been mentioned, but many other Deeside women pursued traditionally male occupations. Girls as well as boys crossed the Fir Mounth, shoes hung about their necks to save the soles, to work

Martha Grant, carrier of Banchory-Ternan and Strachan in the mid-Victorian period. The former town had nine carriers in 1842, but only one in 1877, the railway having arrived in the interim. The total number serving Aberdeen fell by 58 per cent between 1825 and 1900.

The original part of Birkhall, seen in the 1850s and the early 1900s. In the seventeenth century the estate was called Sterin or Steirn, from the Gaelic staircan (stepping-stones), a reference to its fording-point on the River Muick. In 2008, press rumours ran riot that upon the accession of King Charles III, Balmoral will cease to be a royal residence and the court will be based at Birkhall when in the area.

as harvesters down in the Mearns, returning north (shod) at the end of the season. Nineteenth-century Banchory-Ternan had both a female carrier (or courier), Martha Grant, and a postwoman, 'Postie Mary'; both made deliveries using wheelbarrows, the former as far away as Strachan. There was also a female barber, Mrs Webster and we shall soon hear of 'Boaty Maggie' Irvine.

In those Deeside districts where textile- and garment-making remained in people's homes, it was women who led the way in keeping these crafts out of the factory-owners' clutches, and in selling their products directly to the public. Women could also be lairds in their own right from early times, as was the case with Catharine Farquharson, who succeeded to Invercauld in 1806, or Rachel Gordon of Abergeldie, who built the original Birkhall – now one wing in a much larger complex of later buildings – in 1715.

The unusually early socio-economic prominence of Deeside women may be due in part to a population imbalance in their favour. In the wake of the Jacobite rebellions, with all the male deaths and emigrations that they implied, Deeside parishes reported ratios of the sexes as extreme as 57 per cent female to 43 per cent male.

LOST OCCUPATIONS (II): THE DROVERS

Among all their other uses, the Mounth passes of the Province of Mar were a bovine superhighway, along which millions of cattle were driven to market over the centuries. At its end, droving overlapped with the railway age. Its beginning is much less clearly defined. Scholars of an earlier generation often fixed its origin during the Cromwellian occupation of Scotland in the 1650s, or at the Union of the Parliaments in 1707, but this seems to have been based on a questionable assumption that to be economically 'significant', a business must be both international and legal. Certainly, there was a great deal of droving in the fifteenth and sixteenth centuries, but it was then virtually inseparable from crime, to a point that most economic historians ignore it. Even after it became legitimate, however, droving remained a 'rough-and-ready trade', uninhibited 'by any too rigid code of commerical morality'.[67] On Deeside specifically, its heyday seems to have been the period from 1750 to 1830.

Cattle were 'long almost the sole form of realisable wealth' in the Highlands, and branding of beasts to show lawful ownership was recognised and encouraged by the Scottish privy council as early as 1618.[68] In an era when paved roads (where they existed at all) were of gravel, drovers avoided them because they hurt the animals' feet. When such roads could not be avoided, or

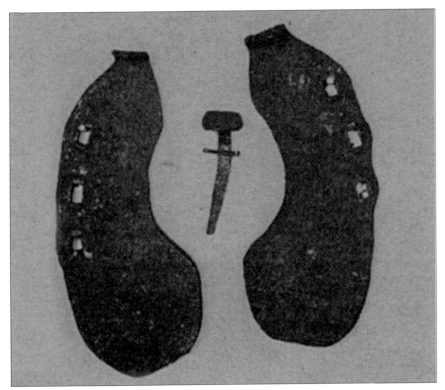

Cattle shoes and shoeing nail, 1860s.

in very bad weather conditions, the drovers arranged for cattle shoes to be fitted. These were similar to horseshoes, but made in two parts due to the animals' cloven hoof. Cattle did not take kindly to the procedure, and as with branding, had to have their feet roped together during it. Even so, one experienced Aberdeenshire smith was able to fit shoes to seventy animals per day.

'The characteristics and qualities required of a successful drover were many', according to A.R.B. Haldane:

Knowledge of the country had to be extensive and intimate, while endurance and ability to face great hardships were essential. The larger and more prosperous drovers owned ponies which they used either for riding on their long journeys to the Lowlands or for carrying supplies for use on the way, or home-made goods which were often taken for sale; but most of the drovers did the whole journey on foot. Resource and enterprise were called for with knowledge of men and tact tempered at times with absence of too fine scruple. Knowledge of cattle was needed and good judgment wherewith to balance the varying factors on which depended the successful completion of the journey[.] . . . Finally, honesty and reliabilty were needed in a drover for the responsible work entrusted to him.[69]

Gentlemen and even noblemen were involved in the trade, but few of the genteel rank actually travelled with the beasts. A few did, however, and were distinguished in the 1720s by their tartan hose or 'trousings', as opposed to kilts, and by the fact that they carried snuff-mulls and pistols in addition to the swords and dirks worn by all drovers at that time. In fact, to be a drover was to be *ipso facto* under imminent threat of armed robbery, and drovers were actually permitted to retain their weapons during and despite the disarming of the Highlands by the British government in the eighteenth century.

Normally, a drove consisted of 200 to 300 beasts, three to seven men, and as many dogs. At the extremes, droves could be as small as 100 and as large as 2,000 head or more, with the number of drovers going up in proportion: roughly by four men per additional 200 animals. Sheep joined cattle only in the last seventy-odd years of this four- to five-century phenomenon.

Because droving depended upon men sleeping out of doors and animals feeding on grass where they found it, the annual season lasted from May to October; but given the high altitudes at which it was pursued, this did not

The village of Strachan's importance in earliest times arose from its position near the convergence of two Mounth roads, the Foggy Road, a.k.a. the Stock Mounth, and the Cairn a' Mount. By the time this photograph was taken, c.1905, organised droving had ceased.

guarantee an absence of snow. At other times of year, drovers worked in agriculture and forestry, among other occupations. Some seem to have been principally pedlars, and even knitted stockings whilst on the march with their animals. Few if any drovers stopped working on Sunday, and into the 1830s, many were prosecuted for Sabbath-breaking as they passed through the southern counties.

By the mid nineteenth century, the dozens of tiny drinking establishments in and around Kincardine O'Neil had been reduced to just one, the Gordon Arms.

By the 1970s, the Gordon Arms – immediately behind the Land Rover – had acquired a 'Highland' log portico and three box-dormers, but it remained otherwise intact and is still in business today. The petrol station has since moved to the western fringes of the village.

On the trail, prepared meat and indeed cookery of any kind were rarely seen. The drover's diet consisted mostly of oatmeal, cheese, onions, and whisky. Though alcohol was taken 'sparingly' when sleeping under the stars, it was a different story at fairs and inns. One gets the impression that during the droving period Kincardine O'Neil was a boisterous place, with virtually every house – and the church – given over to the sale of food and drink, most of the time.

Drovers' promissory notes for cattle taken to market acquired the status of paper money long before the latter became generally available; and 'during the first half of the [eighteenth] century Crieff cattle market was probably the greatest centre of money circulation in the country'.[70] Even so, many drovers went bust at one time or another and, despite inflated claims for their wealth made by Sir Walter Scott and others, their typical daily income increased only from 1s to 4s between the Act of Union and the 1850s. This increase sounds dramatic, but it did not keep pace with rises in the value of cattle over the same period. Increasingly, landowners charged drovers money for the right to put their animals to grass. Bridge tolls, road tolls and market fees also cut into the profits of the trade. Some beasts were swept away when fording rivers, or died of chills afterwards. Deeside drovers crossed the river mostly from Potarch westward, but also at Drum and elsewhere.

Both the economics and the difficulty of droving are illuminated by this anecdote from Col. C.G. Gardyne. A part-time drover in the mid nineteenth century who was also a soldier of the Gordon Highlanders was overtaken on the road by some English tourists who asked him what his beasts would fetch at Falkirk Tryst. When he said £10 a head, they replied, 'Only ten pounds! That's nothing to English prices. If you take them to London, my good fellow, you'll get twenty!' The drover's reply was that, if you took Loch Ness to Hell, you'd get a shilling a glass.[71] The same beasts would have fetched nearer £1 than £2 just a century earlier.

It is an open question how much of the 'cowboy culture' of the south-western USA derived from that of northern Scotland. Woodrow 'Woody' Guthrie, an Oklahoman of North-east Scots extraction and the greatest American folk-singer of the 1930s, referred to a 'well-known famous drover' in his cowboy song 'Buffalo Skinners'. A direct transfer of personnel between the two countries' frontiers is suggested by Rob Gibson's recently published book *Highland Cowboys*. But the greatest contrast to the Americas, as previously mentioned, is that Scottish drovers were almost exclusively walkers.

Unsurprisingly, Deeside drovers – even when anciently old – 'thought nothing of walking for miles to visit relatives for a few hours'.[72] In an ideal situation, a drove would travel only ten to twelve miles per day, but this was not for the comfort of the men – who could have covered thirty miles in a day with relative ease – but to keep the cattle in the best possible condition. Only in the final end-game of droving, at the dawn of the twentieth century, having brought their beasts to market in the time-honoured way, did they deposit their earnings in a bank for transfer back to the North, rather than carrying it back through the lonely Mounth passes. Some of the final generation also returned themselves home by train.

Hardiness, of course, is not always uniform. The drover Donald Lamont, in a famous short story by Sir Thomas Dick Lauder, becomes so footsore that he allows himself to be arrested – even though he could easily prove his innocence – simply for the sake of a free horseback ride to Perth Gaol. Tricks of all sorts are remembered in the drovers' tales of Big Bill Stewart, a last-generation drover born in the late 1850s. These ranged from an apparently sleeping man's 'quick-stand' technique to deter approaching thieves (which worked more often than not) to the elaborate fakery of supernatural phenomena, to humiliate a rival or just pass the time on the roads. Tobacco use seems to have been nearly universal among drovers by Bill's time. The steep decline in the number of licensed premises in the parish of Kincardine O'Neil – from nine to two between 1850 and 1895 – seemingly had less to do with the railway's failure to arrive in the village than with the decline of droving.

The drovers were not the only people using the north–south routes in the relatively peaceful years after 1750. As late as 1795, a man was sent weekly from Braemar down the military road to Coupar Angus for letters and newspapers, because the nearest post office within the shire (at Kincardine O'Neil) was more difficult to reach; further proof, if any were needed, of the relative unimportance of the east–west as opposed to north–south routes through the area in pre-turnpike times. Likewise, the senior Farquharsons – even when living in Braemar – sent most of their correspondence via Marlee near Blairgowrie in Perthshire rather than via Aberdeen. Until after the Second World War, Royal Messengers to and from Balmoral also used the Cairnwell Mounth exclusively, except during the period of the 'Messenger trains' (see *The lost railways*, pp. 232–233).

On Deeside as elsewhere, the height of droving coincided with increased demand for meat during Britain's wars with France. After 1835, the decline of droving has been called 'short, sudden and complete'.[73] It was not that pedestrians – however sturdy and resourceful – could not compete effectively against (primitive) mechanised distribution networks. Rather, it was that they could not operate in a world where 'freedom of passage, freedom of wayside grazing and freedom of nightly stances' had come to be seen as, at best, the alien traditions of a bygone age, or at worst, a new type of theft.[74] More and more roads were paved – and more and more property lines went right up to them, partly due to the new-found quasi-commercialisation of hunting, shooting and fishing. It was finally ruled by the House of Lords in 1848 that drovers' various rights, despite their antiquity, 'constituted a limitation on the ownership of land unknown to the law of Scotland.'[75] The railways, which made no appreciable dent in the already moribund north–south cattle trade until after 1875, merely picked up the pieces. By 1938, 11,000 head of livestock were shipped out of the region via Ballater and Aboyne railway stations alone. It was also at around this time that the last of the drovers, those 'great stalwart, hirsute men', passed away.

LOST OCCUPATIONS (III):
NEARLY EVERYTHING ELSE

A century ago, most of what Deesiders used in their daily lives was produced locally. Smug air-miles types (I am guilty of this myself) who pride themselves on buying shoes made in Northampton rather than China should reflect that within living memory, our smallest hamlets had their own shoemaker and tailor;

Charlestown of Aboyne in the 1850s, looking south-west from the Ballater Road. Note the tailor's shop of Charles Joss at the far left, and the thatched roofs which outnumber slate roofs by two to one. Mature trees and newer houses now completely hide the bridge-toll cottage and (new) bridge from this position – if indeed they were ever visible from this precise angle.

sometimes more than one of each. With a population of less than 900 people in 1793, Cluny parish supported eight weavers, three weavers' apprentices, five tailors, a dyer, eight shoemakers, a shoemaker's apprentice, four blacksmiths, and eight wrights and coopers. Where horn spoons were used, they too were made locally, by 'horners'. Banchory-Ternan, like many other places of similar size, had its own watchmaker (not -repairer) in 1841.

In remoter areas, farmers

> uniting in their person, along with their own profession, that of mason, carpenter, and shoemaker, are, of course, remarkable for a degree of ingenuity and knowledge, to which the common people near the sea-coast, and where the division of labour is established, are strangers.[76]

The raising, buying, selling and daily care of horses seems to have employed more people than the automotive equivalent does today. The railway, too, appears to have employed far more people than modern road-repair and road-safety schemes. Bridge maintenance and road-tax collecting employ virtually no local people, relative to the ferrying and toll-taking which preceded them. The 'carriers' of the nineteenth century and earlier, unlike today's couriers, were well-known and trusted figures in the communities they served, usually for decades on end.

Council workmen surfacing road near Aboyne, 1911, using Aveling & Porter steam-rollers.

'There was no laird's land, however small, without a mill on it'.[77] Birse alone had thirty in the 1840s. While this enormous number of meal mills represented another vanished source of employment (there were four millers and two millwrights in Cluny), it was also indicative of a wider economic structure in which almost nothing that a given person consumed had travelled more than twenty or thirty miles. Among the few exceptions were pins and satin ribbons, the staple products sold by the 'packmen' or pedlars who were once such a prominent feature of Deeside and Scottish life. But even these items were raw materials to facilitate the local, home-based manufacturing of clothing, rather than 'pure' imports to be used up and re-ordered or forgotten. So successfully have we 'automated' or 'outsourced' the basic functions of our society that one in four Scots of working age is now deemed 'economically inactive', and the government pays many of them to stay that way.

Some occupations, of course, were so hazardous that their disappearance should be no cause for hand-wringing. Pearl-fishing was one such, though practised more on the Don: for example, at Kintore in the seventeenth century, though it was also done on the Cluny Burn a century later. The search for Cairngorm stones (smoky quartz) as practised in pre-industrial times was also horribly dangerous. Their colouring can now be achieved through artificial irradiation, though radiation was always the source of the stones' colours. Most so-called Cairngorms now actually come from the USA, Switzerland and Brazil.

CHAPTER 5
STRUCTURES

LOST BRIDGES, FERRIES AND FORDS

Tourists are struck by the loveliness of the white Cambus o' May pedestrian suspension bridge. Dating from 1905, its continued existence would seem to be proof enough of its superiority to the majority of other suspension bridges built on Deeside over the years; but even this one had to be reconstructed in 1988, and some consider the result a 'new' bridge. The 1885 Blaikie Brothers wood-and-iron suspension bridge immediately beside Abergeldie Castle has not been so lucky. It is now rusty and badly warped, and the way to it overgrown with weeds.

I have been unable to locate any specific information on 'Stewart's Bridge' over the Dee in Banchory-Devenick, which one source states was built c.1880 and demolished c.1946. If those dates are correct, it may have been yet another ill-fated pedestrian suspension bridge. The shire council is quite clear there had never been a *road* bridge over the Dee between the Aberdeen Brig o' Dee and Potarch prior to July 1894, when a steel bridge at Maryculter was begun. Severely disrupted by an August lightning storm, the construction of Maryculter Bridge was delayed until the following year.

The first victim of the great flood or 'Muckle Spate' of 3–4 August 1829 was the old bridge at Linn of Dee. The water at the Linn was thirty-three feet above its normal level, which is to say three feet above the walkway, and the old structure shot away like a leaf hit by a fire hose, never to be seen again. A speciously medieval bridge closely modelled on Old Aberdeen's Brig o' Balgownie was – controversially – constructed in its place in 1857 and still stands. Some Victorians loved it, but some preferred the rustic look of the old bridge, while others felt that to have any bridge at the Linn obscured and detracted from the site's remarkable geology.

One of the next bridges carried away was at Old Mar Lodge. The lost bridge was of stone, but its long-term replacement would be of wood. The dining

One of the pre-1857 wooden bridges at the Linn of Dee.

room of the house was filled with mud to a depth of several feet. At Ballater, the water was four feet deep in the streets and six feet deep in some houses; the Thomas Telford-designed five-arched granite bridge of 1807–09, which had cost £3,830, 'with a great noise . . . gave way.'[1] Around Banchory-Ternan, the Dee was up twenty-seven feet. The town's 1798 bridge, of wood and stone, was rendered unsafe and the wooden parts replaced with iron. The Water of Feugh

The second of four bridges built at Aboyne in the last 180 years. This one stood for four decades from 1831, and was 'nearly on the same design' as the 1828 bridge swept away in the Muckle Spate; the two together cost the earl of Aboyne more than £6,000.[2] While most Deeside bridges of this general appearance were true suspension bridges (with the vertical cables parallel to one another), this one appears to have been a cable-stayed bridge (with the cables 'fanning out' from the towers).

rose twenty feet and destroyed its Whitestone Bridge, which was not replaced for decades. Potarch Bridge was 'considerably injured' but survived, and was soon afterwards reinforced with iron. The Beltie Burn (a.k.a. Burn of Canny), meanwhile, 'carried off two bridges completely, and much injured three more, all built of stone and lime'.[3]

The Spate occurred during, and did surprisingly little to arrest, the late-Georgian suspension-bridge fad. 'Suspension bridges are detestable – frail, rickety, trembling under the weight of an ox, and shivering as if they would go to pieces when a coach rattles along them.' So wrote William MacGillivray of the 1830–31 bridge of Aboyne, the 'great flood' of the previous year 'having swept away a previously-erected bridge of the same kind' – which in turn had been put up in 1828 in the wake of a flooding-related fatal ferry accident. Some modern publications assume that a single suspension bridge took from 1828 to 1831 to complete, but this is incorrect. These bridges could be thrown up very quickly and most were simply not very good. The first version of the bridge over the Don at Montgarrie near Alford was 'a suspension bridge of flimsy construction' which, though 'greatly in fashion' was 'too weak to last more than a few years'.[4] Queen Victoria refused to cross one at Crathie on her first visit to the area. The second Aboyne bridge was useless by the 1860s and reconstructed

The Inver Hotel (shown c.1900) and the Boat Inn at Aboyne may typify Deeside inns of mid-Georgian vintage. Their much-bemoaned mock-Tudor elements are fairly superficial, and repeated claims that they are 'Tudor style' tout court tell us as little about that style as about the inns themselves.

beyond recognition – albeit still as a suspension bridge – in 1871. In the 1930s it was rebuilt again. As someone who crosses there two or three times a week, I am glad to report that the suspension gimmick has at last been abandoned.

Notices on Aboyne's and similar suspension bridges of their era advised the cattle-drovers, and drivers of wheeled vehicles, 'to move slowly and gently – cannily . . . or such like'.[5] (Londoners may recollect that the Albert Bridge not only had to be given a major central support in the 1970s, but also still carries a warning to troops: break step before crossing.) Bad as they were, these successive Aboyne suspension bridges very quickly caused the demise of the ferry boat of Bonty, which operated from roughly the site of the present-day Boat Inn, whose name commemorates it, as well as four others that operated within two miles either side. The inn, no longer thatched but retaining much that is old, is even now not the worst place to land boats, of a sort: as the number of kayakers among its summer customers attests.

Not all of the river's suspension bridges were capable of taking vehicles or cattle, however. The Church of Scotland hired John Smith (city architect of Aberdeen) to design a suspension bridge for foot-passengers over the Dee, half a mile above the church of Banchory-Devenick. It was built in 1837 by Charles Barclay, brother of J.W. Barclay MP who would drain Loch Auchlossan a quarter century later. Officially the St Devenick bridge, it was universally known as 'Shakkin' Briggie' for obvious reasons, but put the local ferryman out of

Shakkin' Briggie in better days: 1850s and early 1900s. It was closed for repairs for two years following the floods of 1920, and became irreparable in the 1950s when the river undermined it at the south end. In 1984 the walkway was removed. It remains a listed building.

business nevertheless. It was weakened beyond repair by flooding in the 1950s and stands as a rusting, somewhat creepy, derelict for which no public or private organisation will claim responsibility.

The Crathie suspension bridge, created in 1834 by J. Justice Jr, was deemed inadequate by Prince Albert who commissioned the current un-suspended iron bridge by the legendary English engineer Isambard Kingdom Brunel. The latter was completed in 1858. The iron bridge of Durris, built in 1854 as a means of access to Crathes Railway Station, was twice nearly destroyed by floods whilst under construction. As previously mentioned, Ballater's original granite bridge of 1780s vintage, paid for in part by the Board of Forfeited and Annexed (Jacobite) Estates, fell in an 'uncommon' flood in August 1799.[6] Its second,

The third bridge of Ballater, made from Braemar timber, lasted just over half a century, 1834–1885.

Telford, bridge which was destroyed in the Muckle Spate was replaced after a gap of five years by a wooden bridge. The current stone bridge was created in 1885; and the progression from stone to wood and back to stone again should probably serve as a warning about the nature of progress in general. Each successive destruction of the bridge took several years to rectify, of course, and represented a temporary reprieve to the ferrymen or would-be ferrymen of the town. This is not to suggest, of course, that all Deeside ferry operators were men: one of the last holdouts, Margaret Irvine or 'Boaty Maggie' plied her trade near Maryculter House until 1936. The last river ferry, still in public use in the 1960s, was also owned by a woman, Bella Main. This was at Heathcot (known in earlier eras as Auchlunies), near Blairs.

Additional severe damage was done by the Dee in August 1914, October 1920, and January 1937. During the last-named event, the roadway of the 1895 Bridge of Maryculter was four feet under water. Footbridges were washed away in the Cairngorms in June and July 1956, but that was just a foretaste of the catastrophe to come. On the night of 13 August, the Luibeg tripled in width. Its James A. Parker Memorial Footbridge, Britain's first bridge in aluminium alloy, 'was carried 100 yards downstream and its masonry piers overturned'.[7] It had been built just eight years before.

Still further downstream the Lui and the Dee join. As the headwaters of both had received excessive precipitation, the united stream surged past and over the 'Canadian' bridge above Inverey. This log truss bridge with a central crib had been erected in 1941 by the Canadian Forestry Corps and had recently been given a redecking by the Mar Estate. Despite the fact that the water level was up to two feet *above* the deck the bridge held, but the boulder and gravel fill at each approach was washed out to bedrock leaving it impassable to wheeled transport.[8]

The Canadian Bridge, demolished a few years later, is illustrated in *Lost occupations (I)*, on p. 149.

Earlier in the 1950s, a shanty town of some description which then existed behind the Mill Inn Hotel in Maryculter was cut off from land altogether, and a lifeboat was brought up (by road) to rescue the twenty-odd inhabitants. The highly seaworthy but less-than-'Deeworthy' vessel failed in its mission (!) but local rowboats eventually served the same purpose and apparently no one was killed. In the 1970s, the central iron span of the bridge at Banchory-Ternan (illustrated as it appeared in 1855, p. 23, above) was temporarily replaced by a World War Two-type Bailey bridge, until the completion of the current structure in 1985. The A93 still regularly floods, particularly around Crathes.

No bridges at all were built over the Dee west of the city of Aberdeen between the completion of the city's Bridge of Dee in 1527, and 1752, when the redcoats made the Old Bridge of Invercauld. (It is probably worth mentioning here that, in common with all the 'Wade' bridges and indeed 'Wade' roads of Upper Deeside, Invercauld Bridge was designed several years after Field Marshal George Wade died, in 1748.) The thirteenth-century wooden bridge at Kincardine O'Neil would have been long gone by the 1500s, as would the fourteenth-century wooden bridge over the Clunie in Braemar. References to a bridge of similar date at Durris probably indicate a bridge over the Sheeoch Burn or even the drawbridge of Durris Castle, and almost certainly not another bridge spanning the Dee, as Douglas Simpson maintained. A.R.B. Haldane referred several times to a bridge over the Dee at Banchory-Ternan that existed in 1664, but this was also an error. The original scribe having written bridge of Dye as 'bridge of Dey', the editor of the printed *Records of the Privy Council* corrected this, not to 'Dye', but to 'Dee'; and three centuries later, a wholly imaginary bridge was born.

Ferries charged for their services. The Heathcot Ferry – named for a lost island, Inch of Heathcot, now joined to the river's north shore – cost a penny in the early nineteenth century. They mostly couldn't take anything larger than a horse, or in some cases a horse and empty two-wheeled cart – though Dinnet, unusually, had a second, larger boat suitable for small flocks of sheep in about 1860. So, for those with no money, or who didn't want to spend it, or who were accompanied by a large herd of livestock, or driving any sort of laden wheeled vehicle, the usual option was crossing by a ford. At least thirty-four of these were known on the Dee. The ford of Tilbouries, said to have been built by the Roman legionaries stationed at nearby Normandykes, lasted nearly two millennia. Douglas Simpson noted that he had personally seen it not long before the Second World War, but it had vanished without trace by the 1960s and one wonders if the army did away with it as a German-invasion-hampering measure (on which see also *The Cowie Line: a lost frontier restored?*, pp. 223–224). The marquess of Montrose's army crossed the Dee by a ford at Crathes in September 1644, hoping to avoid a (second) costly and prolonged battle for the Aberdeen Brig o' Dee. The ford of Kincardine O'Neil, plus five others all west of Ballater, were in use in 1968. So useful were they that local people maintained them unasked and apparently without remuneration: John MacLaggan from Torphins reported that 'after a spate, and at intervals otherwise, the inhabitants of the district met and with long poles or hooks, removed all large boulders over a sufficiently broad way in the river.'[9] With the advent of the Land Rover home snorkel kit, they may regain their popularity yet.

In the parish of Kildrummy, and perhaps elsewhere, people in the early nineteenth century walked across the River Don on stilts:

> poles or stakes, about 6 feet in length, with a step on one side, on which the passenger raised about 2 feet from the ground, resting them against his sides and armpits, and moving them forward by each hand, totters through.[10]

Based on the archaeological remains of ancient north–south roads, combined with historical evidence such as the travel itineraries of King Edward I of England, the most important groupings of ferries and fords seem to have been around Aboyne/Dinnet, Kincardine O'Neil, and Drum. The importance of Craigmyle House in earlier epochs is underlined by the fact that it had its own road down to the Inchbare Ferry, and latterly (*c.*1880s) its own private railway platform. It is possible, too, to identify by name the 'seven oldest and most important' fords, from east to west, as follows:

> Foords of Dee at Ruthrieston, near Aberdeen, for the Causey Mounth pass; Tilbouries in the parish of Maryculter for the Elsick Mounth

Durris House was rebuilt on the foundations of the previous structure, which was burned by Montrose in 1645. The current house, birthplace of the antiquarian Cosmo Innes in 1798, was extensively remodelled 1824–38, used as Civil Defence headquarters, and since converted into flats. One of the changes has been the loss (by 1978) of the massive arched entranceway.

route; at Mills of Drum for the Crynes Corse pass; at Kincardine O'Neil for the Cairn a' Mounth route; at Mill of Dinnet for the Fir Mounth; at Tullich for the Capel Mounth pass; and near Braemar Castle, the important ford serving both the Tolmounth and Cairnwell routes.[11]

The section of the modern main road by Potarch Bridge was still known as the 'old boat road' in the 1920s, the original road passing (much more directly) to Kincardine O'Neil behind the hill via Bridge of Canny and Tillydrine.[12] Important as it once was, the ford at Mills of Drum's exact position is not now known. It might have been on the part of the river commanded by the Castlehill of Durris: the site until 1645 of a now-vanished castle on the river's edge, half a mile below Durris church: see *Lost architecture (II)*, pp. 200–209.

Clachanturn, a mile or so east of Easter Balmoral, 'was at one time of considerable local importance, a large market having been regularly held there'. The market, inn and ferry were all gone by 1898, but the blacksmith remained, and was judged competent.[13] Ferry operators did not live by ferrying alone. Despite having two boats, one for people and one for animals, Mr Stephen at Dinnet also kept a pub. This probably lasted until the fraught completion of the

The old bridge over the Clunie at Braemar, which was removed in 1863, and its somewhat more delicate successor, in 1905.

iron girder bridge there in 1862; by 1921, G.M. Fraser reported that 'not a stone is left'.[14] The same bridge led to the demise of the Cambus ford, which vanished even from local memory within sixty years: an important reminder of the sheer speed with which once-vital information is lost along with material objects. The general right to use a ford on private land, for instance on the Abergeldie estate, was considered to lapse after forty years of non-use.

Bridges, and the roads themselves, also could charge tolls. Many toll-takers' cottages survive, and those dating from 1798–1858 are easily identifiable from their semi-circular or half-hexagonal end, usually with three windows, facing the road. Later ones resemble ordinary cottages. Road tolls for the most part ended in Aberdeenshire in 1865 – somewhat ahead of their abandonment in the rest of Britain – and the county's last bridge toll was taken on Park Bridge at Durris in the middle 1950s, when the rate was 3d per car.

LOST POSITION: THREE TOWNS THAT MOVED

As old and quaint as they now seem, it should be remembered that three of Deeside's largest settlements have changed position completely since 1675. These are Banchory-Ternan, Aboyne, and Ballater: by population, the three most important Deeside communities that have not been submerged into Aberdeen city suburbia. These, and all their nearest rivals, are located on the north side of the river; south Deeside falls 'in the cold shadow of the Mounth'.[15] Some of you will object that Ballater was never a town before the late eighteenth century, and in a way you are correct. However, its creation was seen at the time, and for perhaps two generations afterwards, as a movement or rebuilding of Tullich: previously the most important place on that stretch of the river – as attested not least by the size of the guard Farquharson of Inverey was bringing to Tullich market on the fateful day in 1666 when the Baron of Brackley was killed (discussed in *Lost in the retelling*, pp. 56–59).

The prosperity of Ballater was founded on Pannanich water, which was to be drunk for health, in an amount not exceeding two Scottish pints, on an empty stomach before breakfast – but never by the very frail, very young, or very old. The area's goat milk was also being marketed as a cure-all around 1790–95, when belief in spa treatments seems to have peaked nationwide. (The lost community of Milton of Braeloine, in Glen Tanar, was also a centre of goat milk production and consumption until *c*.1860.) Between 1800 and 1820, Tullich lost first its church, then its post office, inn, market, and annual fair, all to Ballater. A desperate rearguard action was fought against this process by Sir Walter Scott, who in 1822 collected or perhaps counterfeited 'proofs' that Tullich had been a royal burgh since the Middle Ages. On the verge of presenting this evidence to George IV, Sir Walter mislaid it all, and was never able or willing to reconstruct it. Perhaps there never was any evidence, forged or otherwise, and Scott hoped that the monarch, hearing of its 'loss', would reconfirm Tullich's 'royal' status out of sheer magnanimity. This did not happen either, 'the final degradation taking place in 1857 when its burgh cross was "dinged doon" and broken up to make road metal'.[16] Half a century later, Tullich was a ghost town. The ghost town in turn has been 'lost' as, like Birsemore, it is reinvented as a vaguely deluxe suburb of nowhere in particular.

The Old Bridge of Tullich continued in use until the coming of the turnpike in 1855. This was not over the Dee but rather the Tullich Burn, on the Old Deeside Road. It was so high-backed that coachmen had to make 'a great rush up that carried them triumphantly over'.[17] Its loss will not be particularly lamented, however, at least not by those drivers who have crossed or attempted to cross the A939's similar bridge over the Gairn at Gairnshiel – which is not so much an arch as a triangle with the point upward.

Aboyne is a much more diffuse affair than Ballater: a huge village green, large expensive houses and no immediately obvious *raison d'être*. The ex-railway station, let by the shire council as shops and half-heartedly signposted, stands in contrast to Ballater Station's fine state of preservation and fairly aggressive self-promotion. As with Ballater/Tullich, however, Aboyne was anciently multi-centred and, if the original parish church site is any guide, mostly east of where it is today. 'Aboyne' is not technically the name of a town but of a parish and a castle. The community located roughly in the heart of the modern town of Aboyne was called Bonty or Bunty or sometimes 'Bounties' until 1676, and thereafter as Charlestown. The latter name, now used locally only in reference to the Green, was until recently adhered to by the BBC's online weather service, which knew not Aboyne, to the consternation of 'Charlestown' dwellers and also, presumably, the people of Charlestown of Aberlour. The explanation for why the town is now where it is seems to have been lost. This is the result of a persistent rumour that there was a medieval castle on the exact site of the current castle. No evidence for this older castle, however, was ever found by the region's leading archaeologist Douglas Simpson, by RCAHMS, or by the Ordnance Survey; and I am inclined to agree with Simpson that scattered references to the 'Castle of Aboyne' in medieval documents might easily be referring to the castle at Coull, just two miles away and at the same general point on the river, on the same side. There are no inescapable references to the current castle site from before the reign of Charles I. My hypothesis, therefore, is that a wholly new castle was constructed in the early seventeenth century to command the strategic ferries and fords of the pre-existing communities of Bonty and Dinnet, as well as the ancient pre-turnpike highway which – unlike the modern one – passed just a few hundred yards from the castle and in full view of it. Not long

Aboyne Castle at its greatest extent, following four different sets of nineteenth-century enlargements. As of 1898 there was even a moat, created by a diversion of the Tarland Burn. In the 1970s, a conscientious pruning away of these miscellaneous additions returned the castle to approximately its original size and vertical shape.

after 1676, when Charlestown was chartered and erected into a market (a mercat cross existed in the 1710s) it simply sucked the life out of the old kirktown of Formaston, half a mile north and east of the eastern extremity of the modern town. The particular Gordons who inhabited the new castle are also known to have inhabited the now-ruined mansion house of Tilphoudie, slightly to the north-east of Formaston. The *coup de grâce* would have been the relocation of the Aboyne parish church from Formaston to Charlestown in 1762.

The name 'Bonty' had passed out of use, and 'Millne of Charletoun' was applied to the most prosperous part of the parish in the poll tax roll of 1696. There, we find there a gentleman with three servants, a merchant, a wright, a tailor, two shoemakers, three weavers, and fifty-six other rateable persons assessed at £31; suggesting that Charlestown was already three times the size of Formaston, and four times the size of Marywell of Birse. This is not to say that the new town was wildly successful. It was still only half the size of Kincardine O'Neil; and during the next century of its existence as a burgh of barony, the number of markets held in Charlestown slumped from one per week to four per year, and the population of Aboyne parish from 1,700 to 1,000. Local historian Jim Cheyne believes that the exact location of Bonty, and the eventual fate of the Charlestown cross, might yet be ascertained. I am less hopeful.

*Above. Banchory-Ternan, looking
west, in 1855. The eighty-foot-high
West Parish Kirk, which now
dominates this view, was not built
until 1879–85; and the Burnett Arms
Hotel (centre), though half its present
size, was the most prominent building
visible. The railway station which
obliterated the medieval town was so
inconveniently far from this, the new
centre of population, that an omnibus
service between the two sites was
offered by the 1890s, and a secondary
passenger platform on Dee Street (out
of frame to the left) was set up in 1961.*

*Right. The mercat cross of Banchory-
Ternan and/or its predecessor
community, Kirkton of Leys. Since this
photo was taken, the cross was moved
to outside the south end of the East
Parish Kirk.*

The town of Banchory-Ternan, in its current position, dates back only to 1805. The position of the old town was again completely to the east of the modern centre, but in this case also much closer to the river. Its eastern edge is indicated by the decidedly eerie churchless churchyard that slopes down from the A93. The kirk, though it had been rebuilt as recently as 1775, was erected on its present site in 1824, to be nearer to the turnpike road built in 1802. The old burgh was a substantial place, with multiple schools and an inn by 1325, and as many as 260 dwelling houses in 1755. All were destroyed, however, in the building of the railway station – of which only the engine sheds remain, in their new guise as the offices of Roy Cowie Garden Machinery.

After a long sojourn in Burnett Park (someone at RCAHMS seems to think it is still there[18]), the mercat cross was moved to its current, third, site in East Parish Church kirkyard, where it is visible from the main road. This terribly plain and uninspiring object is the only survivor of at least five town crosses that rural Deeside once had. Other than the three towns discussed in this section, these belonged to Kincardine O'Neil, from 1511, and Tarland, from 1683. Banchory-Ternan's cross seems to be the main proof that it ever was a burgh prior to becoming a Police Burgh in 1885 (see *The lost policemen*, pp. 150–153),

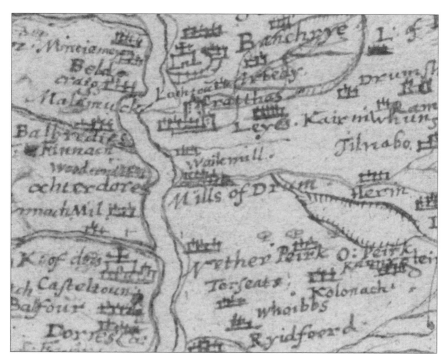

Detail from Timothy Pont's hand-drawn sixteenth-century map showing the relative positions of 'Leyes', 'Banchyre', 'Arbedy' and 'Cratthas'.

evidence which is not universally accepted. It is far from clear that 'Kirkton of Leys', which was given a burghal charter in 1488, is simply an alternative name for Banchory-Ternan, as at least two recent books suggest. A hundred years after the Kirkton of Leys charter was issued, Timothy Pont's manuscript map of Lower Deeside showed 'Leyes' not merely as a different community from 'Banchrye', but with a third village, 'Arbedy', separating them. This adds to the mystery in yet another way, since in direct contradiction to Pont, the Ordnance Survey map of 1868 (like some current road books) depicts Arbeadie *west* of Banchory. Beginning in the 1870s, however, the one-inch Ordnance maps show Arbeadie athwart the turnpike road, just a hair north of the railway station/Kirkton of Leys site. In these later maps, 'New Banchory' is shown immediately north of Arbeadie about a quarter mile, 'Woodside of Arbeadie' immediately north of that, and Banchory proper where it is now generally held to be.

It is just conceivable that Pont meant 'Banchrye' – which he wrote in much larger letters than 'Arbedy', 'Leyes' or indeed 'Cratthas' – as the name of the district or parish only. This would leave open the possibility that Arbeadie in the west and Kirkton of Leys in the east were the *only* two villages that overlapped with the site of modern Banchory-Ternan as of 1600; and earlier mentions of 'Banquoriterne' (however spelled) might be to the parish alone. Not for nothing, one presumes, did the town's provost refer to it as 'New, New-Banchory' in 1828.[19]

The early nineteenth century construction of Banchory Lodge by Gen. Burnett erased one other old hamlet, not depicted by Pont: Cobleheugh. All of this tends to contradict two analyses by Fenton Wyness: 1) in general, that the sites of 'the villages of today' were determined by 'early church sites'; and 2) in particular, that Banquhoriterne, Kirkton of Leys, Arbeadie, 'Town-heid' and Banchory were simply successive aliases of a single town on a single site.[20]

Just how much closer to the river everything in the Banchory-Ternan neighbourhood was, before the 1805 rebuilding, is shown by the locally surviving portion of the old pre-turnpike king's highway. This was renamed Gas Street for a time, and is now called Bridge Street. The present town library, located well below the level of the modern high street, is nevertheless so much *above* the level of the Old Deeside Road that it can only be reached from Bridge Street via several flights of stairs. All trace of this ancient highway in the immediate vicinity of Cobleheugh was obliterated by Banchory Lodge.

That these east–west shifts of whole communities could have happened when they did is a fairly clear sign that the region's current east–west orientation began to manifest itself before the railway was built, and even before the late-

Georgian turnpike road was made. The North Deeside road's non-moving exception that proves the rule now bills itself as 'the Oldest Village on Deeside'. Kincardine O'Neil, located between Aboyne and Banchory-Ternan, is right where it always was. The site of the region's largest church, largest hospital and only cross-river bridge in the 1200s, this once 'illustrious' village was, '[t]hroughout our whole historical period, up, indeed, to the discontinuance of the Old Deeside road (running east and west) and the Cairn-a'-Mounth road (running north and south) . . . an important centre for the North of Scotland'.[21] The Cairn a' Mount, in its northward, non-mountainous configuration, ran through Lumphanan, Cushnie, and Alford to Huntly and thence to the far north from early times until 1817.

The loss of this Kincardine O'Neil–Huntly road was caused by the construction of two new bridges, William Minto's over the Don at Alford (1811) and Potarch Bridge (1814) on the Dee. Not long after the completion of the latter, it was decided that they should be joined by a new road which rapidly super- seded the old. This apparently minor change in the transport network had much farther-reaching effects. So much 'hype' attended the new bridges and the road connecting them that the space at the south end of Potarch Bridge – now a playpark – became the new home of two very important pre-existing institutions.

The 'dockit hoose', a ferryman's house and inn which had its corner cut off to allow the railway to pass: the ultimate symbol of the Deeside region's sudden shift from a north– south to an east–west orientation. The ferry and the railway are both long gone, but this odd structure still stands as a reminder of both.

The first, from north of the river, was Bartle Fair, the main annual fair of the district, previously held near Westertown of Kincardine. The second was Birse Market, until then held at Marywell. Unfortunately, the main economic rationale for the new road or indeed any other north–south-running road on Deeside was cattle droving, a trade that was soon to be undone, as we have seen, by a combination of landlord intolerance and the end of Britain's wars with France. It was in seeking greater opportunity for themselves, to be derived from a traditional north–south road, that both towns died.

LOST UNDER OUR NOSES: GEORGIAN MILESTONES

Though it took me more than a year to first notice one as I whizzed along the North Deeside road at an average fifty miles an hour, Georgian mile-markers form a nearly complete set here. They date back to, but not before, the turnpike period when tolls had to be taken every six miles. Nearly twenty toll-houses were built in Mar, of which more than half were on Deeside *per se*, including those at Culter (demolished about 1894), Mills of Drum, Invercannie, Kincardine O'Neil, Aboyne (where there were two), Tomnakeist, Coillecroich, Inver and Braemar. The turnpiking of the North Deeside Road in the vicinity of Aberdeen was approved in 1795, and authorised to extend west of Kincardine O'Neil in 1800. It reached 'the gates of Aboyne Castle' in 1802 – but there, for five decades afterwards, was where it ended.[22]

In contrast to the road from Aberdeen to Alford via Rubislaw, for instance, no money was given to this expensive project by the city of Aberdeen. Many of the gentlemen who did pay for it – including Irvine of Drum, William Farquharson of Monaltrie, and the earl of Aboyne – are notable for their familial and in some cases personal ties to the revolt of 1745, as well as to Freemasonry. As I mentioned before in reference to the convicted militant Jacobite and great 'improver' Francis Farquharson, the idea that 'improvement' and Jacobitism are inherently opposite can gain little traction on Deeside.

The mile-marker stones are surprisingly complete and intact. Some have, however, been moved. Soon after 1914, when an accused speeder successfully challenged the length of some of the miles, they were re-measured. Of the thirteen examined, one was found to be precisely accurate, and the majority accurate to within five yards. One was lost, and the remainder were inaccurate by not more than seventeen yards. All having been then adjusted as far as the Kincardineshire border, it is possible to say that 'in no county in the British Isles are the milestones set out with greater accuracy . . . than in the county of Aberdeen.'[23] It is the measure of the quality of the design of the original turnpike road that it has moved so little from side to side, and its route is substantially that of the modern A93. The major exceptions are the sections that ran 1) through the built-up area of Banchory-Ternan, as previously discussed; 2) from Potarch Bridge to Kincardine O'Neil; and 3) through the pass of Ballater.

THE 'MOST LOST' ROAD OF ALL

The turnpike was extended westward beyond Aboyne in 1855. The act authorising this also provided that:

> All that Portion of the South Dee Side Road which lies between . . . the House occupied by James Smith near the Eastern boundary of Easter Balmoral in the Parish of Crathie and the South End of the Stone Bridge of Dee called Invercauld Bridge shall cease to be a Public Road, and . . . be closed against all Use for any Purpose whatsoever.[24]

A rare photograph, taken in 1854, of Old Balmoral Castle on the eve of its dismantling. Its original core, a tower-house of c.1550, is easily identifiable at the far right.

Another angle on Old Balmoral. All that remains of this entire compound is a stone marking where the front door once was. Statements in the current Balmoral guidebook, to the effect that both castles coexisted in habitable form for as much as four years (1855–59), contradict the information on the stone itself: that the earlier building was 'taken down in 1855'. In front of the older structure, and therefore directly beneath the modern Balmoral Castle, Lord David Ogilvie's Jacobite troops camped on 19 April 1746.

Some portions of the old king's highways of Deeside that were made redundant by the building of the turnpikes were blocked by gates, or (as in this case) whole farm buildings.

Though the act managed to avoid saying so directly, this was done largely for the royal family's privacy – a measure of how important tourism had already become to the region, and they to tourism. The Old Invercauld Bridge thereafter also carried a public notice, dated 1859, that it had been closed and made private. This notice was removed or otherwise lost in late 1920 or 1921.

LOST ARCHITECTURE (I):
COTTAGES AND CLACHANS

Deeside's ruined medieval churches have already been discussed, but it should be stressed that these churches' roofs were constructed in the same way as most other buildings of the region: with thatch. This roofing material (like so many other features of Deeside's non-fortified buildings) seems to have been in general use from the Bronze Age until the mid-Victorian period. Turf and heather were both used initially, giving way gradually to the near-universal use of heather thatch, which could be seen on Kincardine O'Neil church until 1733 – when a young man shooting pigeons off the roof accidentally ignited it. However, in Birse, where there were no farmhouses with slate roofs in 1790, turf was used not only for roofs but also for the upper parts of walls. The old parish church of Glen Muick was thatched with 'heath' until the day it burned down in 1798. St Bride's, Cushnie, was also heather-thatched into the 1790s. Heather was used, in or by 1725, to replace the roof of Old Glen Tanar Kirk,

Kincardine O'Neil church before 1931, when the ivy was cut down.

which had partly burned in 1696. In Glengairn in 1850, the Protestant church was no longer thatched but the Catholic church still was. At Inverey, 'gradually the old thatched biggins . . . have disappeared and cottages of a modern type have taken their place', A.I. McConnochie noted in 1898. In the same year, he also called the heather thatching of the Episcopal chapel of St Lesmo in Glen Tanar merely an affectation of 'the former style in the district'.[25] Fifty years earlier, however, William MacGillivray visited the Inverey area and praised its 'thatched cottages . . . in the modern style'.[26] While it is highly doubtful he considered thatch to be 'modern' in itself, it was at least not incompatible with modernity at that date. Toward the close of the nineteenth century, half of Inverey's houses were slated, one-third thatched, and the rest in ruins.

The village of Kincardine O'Neil was considered somewhat precocious in its use of slate for roofs in 1842. Torphins's dwelling houses were all 'thackit' in December 1859, when the trains first began passing through. In Lumphanan by the early 1950s, thatching had vanished, but both heather and straw thatch had been used there within living memory. Even in the late-eighteenth-century new town of Ballater, thatch only fully gave way to slate by 1885; and in 1950s Logie-Coldstone it was still seen – along with wooden 'lums' (chimneys).

Up to nine-tenths of stone farm buildings across the North-east region were made using clay as mortar until c.1900, while others had 'solid clay walls finished externally with lime slurry or lime harl', supplemented by lintels and window-surrounds of stone, timber or (after 1700) brick. Not all houses in the nineteenth century used mortar of any kind, many being built of drystone. 'Of course,' remembered J.G. Michie, who was born in such a house in Wester Micras in 1830,

> the wind whistled through such walls with but little let or hindrance.
> This did not matter in summer, for it provided splendid ventilation,
> but it was different in winter when the winds were loaded with snow-
> drift. It became, therefore, a part of the autumn labour, as necessary
> as the 'cocking' (fencing with thorns) of the kailyards to prevent the
> invasion of sheep, to bung the holes in the walls to keep the wind away.
> This was done in the *go-hairst* (after-harvest) by the women and
> children collecting a quantity of moss-crop and inserting it carefully,
> bit by bit, into every external crevice – an operation which was called
> *fogging the wa's*.[27]

A tax levied on the number of bricks produced led to much larger bricks after 1784. Wattle and daub construction was also seen, but known locally as 'stake and rice'. Specialist builders in clay were called 'mud masons'. In Aberdeenshire generally, 'mud work' was often used in the construction of seventeenth-century farmhouses and ministers' manses, which may explain why so few dating from that century have survived. They were cheap to build, windproof and very warm, but all this was achieved at the cost of longevity, and most have literally melted away.[28] In Kincardineshire in 1810, the range of cottage types and the costs of building each were as follows:

Stone and lime, slate roof:	£20–£25
Stone and lime, imported timber roof:	£15–£20
Stone and clay, thatched roof:	£4–£5
Stone and turf, thatched roof:	£2–£3

Thirty years later in the Vale of Alford, thatched and slate roofs were still both being produced, the former costing less than one-fourth as much as the latter (£1 5s as against £5 5s).

Even in the highly 'traditional' pre-1850s period, however, many changes occurred over time. The main evolution in the houses of ordinary people was from round to rectangular. This occurred in stages. First came the rectangle with four rounded-off corners and a chimney in the middle. Later, two corners remained rounded, while the end with the chimney (now built in to an end wall) was left square. The final stage of their evolution was the classic 'but and ben' cottage, with four square corners and a chimney at each end – and often with small windows on three sides instead of one, as before.

A large but otherwise typical Deeside cottage of the pre-1850 period.

Inverey in the 1850s. Some of the structures, especially the one at the far right, seem drawn to indicate that turf rather than thatch was used.

Leaving Home, an engraving by Robert Ross after R.T. Bell, published in 1863. Over the course of the nineteenth century, during which prices generally declined, the wages of male farm servants on Deeside quadrupled, and women farm servants' wages tripled – even as the local population rebounded by 60 per cent or more. Nevertheless, this scene contains only slight evidence of the avalanche of cheap household knick-knacks with which the Victorian era was, and still is, associated.

Like all the rectangular designs, 'but and ben' cottages were of two rooms: in this case designated the kitchen ('but') and parlour ('ben'), though people slept in both, and sometimes in the 'trance' or passage between the two. The very poorest cottars' houses had no 'but', 'except when it was used as an apartment for the fowls to roost in'.[29] Rammed earth floors mostly gave way to planks, and the highly flammable wooden chimneys were replaced by stone ones. Secret Catholic chapels, such as the one on the Auchendryne–Inverey road that was destroyed after the '45, will have differed from these more in purpose than in construction.

Thatching practices also evolved, but out of necessity rather than any desire for improvement. By the mid nineteenth century, the quasi-commercialisation of grouse shooting in the region led to controlled burning of heather. Before burning began, heather grew up to five feet high, and as such was highly suitable for thatching. With burning, it seldom reached a height of three feet, which made thatching so difficult that broom (sometimes called gorse) was used in its place – as it had been in some areas, for instance Peterculter, for some years previously. But broom proved less weatherproof than the 'long' heather, at which

Glas-allt Shiel before 1868.

point the wholesale abandonment of thatch was probably inevitable.

Lastly, it is worth mentioning that Queen Victoria's famous Glas-allt-Shiel on Loch Muick attained its present large scale only in 1868. Previously, it was a one-storey, two-windowed cabin of picturesque but essentially mundane appearance.

LOST ARCHITECTURE (II): LAIRDS' HOUSES, FORTALICES AND CASTLES

The region's main prehistoric hill-fort is the Barmekin of Echt, which was twice occupied in the first millennium BC. After AD 1100, at least six 'motte and bailey' castles were built on Deeside. Requiring no stone for their construction, they consisted of a high, usually man-made earth mound (the 'motte') with a wooden structure on top (surrounding the 'bailey' or inner courtyard). None of these wooden superstructures still exists, but they can be assumed to have been broadly similar in form to later stone castles such as the old tower at Drum. As to the mounds, the most famous are probably the Peel of Lumphanan and Castlehill of Durris; but others can still be discerned at Strachan, Midmar, and Banchory-Devenick. Another, at Coldstone, was completely destroyed at an unknown date after 1659. Mottes remained places of security long after their original buildings had passed away: Coldstone in 1594 had a strong fortalice with 'broad chimneys, stone roof, grated casement and corbelled ramparts'.[30] The house built by Fraser of Durris c.1620 and destroyed by the royalists in 1645 was located atop the Castlehill. Similarly, Thomas Charteris of Kinfauns built a stone house on top of the Peel of Lumphanan, probably about 1490. It was still inhabited in 1702, but dismantled for building stone in 1780. This re-use of mottes was isolated, however, and in the thirteenth century, the fashion passed to all-stone castles that would be motte and bailey in one: most notably, Coull, Drum, and Kildrummy.

It is Deeside's frontier status that serves to explain the area's unique and astonishing proliferation of castles. Continued even long after the permanent cessation of hostilities in 1746, this tradition provides us with an extraordinarily rich and sometimes frustrating legacy of lost monumental buildings. One such frustration arises very quickly, when one attempts to determine precisely which house owned by the earl of Mar played host to John Taylor in 1618. The name 'Kindrochit', now applied only to the ruins of a 1390s fortalice in Braemar village, at one time was applied to some unspecified wider area – perhaps the whole nearby hill known as Cairn na Drochaide (though 'Kindrochit' is inevitably translated as 'bridge-end'). The fortalice's known date is difficult to reconcile with Douglas Simpson's view, that Kindrochit Castle was a place of strategic importance as early as the mid-eighth-century reign of Angus I MacFergus. Taylor's puzzling account maintains that he accompanied the earl

> from his house, where I saw the ruines of an olde Castle, called the Castle of *Kindroghit*. It was built by King Malcolm Canmore (for a hunting house) who raigned in *Scotland* when *Edward* the Confessor, *Harold*, and Norman *William* raigned in England: I speake of it, because it was the last house that I saw in those parts; for I was the space of twelve dayes after, before I saw either house, corne fielde, or habitation for any creature, but Deere, wild Horses, Wolves, and other such like Creatures, which made mee doubt that I should never have seene a house againe.[31]

Could Taylor have meant ruins on the site of the present Braemar Castle, which dates back only to 1628 (i.e. did not yet exist)? Or could Kindrochit proper have been already a ruin, and Taylor's 'house of my good Lord of Mar' an otherwise unknown structure in or around Braemar village – perhaps the same house visited by King Robert II at least five times between 1373 and 1382? Meanwhile, the Victorian tale that Kindrochit, with all its inhabitants inside (including a queen), was destroyed by cannonfire – as a draconian method of containing the plague – has so many things wrong with it that I would not know where to begin.

The region's many unfortified lairds' houses shared a number of features with those of their poorer neighbours, and the MacDonalds of Rineton are known to have provided that property with a thatched roof *c.*1700. The lost mansion houses of Blelack, Monaltrie, Campfield, Inverenzie, Auchintoul, Auchinhove and Auchendryne – all burned by the British Army in the summer of 1746 – may or may not have been thatched at that date. Inverey 'Castle', burned half a century earlier, almost certainly was. Then as now, the main difference between the house of a prosperous farmer and that of a very minor laird seems to have been that the former had three windows on the upper floor on the entrance side, while the latter had five. The least messed-about local examples are Tillyfruskie and Mains of Auchlossan, respectively. The 1735 block of Maryculter House, on the whole a much more elegant structure than Mains of Auchlossan, is nevertheless considered a mere ha' hoose, apparently due to its three-window frontage.

Among the slightly more ornate lairds' houses, the most interesting survival is Balnacraig, and the saddest loss of all is undoubtedly Craigmyle. Craigmyle,

Above and opposite top. Even quite large fortified houses in Mar seem frequently to have had thatch-roofed or part-thatched outbuildings, as recently as the Victorian era. These are Tillycairn (c.1550), Balfluig (1556), and Pitfichie (c.1560), all drawn by James Giles in 1840.

Among the more ornate lairds' houses, Craigmyle has been the saddest loss of all.

which changed hands too often for me to associate it with one family in particular, was a seventeenth-century house that was elegantly and sensitively expanded by Sir Robert Lorimer, then Scotland's greatest architect, in 1904. The barony of Craigmyle was broken up in 1956 and the house deliberately blown up in 1960. Balnacraig (see p. 39) is a time capsule of a once-usual laird's house design, most exemplars of which were destroyed by government troops during the period of Jacobite unrest; its survival is the subject of an elaborate legend,

*Inchmarlo House before and after the mid-nineteenth-century roofline alterations.
Unusually, the changes seem to have been calculated to make Inchmarlo look more, not
less, like what it is: an eighteenth-century house.*

though perhaps the old saying, 'Oot o' the warl' and into Birse' is explanation
enough. Tillyfruskie, also in Birse, is now cited as typifying the ha' hoose *style*,
but in fact the best house in any hamlet, however miserable, might be referred
to as the ha' hoose for that area: as we know happened in the lost eighteenth-
century hamlet of Bellastraid, on the burn of Logie in Cromar.

One of the few mid-Georgian-style mansions of the region, Inchmarlo
House, was built around 1750 for John Douglas of Tilquhillie. Its appearance is
deceptive, however. Prior to remodelling between 1823 and 1850, Inchmarlo –

Coincidence? All four of the Deeside structures shown in this 1930s tourist postcard were either first built or substantially rebuilt after 1746.

now three storeys with a flat roof – was two storeys with high-pitched hip roof.

It would be tempting to agree with Fenton Wyness, that Deeside's Jacobite lairds were directly supplanted by pro-Hanoverian and English incomers, and that the 'essentially native' building work of the eighteenth century gave way directly to 'foreign' styles in the nineteenth.[32] No doubt his ire was fuelled by Queen Victoria's famous comment in the late 1850s that she liked Deeside better, 'now that great and excellent taste has been stamped everywhere'.[33] But as Wyness himself points out, many of the architects and most of the incoming landlords during the eighty-odd years after Culloden were Scots.

For Wyness as for others, the lightning rod of this controversy is the Glen Tanar estate, and certain portions of the town of Aboyne, as built or rebuilt by the English banker Sir William Cunliffe Brooks between 1888 and 1899. It is clear, Wyness writes, that Sir William 'failed to appreciate that Scotland possessed any architectural tradition'.[34] This is quite unfair. First of all, Glen Tanar's buildings, while not inescapably part of a previously known Scottish tradition, are not simply English imports. Most are built of pink granite, and feature gloss-green-painted exterior woodwork and/or crowstep gables. Like Cunliffe Brooks himself, they are altogether weird. In the buildings' case, this is manifested as an attempt to imagine what a Scottish vernacular architecture *might have been,* had the field not been utterly taken over (e.g. at Blackhall) by degenerate versions of the new Balmoral Castle, itself a badly out-of-scale version of a sixteenth-century chateau. Secondly, the workers' houses on the Glen Tanar estate are of admirable quality, and the whole rebuilding scheme seems to have been rooted as much in concern for the welfare of the Glen Tanar community as in a sheer desire for self-aggrandising Anglicisation, as is so often claimed. The estate should be seen, rather, as a far-northern exemplar of the same 'benevolent-proprietor' planning movement that produced Bournville and Saltaire. In his lifetime, it was remarked of Cunliffe Brooks that he 'has . . . directed special attention to the introducing of an ample supply of the purest water, erecting healthier houses for the tenants and workmen on his estate, and making good roads, and thus greatly improving . . . sanitary conditions'.[35] All of these measures were continued by Cunliffe Brooks's successors and are still in evidence. By the 1950s the Glen Tanar Home Farm was organic, and the laird had built an electric car, capable of getting to Aboyne and back on a single charge, albeit 'at very modest speed'.[36] Though not a native myself, I suspect that nativist ire could be more sensibly directed elsewhere.

Far greater damage to our built heritage was done by the nineteenth-century fashion of expanding nearly every place designated a 'castle' to massive, Fyvie-like proportions. This began in 1801 in the case of Aboyne Castle, which is illustrated at its maximum extent in *Lost position*, p. 187. It was reduced to more or less its original form in 1975. Though a century older, Abergeldie Castle underwent a very similar sequence of nineteenth-century alterations and

The 'Queen Anne' version of Invercauld House, some twenty years before the massive expansion of 1875.

*Skene House, whose private library rivalled that of King's College, Aberdeen, in both
quantity and quality, is shown here in 1839 in the last blush of its 'organic' development.
A decade later, Skene was 'baronialised' by the Aberdeen architect Archibald Simpson,
and might now be mistaken for a scale model of Yale University.*

twentieth-century 'de-alterations': with the additions by James Henderson being
demolished in or after 1969. Invercauld and Old Balmoral Castle differ from
this in that their expanded forms remained: Old Balmoral's (dating from 1834–
38) lasted until it was razed to the ground in 1855, and Invercauld's (dating from
1875) until the present day. Midmar Castle's 'footprint' has doubled since it was
first completed in 1550. Only a fraction of Skene House's fourteenth-century
core is still visible, amid 1740s and 1840s additions eight or nine times its original
size. (It also underwent a 1680 'facelift'.)

Of all such projects, only Drum can be considered an unqualified aesthetic
success – chiefly because no attempt was made either to hide the thirteenth-
century keep, or to hide the fact that it was older than the rest of the complex,
when major extensions were made in 1619 and since. The 1619 block is, indeed,
a glorious building in its own right and ripe for emulation. Dunecht House,
meanwhile, is an extreme case of an early-modern structure little better than a
farmhouse being transformed into a Victorian structure little worse than a
palace.

Early Victorian depiction of Crathes Castle, by R.W. Billings.

Even the best-preserved castles in the region have undergone some alterations and taken some damage. Crathes has seen some of its windows and at least one gun-loop filled in, and other windows punched through. Its well and a staircase have been blocked up and later reopened. An eighteenth-century extension burned, in 1966, and was rebuilt with significant changes. Craigievar was harled with cement rather than lime in the 1970s, which caused humidity inside to reach unsustainable levels, and a near-collapse of several ceilings in 1990. Restoration has left the upper level structurally sound but internally rather plain, and such ornaments as there are include several replicas.

Castles' names, now seemingly part of the landscape, also changed with the fashion of the times and the owners' whims. The place we know as Midmar Castle was called Ballogie in 1593, Midmar in 1700, then Ballogie again, then Grantsfield, and ended up as Midmar again by 1780. Because Deeside would not be Deeside without two of everything, there is a second Ballogie, on the other side of the river: an eighteenth-century laird's house which was known as Tillysnacht, until built over in 1856 in a style that was not quite Georgian, and renamed Ballogie for reasons not now clear. It was built over again, *definitely* as Georgian, in 1983.

Crathes's Queen Anne wing before the 1966 fire. The original windows were much smaller than those of the present structure, and the chimney-stacks much larger: a reflection of the building's pre-1951 role as a family house?

*Above. Ballogie/Tillysnacht as it appeared
between 1856 and 1982.*

*Right. This sixty-foot-high granite obelisk on top
of Mortlich, a memorial to the tenth marquess
of Huntly, was put up in 1868 and collapsed on
6 November 1912.*

The Fall of Morlich Monument.

Keen regret was felt in the Aboyne district yesterday at the collapse of the monument on the Hill of Mortlich. The familiar obelisk was a prominent landmark. Built of granite, it was 60 feet high, and stood on the crown of the hill, itself 1258 feet. The hill is about a mile north from the Loch of Aboyne, and, being the highest point in the parish on the north side

of the Dee, was conspicuous, and was seen from many places in the district.. The monument, which was surmounted by a cross, was erected in 1868, and bore the inscription:—

Charles, 10th Marquis of Huntly. Died, 18th Sept., 1863. Erected by Mary Antoinetta, his widow, and the tenantry of Aboyne.

The structure was erected by Robert Dinnie, father of Donald Dinnie, the famous athlete.

LOST ORIGINS:
BLACKHALL CASTLE

Joseph Farquharson RA's wife Violet Hay was also his neighbour, born on the adjoining estate of Blackhall – which her husband's distant forebear the 'Wild Laird' Archibald Farquharson had owned and, in 1829, lost. This structure, or rather succession of different structures, is quite mysterious. What is perfectly clear is that the last iteration of the castle – having served as the rural refuge of St Margaret's School, Aberdeen, during the Second World War – was demol-ished in 1946, and some of its stones used to repair bomb damage to the Houses of Parliament in Westminster. It is also reasonably clear that this version of the castle was built, replacing an older structure, probably in 1884 but certainly during the lifetime of Violet's father James Tonor Hay, autocratic heir to a Leith rope-making fortune.

It is with the immediately preceding version of the castle that we run into difficulty. W.M. Farquharson-Lang, fourteenth laird of Finzean, states unequiv-ocally that his forebear the eighth laird 'built and occupied a splendid castle at Blackhall near Banchory'.[37] The eighth laird of Finzean was born in 1793 and married into the Russells of Blackhall aged twenty-one, so his building on their estates could not have commenced before 1814 – probably, before 1816, when a J. Russell 'of Blackhall' was alive enough to subscribe to a new edition of Ossian's *Poems* printed in Montrose. The Farquharson building also must have been completed well before 1826, when the eighth laird retired from parliament,

Blackhall Castle in its final form, 1884–1946.

This uncharacteristically murky 1850s illustration by Gibb seems to be the source of the contention that Blackhall was a sixteenth- and seventeenth-century structure which lasted until the rebuilding of 1884, and that no comprehensive rebuilding took place either in the 1770s or the 1820s.

having previously thrown parties at Blackhall for several seasons.

Unfortunately, this *c.*1820 building is completely unknown to the Ordnance Survey, who in 1864 thought the then castle was from 1771. RCAHMS dispute this date, but in its place they offer only a vague suggestion that the castle was 'early', by which they usually mean pre-Civil War. Still others claim, more specifically, that a seventeenth-century house of two storeys was added on to a sixteenth-century crenellated and turreted keep of four or five storeys.

That a house built in stages in the 1500s, 1600s and 1800s could be mistaken for one of 1771 is conceivable, but unlikely. It seems to me more plausible that the *c.*1820 house, which Farquharson-Lang called 'modern', 1) obliterated any previous houses on the site; and 2) was mistaken by the surveyors as fifty years older than it really was – perhaps due to the re-use of an old-ish dated stone from an entirely different building: a common Aberdeenshire practice. The current Bridge of Ess at the north end of Glen Tanar, for instance, was built in 1894 but carries a (genuine in itself) date stone which reads 1779; similarly, the nineteenth-century bell of Birse Kirk, like the bell it replaced, was given the date '1675'.

Into the twentieth century at Blackhall, 'A goat (the Russell crest), life size'

The old 'goat gate' of Blackhall Castle, drawn in the 1850s. The symmetry of the site was foiled by the later addition of a polygonal gatehouse with two 'witch's hat' turrets at the left-hand side.

could be seen 'upon the top of each of the two principal pillars of the gateway, prettily cut in stone, with the motto – CHE SARA SARA (What will be, will be)'.[38] This just adds more layers to the oddity of the castle, since the crest-and-motto combination described pertains to the duke of Bedford, with whom the Blackhall Russells are not known to have had any connection. If the goat was put up without proper heraldic authorisation, it could have been taken down by order of the Scottish heralds, which might explain why it disappeared from the site before the castle itself. A small modern dwelling house has now been built directly on the site of Blackhall Castle, so further investigation using archaeological methods may be deemed more trouble than it is worth.

LOST ARCHITECTURE (III):
CIVIC AND PUBLIC ARCHITECTURE OF THE BURGHS

As previously mentioned, Deeside proper can boast only one very plain and fragmentary market cross, that of Banchory-Ternan (in its Kirkton of Leys incarnation). Tullich's is known to have been destroyed, while on South Donside, I have been able to find no record of a town cross in use in the royal burgh of Kintore. Charlestown of Aboyne's courthouse and tolbooth, presumably dating from the Restoration period when the burgh was chartered, were located on the site of the present Victory Hall, designed in 1920 by A. Marshall Mackenzie & Son. The tolbooth may or may not be the same as the 'Bonty' tolbooth which was pulled down a little before 1800. No information seems to exist on the public architecture of Kirkton of Durris, which even the greatest scholars of the region seem to forget was erected into a burgh of barony in 1540 or 1541.

Banchory-Ternan had, in the 1840s, a wooden post office located in Watson Street, as well as a gaol. It also had its own slum: Hammerman Square, described in a lengthy mid-Victorian poem, ostensibly written by a visiting Ross-shire navvy.

> And then for the beds and the lodgings they keep,
> You may go to repose, but you get little sleep,
> For the rats and the varments that that dance but and ben
> Would make you as nervous as granny's grey hen!
> At church or at chapel they never appear,
> Their God is their belly, their pleasure is beer,
> And blind silly 'flats' are soon snapped in a snare
> If they mind not the dodges of Hammerman Square.
> They kick up a row, and they swear, drink and fight,
> And like tigers they roar till the morning grows bright.
> 'Tis a rare habitation – deny it who dare;
> 'Tis a hell upon earth in the Hammerman Square.

It has since been built over and renamed St Ternan Place.

I have been unable to find any information on the exact location, external appearance or final fate of the 'spacious' Banchory Grammar School, which was endowed by Sir Thomas Burnett of Leys, Bt, in 1651. In addition to the school, the building contained a hospice for the poor and infirm (two males, two females and four attendants) located in the 'four arched vaults below'.[39] Presumably in or near the kirktown, it or its remains may have been destroyed there along with so much else in 1853. A girls' school was set up, also about 1650, but cannot now be identified either – except to the extent that it is not the same girls' school which operated from 1750 to 1912, latterly occupying the Burgh Buildings. Echt was also noted as having two private schools in 1842.

Tarland was a burgh of barony, coeval with Charlestown of Aboyne but chartered by the Irvines of Drum. It too had a tolbooth and market cross but

The new town of Torphins mimicked the market crosses of yore with its Queen Victoria Jubilee Fountain.

these, and everything else from the Restoration period, are gone now. The original site of Lumphanan is no longer in use either: a casualty of the decision to site the Lumphanan railway station half a mile to the east of it.

LOST ARCHITECTURE (IV):
COMMERCE AND INDUSTRY

A major category of lost architecture of the Deeside region can be classified as water-powered industry. Despite the furious unpredictability of the Dee itself, milling of one sort and another was conducted on its tributaries, and many of the original buildings still exist as private houses, restaurants, or ruins. The Gairn and the Muick had ten water-mills between them in 1842. The Water of Feugh, the Dee's largest tributary, had seven mills at one time, but of these only three survive: Clinter, Bucket, and Perciemuir. The Loch of Loirston, in Nigg, boasted a sawmill, a meal-mill and a bone-mill in 1838. A Victorian horse-powered mill, one of the region's very few, lives on as a restaurant by Crathes Castle.

The great majority of mills were for foodstuffs, but some of the products of these early factories are no longer used at all. William Leith, a private in Moir of Stoneywood's Aberdeen Jacobite regiment, gave his occupation as snuff-grinder; a century later, William McCombie, Esq., of Easter Skene was operating a snuff-mill on the Culter Burn. This was 'a small low square thatched building . . . driven by a water wheel of eight horse power', which allowed a lone employee to grind three hundredweight of snuff per week. In the same parish, a paper mill established by Bartholomew Smith in 1750 was still in operation a century later,

Extremely rare photos, courtesy of Colin Narbeth, of rarer banknotes: the Aberdeen Bank's £20 and 5s notes, made in the 1790s using paper produced at Culter.

powered by two very big waterwheels. Among other things, it made cartridge paper (no longer used since the transition to brass cartridges in the 1860s) as well as very fine papers for the banknotes of the Aberdeen Bank: forgotten products of a lost institution. Smith's firm held a 114-year lease from Patrick Duff of Culter,

Culter Paper Mills, drawn c.1850 by Gibb, and photographed c.1900.

for the former site of the waulkmill of Craigton. It was the first operation of its kind in northern Scotland but had a very small output at first. It descended in the Smith family until 1820 when it passed to Alexander Irvine, thence in 1837 to Arbuthnot & McCombie, then to Pirie's of Stoneywood in 1856, becoming at last the Culter Mills Paper Company Ltd in 1865. The water-wheels seem to have been replaced by steam power by 1895. A conservative organisation, the Culter Mills retained their Musgrave tandem compound steam engine as a backup power source, apparently into the 1970s, and acquired a small, thirteen-year-old steam locomotive in 1954. This was the firm's third loco and the second built by Peckett of Bristol. As can be surmised from this, the Culter Mills was one of the major freight customers of the Deeside railway line (*The lost railways*, pp. 226–232), taking in vast quantities of coal as well as wood, and also sending forth its finished products principally by rail. The firm closed its doors in 1981 and its buildings, including the 200-foot lum, were demolished in the same year. The site is now covered by private dwellings.

The early nineteenth century saw the establishment of parish savings banks. These were inspired by Henry Duncan's successful experiment with one, begun in the Borders parish of Ruthwell in 1810, and popularised through his 1815 tract *On the Nature and Advantages of Parish Banks; together with a Corrected Copy of the Rules and Regulations of the Parent Institution in Ruthwell.* By the following year, a parish bank had been established in Braemar. A quarter century later, there were others in Maryculter, Banchory-Devenick, Birse, Ballater, Tarland and Kintore, and in Strachan one was planned; the Braemar bank's capital had risen above £2,000. In Banchory-Devenick the average depositor's savings was £25, and in Kintore, deposits reached £4,000 within five years. Surprisingly strict limits were set on monthly depositing and total deposits: the Tarland savings bank established in the mid-1830s under the patronage of the earl of Aboyne had both a maximum monthly deposit of £10, and a maximum total deposit of £60. If the Ruthwell plan was adhered to strictly, there would also have been a minimum annual deposit of four shillings, and interest rates that went up (to as much as 5 per cent) the longer a customer stayed with the bank. The whole scheme aimed to alleviate poverty – and thereby, 'French' radicalism – essentially by making poor people's money more difficult for them to spend. In Alford, no. 2 Bank Terrace, a dwelling house since 1859, may commemorate such an institution; but for reasons not now clear, few if any surviving purpose-built banks in the Mar region date to before the mid-1860s.

Lead was almost certainly mined in the area by the 1740s, when Thomas Laing, an Aberdeenshire soldier serving in Roy Stewart's Jacobite infantry regiment, gave lead mining as his occupation. Abergairn in particular seems to have been mined extensively: lead was found there 'in some quantity', but this was 'many years ago' and the workings 'now ploughed over', William MacGillivray noted in 1852.[40] The experiment was tried again by a Mr Belt, at the behest of the marquess of Huntly, in or about 1875. While initially promising, this too was rapidly abandoned. There was a small but relatively productive silver mine on Craig of Proney in the eighteenth century. From Monymusk in 1791 and again in 1840 a potentially productive iron mine was reported, but its ore was not wrought due to the general shortage of fuel. Diatomite, a naturally occurring but rare ingredient of dynamite, was found in the eastern part of Dinnet Moor and extensively exploited during the First World War, a special camp being erected for the purpose. The camp's buildings and bogie-tracks were seen in a derelict condition there for many years after the war ended, but had been removed by the 1960s.

Perhaps the oddest episode involving mining on Deeside was an attempt

Stagecoaches ran to Castletown of Braemar from wherever the railway line ended: i.e. all the way from Aberdeen until September 1853; thereafter from Banchory-Ternan until 1859; then from Aboyne until 1866; and then from Ballater, until their final replacement by motor-coaches and cars. This drawing shows the Burnett Arms Hotel, Banchory-Ternan, during that town's short period as the railway's western terminus. The inn's coaching tradition died hard: even forty years later, it still advertised carriages, broughams, gigs, dog-carts, and job- and post-horses, as well as an omnibus to and from the local railway station.

by the South of Scotland Electricity Board to find uranium. In 1977, commercially viable quantities of the highly radioactive metal were believed to lie within the Hill of Fare, as well as south by south-west of Kirkton of Durris on the other side of the river. This led to a storm of controversy including a protest song to the tune of Scott Skinner's 'Bonnie Banchory, Oh!', whose verdict on uranium was, 'we nivver felt the wont o't, and we'd rather dae withoot'. Perhaps most disturbing was the thought that if mining were approved, the Hill of Fare would be substantially destroyed, and in its place would be left three 'tailings lagoons' of up to two square miles, for an unspecified but lengthy period. Friends of the Earth (Aberdeen) produced a short book arguing against the plans, and calling each of the tailings lagoons 'a potential avalanche of toxic mud'. Citing precedent from the Orkney Islands Council, the Friends argued that 'there is no point in granting permission for exploratory drilling unless eventual exploitation of a confirmed ore body is also acceptable.'[41] Clearly it was not.

In contrast to castles new and old, Deeside's hotels have been getting wider.

219

Banchory Station before, during and after the rebuilding of 1902. Only the engine sheds remain.

The current wildly asymmetrical appearance of the Burnett Arms Hotel in Banchory-Ternan contrasts with that of 1855, due to the addition of two new wings, stepping southward and eastward up and into the street, the outermost looking not unlike a lost piece of an Edwardian London department store. Similarly but less dramatically, the west front of the Huntly Arms Hotel, Aboyne, has expanded southward, nearly doubling its width. Invery House, long a hotel, is now a private house again; and of course, we have lost the overwhelming majority of the numerous small inns, often operated by ferrymen and -women, which once catered particularly to Excise men, drovers, and floaters.

The architecture of the region's railway stations was relatively varied. Though most stations of the Deeside line were wooden structures, built to a simple pattern first established at Park and Crathes, others were more elaborate. Banchory Station, initially constructed of wood like most of the others, was rebuilt in masonry in 1902. Though Aboyne Station was considered 'commodious and imposing . . . the last word in design' in the 1860s,[42] it was also rebuilt in 1890, to 'match' the other parts of the town as remodelled by Sir William Cunliffe Brooks. In contrast to most of the Great North of Scotland Railway network, which had simple but attractive station overbridges built in a uniform style with a distinctive pattern of 'x'-shaped cross-bracing, the overbridge at Aboyne was roofed.

Both Aboyne and Banchory had very briefly served as the western terminus of the line, but that was a generation earlier and does not by itself explain the rebuilding urge. Ballater Station, which was the western terminus for a hundred years (1866–1966), was not initially intended to be so. The construction of the famous royal waiting room there was done at the suggestion of a public-spirited resident of Glen Muick, Mr J.T. Mackenzie. Mackenzie's offer to provide the building materials for free, if the railway agreed to rebuild the station in stone, was ignored. Hopes that the line would be extended to

X-type GNSR bridge and typical wooden station house.

Walker's Shortbread's original site in Torphins.

Braemar village, to a site 'about a quarter of a mile below the Invercauld Arms Hotel and on the same side of the road', were also dashed (see *The lost railways*, pp. 226–237).[43]

Of at least twenty-five stations and halts that existed on the Deeside line at one time or another, fewer than half have left more than faint traces. Ballater's station is a museum; Aboyne's is council-owned and tenanted by shops. Businesses and workshops of various sorts now also occupy former station buildings at Cults, Park, Dess and Dinnet. Conversion to private housing occurred at Pitfodels, Murtle, Crathes, Glassel and Cambus o' May. At Lumphanan and Torphins, however, 'it is difficult to realise that the railway ever existed'; the latter village has even resumed its pre-railway-age road layout.[44] At Culter, all that remains is one platform and a rather bent sign. All others in the suburban zone were completely destroyed.

As elsewhere in Britain, so many beloved small shops have closed just in the last thirty or forty years that it would be impossible to name them all in a narrative fashion. It is not now widely remembered that the mighty Walker's Shortbread empire originated as a small business in Torphins. Two other very sad losses are D'Agostino's ice cream shop in Banchory-Ternan (now a Royal Bank of Scotland branch), and the Northern Cooperative, which following a £7 million loss in 1992 shed 1,200 of its 2,000 staff, and closed the following year. The 'Coopie' is particularly missed in Culter, where it provided a focus of sorts for the community in the decade following the closure of the paper mills.

THE COWIE LINE:
A LOST FRONTIER RESTORED?

Other than the 'star fort' and English-style crenellations applied to Braemar Castle by the British Army, and the bridges of Invercauld and Gairnshiel, Mar has seen few examples of purpose-built military architecture in modern times. The great exception was the Cowie Stop Line.[45]

By the end of June 1940, the British Expeditionary Force – minus most of its anti-tank artillery – had been evacuated from the Continent, and the Nazis had conquered France, the Low Countries and, most importantly from our point of view, Norway. It was thought, erroneously as it happens, that the enemy had an aircraft capable of transporting one or more Panzerkampfwagen I tanks, or captured Polish tanks, or armoured cars; so anti-tank defences were considered necessary throughout the country. Running seventy miles westward from Stonehaven along the southern edge of the Mounth, the Cowie Stop Line was one of eleven defensive lines that were built or planned in eastern Scotland at this time. The Mounth remained such a formidable obstacle that only twenty-five miles of the seventy-mile line had to be actively fortified, the rest of the area being deemed inherently impassable to enemy mechanised forces.

Construction lasted from June 1940 to June 1941, and was performed largely by the 98th and 217th Pioneer Companies, about 550 men in all, though they may have been assisted by infantrymen of the 9th (latterly 51st) Highland Division[46] as well as civilian contractors and council workmen. Consisting of twelve pillboxes, three miles of ditch-and-bank anti-tank barriers, nine groups of concrete anti-tank cubes, slit trenches, weapons pits, barbed wire, roadblocks made from old railway rails, and the planned demolition of six bridges including the Bridge of Dye on the Cairn a' Mount road, it was considered a 'strong obstacle' by the army as of April 1941. Pillboxes were mostly hexagonal, with three-foot-thick walls and twelve-inch-thick roofs; one, defending a now-bridged ford on the Crynes Corse Mounth road, was so well camouflaged with earth and vegetation that it could not be seen from thirty feet away. Pillbox walls were deemed bulletproof at eighteen inches and tank-gun-proof at forty-two inches; but these numbers would need adjustment in the case of pillboxes constructed of coursed granite (as several were here) rather than reinforced concrete.

Although the beaches between Aberdeen and Fraserburgh were considered one of the likeliest places for a German invasion from Norway, northern Aberdeenshire behind the beach defences was a strategic write-off. It was 'so extensive and so open and had so many roads', according to an army memorandum of 9 June 1940, that all that could be hoped for was containment of the Germans to the north of Angus. To this end, the fight for the Cowie Line was to be a fight to the death.

The beach defences were quite insecure. The 10,000-odd men of the 9th/51st Division – including the 7th (Mar and Mearns) and 9th (Donside) battalions, Gordon Highlanders – were in theory responsible for the defence of the whole east coast from Easter Ross to Grangemouth; but in practice, most of them were guarding naval installations as far away as the Northern Isles. Chief responsibility for defending the Cowie Line itself – and all of Deeside west of Culter – therefore fell to the 3rd South Aberdeenshire and Kincardineshire battalion of the Home Guard, with assistance from the 9th/51st Division's engineers. Engineer Lt Cooper and seven sappers actually manned the demolitions in the Cairnwell Mounth during an invasion scare on 7 September 1940. Though their pillbox has not survived postwar road improvements, many anti-tank cubes are still there, and the line as a whole is remarkable for how much of it has withstood afforestation, beautification and agricultural improvement schemes since the war's end. However, it should be noted that many of the North-east's hexagonal pillboxes, such as the ones on the A93 just west of Aboyne and on the A947 at Fyvie, were not considered part of the Cowie Line or any other defensive line.

The soldier-lumberjacks of the Canadian Forestry Corps (*Forgotten heroes*, pp. 142–150) were implicitly part of the scheme for defending the Mounth against attack from the north, insofar as they were for long periods the only regular army troops stationed between the Royal Scots Fusiliers and Black Watch at Banchory-Ternan, on the one hand, and the Lovat Scouts at Balmoral, on the other. Though on paper a single, incomplete battalion, the CFC was always over-strength at a given unit size, and the Abergeldie–Blackhall sector had as many men as any two British infantry battalions. Nevertheless, one of the CFC's two companies in Birse was issued no rifle ammunition for a period of five months.

THE LOST OBSERVATORY

The great Dunecht (or 'Dun-Echt') Observatory was founded in 1872 by James Ludovic Lindsay, then Lord Lindsay and later the 26th earl of Crawford. Its exact location on the Dunecht estate is not now clear, with some sources claiming it was located on the Barmekin, an ancient hill-fort, and others that it was within Dunecht House. Perhaps both sites were used. Requests for information to the Dunecht estate office have not been answered, but photos, drawings and information provided to me by Karen Moran of the Royal Observatory, Edinburgh, indicate 1) that the three domes and library of Dunecht's observatory were connected by gravel paths through grass in a gently rising, treeless area, which may or may not have been a hilltop; 2) that whichever of these domes housed the transit circle had been removed by 1982, the site now being rough grassland; 3) that Dunecht's photographic solar laboratory and siderostat were located in two other, probably wooden buildings on completely flat ground near a coniferous woodland; and 4) that astronomical observations were also made from the roof of the resident astronomer's three-bay, two-storey stone-built house. In short, at least seven structures – located at up to three very different sites, not including Dunecht House – collectively made up the observatory complex.

Using Otto Struve's catalogue of the contents of the Imperial Russian Observatory at St Petersburg, then the finest institution of its kind, Lindsay assembled a collection of more than 11,000 astronomical books – 2,500 of them previously owned by Charles Babbage, father of the computer – and instruments which the Royal Observatory describes as 'priceless' and 'one of the great scientific collections of the world'.[47] In 1872 alone, £8,300 was spent on equipment, and within the British Empire by 1876, Dunecht's instrumentation was outshone only by that of Greenwich. Dunecht's vastly important printed book collection, with items dating back to 1478, included a first edition of Isaac Newton's *Principia Mathematica*.

Lindsay was assisted by David Gill, a watchmaker who had studied under James Clerk Maxwell at Marischal College, Aberdeen, but had not graduated. Gill first came to the attention of astronomers when he and the young George Washington Wilson took some excellent long-exposure photographs of the moon, through a twelve-inch reflecting telescope of Gill's own design. He was succeeded as director of Dunecht by Ralph Copeland, a Lancashire farmer's son and sometime shepherd, who had become interested in astronomy while caught up in the Australian Gold Rush of the 1850s. Returning to Europe, Copeland obtained a PhD in astronomy in Germany, and served in Capt. Carl Koldeway's German Arctic expedition of 1869–70, for which he was knighted by Kaiser Wilhelm I. After Dunecht was wound up, Copeland stayed with its contents, becoming Astronomer-Royal for Scotland and professor of astronomy at Edinburgh University. Gill was elected to the Royal Society in 1883 and given a (British) knighthood in 1900.

Arguably the crowning glory of Aberdeenshire's private-museum movement, the Dunecht Observatory survived there for less than twenty years. However, this was for patriotic rather than tragic reasons. When the much-inferior Royal Observatory in Edinburgh was threatened with closure, Lindsay rushed to its rescue, donating to it Dunecht's entire contents. There they remain, as the nucleus of the United Kingdom Astronomy Technology Centre. After the opening of the new purpose-built facility on Blackford Hill, Edinburgh, in 1896, Lindsay apparently never set his hand to a telescope again, and after 1898, he lived almost exclusively at sea.

Gill, Lindsay and Copeland were not Deeside's only great astronomers, however. In addition to these men, and James Gregory of the reflecting telescope, and David Gregory, Oxford chair of astronomy and friend of Edmund Halley (see *Lost heroes*, pp. 132–134), the valley produced Johann von Lamont. Born John Lamont at Corriemulzie in 1805, he was sent to a Catholic college in Germany at the age of twelve. Not feeling himself called to the priesthood on graduating, he became an assistant at the Royal Observatory of Bavaria in Brögenhausen aged twenty-five, its director at thirty. Eventually, he was given a professorship of astronomy at Munich University, and received the honour of knighthood from the King of Bavaria.

THE LOST RAILWAYS

I use the plural of 'railways' advisedly. For a relatively short, single-track line,[48] Deeside boasted an impressive, not to say bewildering, variety of train operators and shell companies. The initial 1845 flotation of the Deeside Railway, £100,000 at £50 a share, was fully subscribed in one week. The projected terminus was almost immediately moved from Banchory-Ternan to Aboyne, and the stated capital requirements more than doubled – due to the assumption, wrong as it happened, that the line would have to cross the Dee in two places. In the general atmosphere of railway euphoria, the new shares were oversubscribed sixfold.

The business plan was simple, even simplistic. Annual running costs of £5,000 would be met entirely by the fares of tourists and others who had never been up the valley before. Meanwhile, the business of the turnpike roads (worth £7,000 a year) and timber floating (£2,000 a year) would be immediately destroyed, and their combined annual value of £9,000 handed directly to the railway as profit.

The Deeside Railway Act received the royal assent in July 1846. Then the problems started. Wishing to share heavy equipment with the separate Aberdeen Railway, then in financial difficulties, the Deeside Railway lent them £16,000. After a year of inactivity, this inter-company loan led to shareholder unrest, and eventually, to the debtor company taking a controlling interest in the lender company, if only temporarily. The new board scrapped plans to extend the line past Banchory-Ternan, which required a new Act, passed in 1852.

There were few problems with the actual building of the line, despite this seven-year period of delay and muddle. The first turf was cut at Mains of Drum in July 1852 and the line opened for business on 8 September 1853, when three trains ran from Aberdeen to Banchory and back, the first leaving the city at 7 a.m., and the last departing Banchory at 6.30 p.m. In each case, the whole journey took sixty minutes, and the intermediate stops were Cults, Murtle, Culter, Park, and Mills of Drum. (Mills of Drum Station had disappeared by 1921, replaced by Crathes Station, a different site. This in turn is not to be confused with the private *platform* maintained for Crathes *Castle*, or the modern tourist station Milton of Crathes, now under construction.)

The hoped-for locomotives from Hawthorn's of Leith could not be ready in time for the opening of the line, so both the engines and the carriages were initially rented from the Scottish Central Railway and the Aberdeen and Scottish Midland. These rental agreements broke down irretrievably, but fortunately, not until after Hawthorn's got their act together in early 1854. Also in 1854, the Aberdeen end of the line moved from Ferryhill to Guild Street. A notionally

DEESIDE RAILWAY.

OPENING OF THE LINE FOR TRAFFIC.

ON and after THURSDAY the 8th SEPTEMBER, and until further notice, Trains will leave ABERDEEN and BANCHORY at the Hours undernoted:—

Departure from Aberdeen.

Miles.	TRAINS LEAVE	1. CLASSES 1 & 3.	2. CLASSES 1 & 3.	3. CLASSES 1 & 3.
	Aberdeen ....depart	7 0 A.M.	11·0 A.M.	4·39 P.M.
3¼	Cults	7·12 ,,	11·12 ,,	4 42 ,,
4¾	Murtle	7·18 ,,	11·18 ,,	4·48 ,,
7	Culter..................	7 26 ,,	11·26 ,,	4·56 ,,
10¼	Park	7·38 ,,	11·38 ,,	5·8 ,,
12½	Mills of Drum	7·46 ,,	11·47 ,,	5·17 ,,
16¼	Banchory . ...arrive	8·0 ,,	12·0 ,,	5·30 ,,

Arrivals in Aberdeen.

Miles.	TRAINS LEAVE	1. CLASSES 1 & 3.	2. CLASSES 1 & 3.	3. CLASSES 1 & 3.
	Banchory ....depart	8·30 A.M.	1·0 P.M.	6·30 P.M.
3¾	Mills of Drum	8·44 ,,	1·13 ,,	6·43 ,,
6	Park	8·53 ,,	1·22 ,,	6·52 ,,
9¼	Culter..................	9·5 ,,	1·34 ,,	7·4 ,,
11½	Murtle	9·13 ,,	1·43 ,,	7·12 ,,
13	Cults	9·18 ,,	1·48 ,,	7·18 ,,
16¼	Aberdeen ....arrive	9·30 ,,	2·0 ,,	7·30 ,,

Opening-day timetable of the Deeside Railway, 1853.

The first locomotives were from Hawthorn's of Leith, painted in a distinctive mid-blue with black details, and gloriously open to the sky.

independent 'Deeside Extension Railway' absorbed the risks of extending the line from Banchory to Aboyne, beginning in 1856; after Aboyne was reached, a third company, the 'Aboyne and Braemar Railway', was similarly set up. The Deeside Railway itself was always profitable, paying a dividend of up to 7.5 per cent, whereas its shell companies' dividends never reached 3 per cent.

This early, 'cowboy' phase came to an abrupt end in September 1866, when the Great North of Scotland Railway leased the Deeside Railway for 999 years. Because this occurred more than a month before service commenced from Aboyne to Ballater, neither the Deeside Railway itself nor the 'Aboyne and Braemar' ever ran a train on that stretch of the line. GNSR's outright ownership of the Aberdeen–Aboyne line followed in August 1875, and Aboyne–Ballater in January 1876.

Though superseded by London and North Eastern (in 1923) and British Railways (in 1947), it is GNSR that is most associated with the Deeside line in its heyday – as well as with the branch line that connected Alford to Kintore Junction on the Aberdeen–Elgin line, opened by/as the Alford Valley Railway in 1859. Despite the lack of local competition, GNSR is remembered as a 'good' railway company which gave the Deeside line 'more than a fair share of publicity'. Its successor LNER, in contrast, was a giant 1920s conglomeration of four English and two Scottish railways, and is held responsible for 'the first stages of running-down the Deeside line' – not least through its 'financial interest in the competing bus company'![49] The overall level of activity on the line achieved by GNSR in the last days of peace before the First World War was never equalled again.

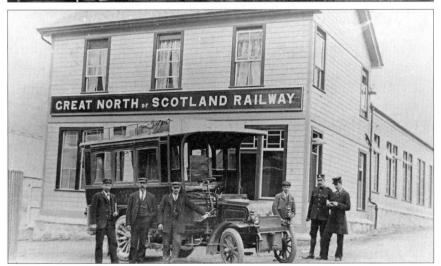

Top. GNSR locomotives clearing snow on the Alford line, 1907. Middle. A busy Alford Station in 1910. Bottom. The extant but abandoned Braemar bus station, 1910.

LNER bus in Ballater, interwar period.

The Victorian-era Deeside line could not easily be connected to the south through the Mounth, which was simply too steep for trains of the time to negotiate.[50] (Average speed on the line between 1866 and 1879 was 17 m.p.h.; the 'Deeside Express' trains instituted in 1880 achieved 28 m.p.h.) At one time, it was proposed that the line be extended via Braemar to Blair Atholl in Perthshire. To connect it with the north was more plausible, but at least seven such schemes nevertheless all failed. They included 1) Banchory–Lumphanan–Cushnie–Alford; 2) Coalford[51]–Echt–Tillyfourie–Alford; 3) Cambus o' May–Nethybridge; 4) Dundee–Ballater–Inverness; 5) Aberdeen–Culter–Kintore; 6) Ballater–Braemar–Kingussie; and, last but least ambitious, 7) Aboyne–Coull–Tarland. There were also various unexecuted plans for steam-powered trams, one of which would have run from Belmont Street, Aberdeen, to Midmar via Echt (1877); similar proposals included Bayview in Aberdeen to Echt, with or without a branch to Skene (1896), and Woodend in Aberdeen to Echt, with a branch to Waterton (1900).

It was generally assumed that the Deeside line itself would extend past Ballater to Braemar, but this was reduced to 'goods only'. The company position on this until 1921 was that, when the goods in question turned out to be timber from Ballochbuie Forest, the need disappeared, because Ballochbuie was not logged once in royal ownership. In fact, Queen Victoria had secretly vetoed any extension of rail service past Ballater – and would not even allow the completion of the track-in-progress as far as the east bank of the Gairn.

Despite these setbacks which might have left the Deeside line a proverbial 'road to nowhere', a combination of commuting (within ten miles of Aberdeen) and tourism (from Banchory westwards) kept it in decent shape financially. In its six years as the western terminus, Banchory socked away Aberdonian tourist revenue, using it to become – and indeed remain – Deeside's most important country town.

Suburbanisation of Aberdeen was train-led, more or less in a straight line out Deeside to a distance of nearly ten miles: not bad going for a city of just 153,000 people (as of 1901). Not suburbs merely, they now contain some of the most valuable, or at any rate expensive, properties on the planet. Lumphanan, though too far from the city to become a suburb, nevertheless 'boomed' during the railway era as the result of the decision to run the line through it (and Torphins, Dess and Glassel) rather than through Kincardine O'Neil. Torphins became a town virtually *ex nihil*; the measure of its success was that the Aberdeen–Ballater express trains that were laid on in 1914 made intermediate stops only in Torphins and Aboyne. (However, two carriages were disconnected at Banchory and allowed to coast to a stop while the rest of the express passed on!) The roads between Banchory and Aboyne via Torphins were so poor, even in the interwar years, that that portion of the railway thrived as a direct result. Conversely, rail travel may have suffered later due to the major road-improve-

A post-electrification city tram and a GNSR steam train pass simultaneously across and below Aberdeen's Union Bridge. The tram's lack of horses and the absence of His Majesty's Theatre place this after 1898 and before 1907.

ments that were wrought by or on behalf of the Canadian army (*Forgotten heroes*, pp. 142–150).

Four bridges including Milltimber's were built specifically to facilitate access to the line from the south side of the Dee. The development of the motor bus industry was spurred, indirectly, by the unexpected failure of the trains to connect with Braemar. LNER's bus interests have already been mentioned, but even GNSR operated a fleet of buses as early as 1904. These were mostly Milnes-Daimlers, but a Durkopp was also used. The extant Braemar 'Bluebird' office was in fact purpose-built as a motor-coach depot, by GNSR, at about this time. A Culter Station–Midmar bus service was less successful, however, and lasted only from 1905 to 1906.

Several negative economic effects of the railway have already been noted throughout this book. There were others. 'The railway has drawn to itself the traffic on both sides of the Valley, and the turnpike roads are comparatively little used', one observer noted in 1895.[52] Writing three years later, A.I. McConnochie thought that because the railway bypassed it, going through Lumphanan instead, the portion of the Dee from Aboyne to Banchory was the most 'sequestered' and the least known to outsiders.[53] One of the specific casualties of this was the inn at Bridge of Canny, which failed even before the North Deeside road was moved out of its way. The reverse is surely now true: I visit Aboyne or Banchory almost every day, and Ballater or Kincardine O'Neil once a month, but I had lived on Deeside for a year before passing through Tarland (without stopping), and never once had call to visit Lumphanan until I began researching the present book.

One of the great events on Deeside was the passing of the Royal Train. Until 1923, soldiers and policemen were posted within sight of each other along the train's entire route – from Windsor, if need be. The Messenger service, which included the only Sunday train ever run by GNSR, was introduced in 1865. Subsidised by the Treasury at £9 2s per day, it was at first a single-carriage affair for the exclusive convenience of the Queen's Messengers, who until that date reached Balmoral by road, through the Cairnwell Mounth pass. A second carriage was later added for 'VIPs'. An unconfirmed tale exists that the first Messenger Train 'was painted all over in Royal Stuart Dress tartan'.[54] Certainly, Ballater Station was temporarily repainted black and gold for the visit of Tsar Nicholas II in 1896.

Neither the Royal Train nor the Messenger Train should be confused with the Royal Saloon, a railway carriage built in Kittybrewster and used intermittently on the Deeside line between 1898 and 1964. It had a drawing room, smoking room, servants' quarters, steam heat, electric light, and a clerestory roof, and 'was panelled throughout in walnut, mahogany and oak in a most

The Scots Greys cavalry regiment greets Nicholas II at Ballater Station in 1896. The Tsar was roundly hated in Britain and the government feared an attack by Nihilists.

attractive style'. It was royal only in that it was sometimes used by King Edward VII; before and after his relatively brief reign, it was available 'for hire to special parties and for the use of the directors'.[55]

In 1883, Sir Robert Burnett of Leys sued GNSR because the Messenger trains were not stopping at Crathes Castle. The case reached the House of Lords, which ruled that the Messenger trains *did* need to stop at the castle – but that ordinary excursion trains did not. In fact, all trains stopped at Crathes Castle from then until 1914, when the Burnett family waived their right to a private platform. The Messenger train service was discontinued in 1937, and the Cairnwell Mounth was again used by the Royal Messengers – now in motor cars – until helicopters were made available to them in or about 1949.

The Deeside line was scheduled for closure by British Rail in 1964, though local activism delayed the final closure by two years. The closure is nowadays recollected as sudden and capricious, but it was in fact a rational decision that was a very long time in coming. Drum Station, which had sold 6,600 tickets in 1864, sold just 400 in 1938. It was closed in 1951. Indeed, by the time the last train ran in 1966, almost as many stations on the Deeside line had been closed over the years as there were stations remaining. The pre-1960s station closures included Milltimber, Murtle, Bieldside, West Cults, Pitfodels, Ruthrieston and Holburn Street (all 1937); Cults (1953) and Crathes (1954). The Alford–Kintore line was closed to passengers *en bloc* in January 1950, and the closure of the entire Deeside line was contemplated as early as November of the same year. Under BR's mismanagement, tourist use of the line effectively ceased: despite

The shape of things to come: Deeside Omnibus in Aboyne.

the city of Aberdeen receiving 750,000 summer visitors annually, half of them without cars, the same number of people used the Deeside railway in summer as in winter.

Even in terminal decline, the line saw some interesting innovations. Something akin to the static-caravan holiday was developed using old, worn-out LNER carriages beginning in 1935. Two were provided for holidaymakers at Banchory Station, and one carriage each at Murtle, Crathes, Cambus o' May, Torphins, Aboyne, and Ballater. Holding up to six people apiece, they were lit with paraffin. These arrangements lasted until 1955, except at Aboyne, where the clever Depression-era expedient soldiered on for another five years. With the end of steam in 1958, a bolder experiment was tried: the £50,000, 117-seat Battery Railcar, the first such vehicle to be used in Britain. Recharged at each end of its journey, it was virtually silent, and known to locals as 'the Sputnik'. After its immature battery technology led to a series of small fires, it was withdrawn in 1962. After a circuitous 39-year journey taking in Inverurie, Glasgow, Derby, Yorkshire, and Lancashire, it returned to Deeside in 2001.

A remarkable dossier of documents, released to the Public Record Office in 2002, details the final end-game of the closure of the Deeside railway line.[56] Five years after the last trains ran, much of the railway's land had not been sold. On 6 September 1971, BR's Property Board Minute No. 192 recorded that a previous plan to sell the disused line to Aberdeenshire Council for £67,000 had fallen through. Within this price, the Peterculter Station area had been valued

Like something from Dan Dare, Pilot of the Future, *the Battery Railcar passes silently beneath a characteristically shabby LNER-built station overbridge, at Dinnet.*

at £14,400 and the Torphins Station area at £3,275. A related £7,000 sale to Kincardine County Council had also fallen apart. Banchory Town Council, another lost institution, was on the hook for £11,500, and railway land within the city of Aberdeen was worth another £2,700. Together, these parcels included nine or more houses.

Aboyne Goods Yard had closed on 18 July 1966 but was not marked 'non operational' by BR until mid-1971; its two tenants at the latter date were the 'major local coal company', Ellis & McHardy, and the shire council, who used their (granite and slate) half as a vehicle garage. The combined rent of both premises was £431 – a year. BR foresaw almost no demand for land in Aboyne, either for industrial or residential purposes. As such, it identified the shire council as the only plausible buyer, since the council's role was 'to stimulate the demand for industrial sites'. Mostly, BR was less interested in gaining money than in ridding itself of hassle: 'By the sale of this Branch, the Board will be relieved of the maintenance of: (a) 67 under-bridges (b) 31 over-bridges (c) 1 viaduct (d) 80 miles of fencing.' At this time, they wrote,

> The former station houses at West Cults, Bieldside, Murtle and Milltimber have all already been sold as have the station buildings at Bieldside and Murtle which have been converted into small residences. All other buildings [between Cults Station and Peterculter] . . . have been demolished.

No buildings remained at Drum Station, which was deemed 'incapable of development . . . owing to the lack of an adequate water supply in the area'. Water-supply problems also made the possibility of development 'negligible' at Crathes, though the stationmaster's house, a cottage, and the station building were still standing. They may have been quite basic, however: at Glassel, the stationmaster's house had no gas or electricity supply, and its water was from a well. Demand for land at Glassel was 'very poor'. The house was assigned a gross value of £20, and its tenant had asked to be moved to a council house.

Cambus o' May 'would be ideal for development in connection with the tourist industry if an adequate water supply could be obtained'. The line between Aboyne and Dinnet was deemed to have little or no agricultural value. Dinnet shared the water problems of other sites, and indeed, all villages in the area had 'continual difficulty in maintaining water supplies'.

BR's only really positive suggestions, both of which were ultimately implemented, were 1) that Ballater Station be 'developed in connection with the tourist industry', and 2) that the line itself, newly free of rails and sleepers, be used 'to form public walkways or tracks for pony trekking' through 'some of the most beautiful countryside in the North of Scotland'. Throughout their discussions, BR reiterated 'the lack of demand for land for development of any kind in these areas'. Following two decades of speculative mania that have seen the most dubious plots of land surpass and indeed replace gold as the basis of the world economy, this is both funny and sad: a 'bizarro world' version of the Deeside of today, where all the oil money on earth seemingly cannot cure a basic lack of residential space.

After extensive planning, the Alford Valley Railway was successfully re-created as a narrow-gauge tourist attraction in 1979–80. It now has regular steam services at reasonable prices, and a seemingly symbiotic relationship with its neighbour, the excellent Grampian Transport Museum. The Deeside line has been less fortunate: a petition against closure garnered just 577 signatures, which may indeed have represented most of the people who still used the service regularly (fewer than 300 per weekday). BR received 'only three enquiries about the acquisition of the line for use as a private railway' in the four years to October 1969; and 'each eventually withdrew their interest'.

One of these approaches may have been the public appeal launched by James Davidson, Liberal MP for West Aberdeenshire, 'to buy the line . . . and operate it as a private concern'. It was estimated that this would cost £250,000. 'Mr Davidson admitted that there was no evidence of a great deal of enthusiasm in the area to save the line, but he wanted to give people a last chance to act', the *Glasgow Herald* reported on 18 September 1969. A quarter of a century later,

> British Railways Board
>
> PUBLIC NOTICE
>
> Transport Act, 1962
>
> # WITHDRAWAL OF
> # RAILWAY PASSENGER SERVICES
>
> The Minister of Transport having given approval under powers conferred by the Transport Act, 1962, the Scottish Region of British Railways announce the withdrawal of ALL railway passenger train services between ABERDEEN and BALLATER on and from MONDAY, 28th FEBRUARY, 1966
>
> From the same date the following stations and halts will be closed to passenger traffic:—
>
> | CULTS | DEE STREET HALT | ABOYNE |
> | CULTER | GLASSEL | DINNET |
> | PARK | TORPHINS | CAMBUS O' MAY |
> | CRATHES | LUMPHANAN | HALT |
> | BANCHORY | DESS | BALLATER |
>
> The following alternative services by road passenger transport will be available:—
>
> OPERATED BY:
> MESSRS W. ALEXANDER & SONS (NORTHERN) LTD.
>
> Table Service
>
> | No. | No. | |
> | 1 | 1 | ABERDEEN-BALLATER/BRAEMAR via Cults, Culter, Banchory, Aboyne, Dinnet and Crathie. |
> | 3 | 1B | ABERDEEN-GLEN O' DEE HOSPITAL. |
> | 4 | 1C | ABERDEEN-BANCHORY via Cults. |
> | 6 | 1E | BANCHORY-BALLATER via Glassel Station, Torphins, Lumphanan, Dess and Aboyne. |
> | 7 | 2 | CULTER/KEPPLEHILLS/STONEYWOOD-DYCE. |
> | 21 | 14 | ABERDEEN-ABOYNE via Torphins and Lumphanan. |
>
> These tables include certain additional services which are required by the Minister of Transport as a condition of consent to the withdrawal of the passenger train service.
>
> A pamphlet giving full details of the alternative services will be available shortly at stations.
>
> PARCELS TRAFFIC
>
> Parcels and other passenger-rated Merchandise traffic will continue to be dealt with meantime at ABOYNE, BALLATER, BANCHORY and CULTER. Collection and delivery arrangements will be as follows:—
>
> ABOYNE for BALLATER, DINNET, GLASSEL, LUMPHANAN and TORPHINS.
>
> ABERDEEN for BANCHORY, CULTER, CRATHES, CULTS and PARK
>
> Further information may be obtained from the Station Master at Aberdeen.

Public notice that the Deeside line would be closed, 1966.

something was finally done, and the Royal Deeside Railway founded as Scottish charity no. SCO27686. It is a sad comment on the thoroughness of the original railway's destruction that the new company has needed to build a wholly new station on a site not previously so used (Milton of Crathes), to serve a line not now expected to exceed three miles in length. To the best of my knowledge it has not yet run a steam service, or rendered the Battery Railcar operable, despite owning it for nine years. I sincerely hope that whatever obstacles it is facing will soon be overcome.

LEST WE FORGET:
LOST HISTORIES IN THE MAKING

The current Inverey House is very convincing as Queen Anne style (or somewhat earlier), but was in fact built by Oliver Humphries in 1983. The same year saw the 'Georgianisation' of Ballogie/Tillysnacht, previously alluded to. I have also mentioned that Birse Castle was transformed from a ruin to a livable house in 1905; in fact, work there in 1930 and since has transformed it into an arguably new structure, albeit a very nice one.

Strathieburn and Balfour Tower, despite their seventeenth-century appearance, were both conceived in the last thirty years. Strathieburn, built by architect Ron Gauld for his own use in 1986, is the more exciting of the two, incorporating much recycled stonework, including some from the Queen Anne wing of Crathes Castle, lost to fire in 1966. (Sharp-eyed readers will already have noted that the current 'Queen Anne' wing at Crathes is from after 1966.) A whole Georgian facade for Strathieburn was salvaged from Culter Paper Mills, demolished in 1981, and recycled antique panelling and beams have been used inside.

For Balfour Tower, architect Michael Rasmussen had a very different brief in 1991: 'to produce a tower house . . . for the same cost as an up-market executive home, with all modern conveniences'. This was achieved, and the finished building has been praised as 'honest and effective'.[57]

LAST THOUGHTS

'Let us then humble ourselves,' William MacGillivray wrote not long before his death in 1852, 'that in contemplating God's works, we may ever see Him in the midst of them. If, in this temper, we traverse the valley of the Dee, and ascend the mountains from which the sources of that beautiful river gush forth, even if we discover little that may be of interest to science, we shall find much that may benefit our spiritual nature. And what would it profit a man were he to solve half the mysteries of external nature, and yet be ignorant of the higher relations of his own being? Strange adventures, perils among rocks and floods, wonderful discoveries, or magnificent theories – cannot be expected from a quiet journey to be made in one pair of shoes.'[58]

ACKNOWLEDGEMENTS

I would like to thank all of the National Trust for Scotland personnel who helped me in the research for this project, including especially Diana Robertson at Drum Castle and Gillian Wilson in Charlotte Square. I would also particularly like to thank Eleanor MacCannell, Peter Davidson, Jane Stevenson, Sir Moir Lockhead and Lady Lockhead, Jane Geddes, Anna Brown, Max Edelson, Dean and Juliet MacCannell, Marc and Karen Ellington, Andrew Elrick, Alan MacDonald, Barry Robertson, Michael Rasmussen, Ken Glennie, Jackson Armstrong, Vicky Dawson, Colin Narbeth, Peter Donaldson and all the volunteers and staff of the Grampian Transport Museum, Karen Moran of the Royal Observatory, Edinburgh, scottishpoliceinsignia.com, Fiona-Jane Brown of the Grampian Police Museum, and all the empoyees of Banchory Library, Aberdeen City Library, the National Archives at Kew, the Library of Congress, and Aberdeen University. Any errors in the book are, however, my responsibility alone.

FURTHER READING

In my opinion, the three best books about Deeside's losses are William MacGillivray's *Natural History of Dee Side and Braemar* (1855), John Grant Michie's *Deeside Tales* (1908), and G.M. Fraser's *The Old Deeside Road* (1921). For buildings that are still in existence (and a few that aren't), I can also highly recommend Jane Geddes's *Deeside and the Mearns: an illustrated architectural guide* (2001).

In a second tier of excellence, I would place Fenton Wyness's *Royal Valley* (1968) and Douglas Simpson's *The Province of Mar* (1944). The *Old Statistical Account* and *New Statistical Account* entries for this part of the country vary tremedously in style and content, but all are useful to a degree. For additional reading suggestions, please refer to the endnotes.

NOTES

CHAPTER 1

1. Sir Samuel Forbes of Foveran, 'Description of
   Aberdeenshire', in Gavin Turreff, ed., *Antiquarian
   Gleanings from Aberdeenshire Records* (Aberdeen,
   1871), 30–43, 33.
2. W. Douglas Simpson, *The Province of Mar: Being the
   Rhind Lectures in Archaeology, 1941* (Aberdeen, 1944),
   132.
3. Alex Inkson McConnochie, *The Royal Dee: a
   description of the river from the wells to the sea*
   (Aberdeen, 1898), 50.
4. Samuel Martin, hatter, of Aberdeen, quoted in A.D.
   Farr, *The Royal Deeside Line* (Newton Abbot, 1968),
   11.
5. Website of the Royal Commission on the Ancient and
   Historical Monuments of Scotland (hereafter,
   'RCAHMS').
6. Quoted in W.M. Farquharson-Lang, *The Manse and
   the Mansion: The Langs and the Farquharsons of
   Finzean 1750–1950* (Edinburgh, 1987), 72.
7. John Grant, *Legends of the Braes o' Mar* (Aberdeen,
   1876), xi.
8. Grant, *Legends*, 201; NLS MS 976 (1718). The kirkyard
   of Tullich was allegedly once the scene of a wild
   Sunday dance by the entire community – memori-
   alised by John Skinner as the 'Reel o' Tullochgorum' –
   which was successfully passed off as an attempt to
   keep warm; but surely it was also an act of protest at
   a time when the Kirk made dancing on the Sabbath
   punishable by a fine or imprisonment or worse.
9. John Grant Michie, *Deeside Tales*, ed. Francis C.
   Diack (Aberdeen, 1908), xix, describing his own
   experiences in the 1830s.
10. Another under-Dee tunnel was legendarily said to
    connect Knock Castle to Abergairn.
11. Cuthbert Graham, *Portrait of Aberdeen and Deeside*
    (London, 1972), 105.
12. Fenton Wyness, *Royal Valley: The story of the
    Aberdeenshire Dee* (Aberdeen, 1968), 38.

CHAPTER 2

1. A claim that 'Cennakyle and Ballatrach in
   Inchmarnoch' were owned at one time by Donald
   Farquharson of Tillygarmont (d.1619) remains to be
   investigated.
2. Hugh Cheape, 'The Printed Book in Scottish Gaelic',
   Papers from the ILAB Congress in Edinburgh,
   September 2000.
3. Michie, *Deeside Tales*, 108.
4. Michie, *Deeside Tales*, 109.
5. Chrissie Gibson, *Memories of Finzean: Schooldays
   1925-1933*, ed. R. Gibson Forbes (n.p., 1997), 130.
6. Quoted in Adam Watson and R.D. Clement,
   'Aberdeenshire Gaelic', *Transactions of the Gaelic
   Society of Inverness* 52 (1983), 373–404, 399.

7. Watson and Clement, 'Aberdeenshire Gaelic', 391.
8. Manuscript number 3617.
9. http://canmore.rcahms.gov.uk/en/site/32472/
   details/house+of+glenmuick/, accessed 1 July 2010.
10. McConnochie, *Royal Dee*, 39; see also John
    Mackintosh, *History of the Valley of the Dee from the
    Earliest Times to the Present Day* (Aberdeen, 1895),
    193.
11. John Taylor, *The Pennyles Pilgrimage Or The Money-
    lesse perambulation* (London, 1618), sig. [E4]v.
12. *Pennyles Pilgrimage*, sig. Fv.
13. Thomas Douglas, earl of Selkirk, *Observations on the
    present state of the Highlands of Scotland, with a view
    of the causes and probable consequences of emigration*
    (London and Edinburgh, 1805), 19.
14. C.G. Gardyne, *The Life of a Regiment: The History of
    the Gordon Highlanders from its Formation in 1794 to
    1816* (London, 1929), 2.
15. Stuart Maxwell and Robin Hutchison, *Scottish
    Costume 1550–1850* (London, 1958), 155.
16. Maxwell and Hutchison, *Scottish Costume*, 132.
17. All data and quotations in this paragraph are from
    the *Old Statistical Account* (hereafter '*OSA*') and *New
    Statistical Account* (hereafter '*NSA*') for the parishes
    named.
18. A.C. O'Dell *et al.*, *The North-East of Scotland*
    (Aberdeen, 1963), 84.
19. Farquharson-Lang, *The Manse and the Mansion*, 110-
    111.
20. Taylor, *Pennyles Pilgrimage*, sig. [E4].
21. Michie, *Deeside Tales*, 342.
22. Farquharson-Lang, *The Manse and the Mansion*, 150.
23. Wyness, *Royal Valley*, 110.
24. T.F. Torrance, quoted in *Oxford Dictionary of National
    Biography* online edition (hereafter '*ODNB*') for
    Patrick Forbes of Corse.
25. Stuart Reid, *Scots Armies of the English Civil Wars*
    (Oxford, 2003), 48.
26. *The Spirit of Slander Exemplified*, AUL MacBean p
    Cal.
27. Wyness, *Royal Valley*, 146.
28. *OSA* for Nigg.
29. *OSA* for Cluny.
30. *OSA* for Nigg.
31. John A. Henderson, *Annals of Lower Deeside*
    (Aberdeen, 1892), 24.
32. Margo Todd, 'Profane Pastimes and the Reformed
    Community: The Persistence of Popular Festivities in
    Early Modern Scotland', *Journal of British Studies*
    39:2 (April, 2000),
    123–56, 123.
33. J.G. Michie, ed., *The Records of Invercauld* (Aberdeen,
    1901), 397.
34. Alastair Livingstone *et al.*, *Muster Roll of Prince
    Charles Edward Stuart's Army, 1745–46* (Aberdeen,
    1984), 125.
35. Alexander Allan Cormack, *Two Aberdeenshire Spas:
    Peterhead and Pannanich* (Aberdeen, 1962), 18.

36. Cormack, *Two Aberdeenshire Spas*, 17.
37. Turreff, *Antiquarian Gleanings*, 193.
38. *ODNB* for Laurence Oliphant of Gask (1691–1767).
39. Timothy Mowl, 'A Roman Palace for a Welsh Prince: Byres' designs for Sir Watkyn Williams-Wynn', *Apollo* (November, 1995), 33.
40. Peter Davidson, 'James Byres of Tonley: Jacobites and Etruscans', in *Recusant History*, vol. 30, no. 2 (October 2010), pp.261–74.
41. Mackintosh, *History*, 167.
42. *ODNB*.
43. 'The MacBean Collection, the Pitsligo Papers and other Jacobite holdings', in Iain Beavan, Peter Davidson and Jane Stevenson, eds., *The library and archive collections of the University of Aberdeen: an introduction and description* (University of Aberdeen and Manchester University Press, 2011).
44. Preface to *Leven and Melville Papers*, ed. William Henry Leslie Melville (Edinburgh, 1843), xxxvi.
45. *Ibid.*, xxxvii.
46. *OSA* for Maryculter.
47. *OSA* for Kemnay.
48. *Aberdeen Journal*, quoted in Cormack, *Two Aberdeenshire Spas*, 50.
49. *OSA*.
50. John D. Hargreaves, *Aberdeenshire to Africa: Northeast Scots and British Overseas Expansion* (Aberdeen, 1981), 15, 16, quotation at 15.
51. Aberdeen University MS 30/2/561.
52. Donald I. Stoetzel, *Encyclopedia of the French and Indian War* (Westminster, Maryland, 2008), 152.
53. Sir Thomas Mitchell, 'Preface', in Canadian Legion Educational Services, *A Course on the Industry and Character of North-East Scotland for Candians on Leave* (Aberdeen, 1944), 2–4, 4. He may have been misinformed: the Hondurans seem to have been deployed largely to the north of Inverness.
54. Grant, *Legends*, 109.
55. Grant, *Legends*, 41, who calls the hill Creag-an-aibhse.
56. Robert Smith, *Land of the Lost: Exploring the Vanished Townships of North-East Scotland* (Edinburgh, 1997), 17.
57. V.J. Buchan-Watt, *The Book of Banchory* (Edinburgh and London, 1947), 178.
58. Grant, *Legends*, 98.
59. William MacGillivray, *Natural History of Deeside and Braemar*, ed. Edwin Lankester (London, 1855), 246, 279, 333.
60. MacGillivray, *Natural History*, 281.
61. Peter Marren, *Grampian Battlefields: The Historic Battles of North East Scotland from AD 84 to 1745* (Aberdeen, 1990), 2.
62. Marren, *Grampian Battlefields*, 61.
63. Marren, *Grampian Battlefields*, 80–81.
64. McConnochie, *Royal Dee*, 27.
65. F.J. Child, ed., *The English and Scottish Popular Ballads* (Edinburgh, 1965), vol. 4, 83.
66. *NSA* for Peterculter.
67. Mackintosh, *History*, 85.
68. http://canmore.rcahms.gov.uk/en/site/17127/details/mill+of+brux/, accessed 1 July 2010.
69. *NSA* for Coull and Leochel-Cushnie, respectively.
70. G.M. Fraser, *The Old Deeside Road: Its Course, History, and Associations* (Aberdeen, 1921), 132; McConnochie, *Royal Dee*, 130.
71. McConnochie, *Royal Dee*, 77.
72. McConnochie, *Royal Dee*, 78.
73. Simpson, *Province of Mar*, 51.
74. Henderson, *Annals of Lower Deeside*, 36.
75. McConnochie, *Royal Dee*, 137.
76. Aberdeen University MS M361/2, letter from Jonathan Troup, 14 August 1796. RCAHMS considers the surviving portion of the chain to be now lost, but my understanding is that it is still owned by Marischal Museum.
77. *OSA*.
78. Jane Geddes, *Deeside and the Mearns: an illustrated architectural guide* (Edinburgh, 2001), 134.

79. Simpson, *Province of Mar*, 40.
80. F.L.P. Fouin, *Glen Tanar: Valley of Echoes and Hidden Treasures* (Inverrurie, 2009), 114. RCAHMS's information that the c.1880 structure 'was converted into a museum in 1912 to house the oak canoes etc found in the area' cannot be correct, since McConnochie was aware in 1898 that the museum's goods – including the canoes – had recently been destroyed.
81. Mackintosh, *History*, 18.
82. *NSA* for Tough.
83. MacGillivray, *Natural History*, 193–94.
84. Mackintosh, *History*, 65.
85. *ODNB*, as also all earlier quotations regarding Meston in this section.
86. MacGillivray, *Natural History*, 63.

CHAPTER 3

1. Quotations from O'Dell *et al.*, *North-East of Scotland*, 54. I am grateful to Professor Richard Oram of the University of Stirling for a very interesting discussion of this point.
2. MacGillivray, *Natural History*, 390.
3. MacGillivray, *Natural History*, 60.
4. MacGillivray, *Natural History*, 326.
5. MacGillivray, *Natural History*, 173.
6. McConnochie, *Royal Dee*, 77.
7. MacGillivray, *Natural History*, 135.
8. MacGillivray, *Natural History*, 136n.
9. Turreff, *Antiquarian Gleanings*, 254.
10. *NSA* for Drumoak.
11. MacGillivray, *Natural History*, 17. He later made clear his position that there was one (but only one) pine species native to Deeside, but he did not specify which one: *ibid.*, 136.
12. MacGillivray, *Natural History*, 69.
13. *OSA* for Birse. It should be noted that 'mountain ash' is not an ash at all but an eighteenth-century and US term for rowan.
14. McConnochie, *Royal Dee*, 57.
15. Fraser, *The Old Deeside Road*, 175n. At that date and possibly from the first use of the wells there medicinally, the 'fashionable' hotel was Pannanich Lodge, located 'on the low ground west of the present [1921] hotel': *ibid.*
16. *NSA* for Echt.
17. MacGillivray, *Natural History*, 28.
18. McConnochie, *Royal Dee*, 52.
19. Quoted in Hargreaves, *Aberdeenshire to Africa*, 45.
20. O'Dell *et al.*, *North-East of Scotland*, 112.
21. Buchan-Watt, *The Book of Banchory*, 6.
22. *OSA* for Braemar and Crathie.
23. *NSA* for Banchory-Ternan.
24. D. Jenkins and M.V. Bell, 'Vertebrates, except salmon and trout, associated with the River Dee', in D. Jenkins, ed., *The biology and management of the River Dee* (Abbotts Ripton, 1985), 83–93, 84.
25. Jenkins and Bell, 'Vertebrates', 84.
26. *NSA* for Banchory-Ternan.
27. *NSA* for Nigg.
28. Jenkins and Bell, 'Vertebrates', 83.
29. MacGillivray, *Natural History*, 20.
30. Alexander Bremner, *The Physical Geology of the Dee Valley* (Aberdeen, 1912), 35.
31. MacGillivray, *Natural History*, 284n.
32. *OSA* for Alford.
33. *NSA* for Drumoak.
34. 'The Otters of Drum', *Drumoak and Durris Newsletter* 50 (March 2007), 1–3, 2.
35. Bremner, *Physical Geology*, 39.
36. http://www.scotlandsplaces.gov.uk/search_item/index.php?service= RCAHMS&id=36627, accessed 15 June 2010; Fraser, *Old Deeside Road*, 109n; Wyness, *Royal Valley*, 148–49.
37. News report of 1810 quoted in Buchan Watt, *Book of Banchory*, 19.
38. *NSA* for Strachan.

39. Michie, *Deeside Tales*, 263.
40. *NSA* for Drumoak.
41. Wyness, *Royal Valley*, 326n.
42. The original, a whaling ship's figurehead, had to be provided with legs and shoes. This was replaced in 1865 but shot up by the army. The third version, which eventually deteriorated due to weather, was installed in 1926.
43. George Sim, *The Vertebrate Fauna of 'Dee'* (Aberdeen, 1903), 264.
44. http://www.riverdee.org.uk/projects/theculterburn.asp, accessed 15 June 2010.
45. G.H. Martin, 'Road Travel in the Middle Ages', *Journal of Transport History*, New Series, 3:3 (Feb 1976), 159–178, 161–62. Similar conclusions were reached (independently) in the 1880s by J.C. Blomfield, J.H. Wylie, and J.E.T. Rogers.
46. Simpson, *Province of Mar*, 59.
47. *OSA*.
48. *OSA*.
49. *NSA* for Durris.
50. Fraser, *Old Deeside Road*, 138.
51. Quoted in Fraser, *Old Deeside Road*, 136.
52. Taylor, *Pennyles Pilgrimage*, sig. [E4].
53. Taylor, *Pennyles Pilgrimage*, sig. F2.
54. Fraser, *Old Deeside Road*, 60–65; Wyness, *Royal Valley*, 345.
55. Fraser, *Old Deeside Road*, 63.
56. Fraser, *Old Deeside Road*, 101.
57. *OSA*.
58. McConnochie, *Royal Dee*, 156.
59. James MacDonald, *Place Names of West Aberdeenshire* (Aberdeen, 1899), 345–346.
60. Grant, *Legends*, 16.
61. Gibson, *Memories of Finzean*, 152.
62. *OSA* for Peterculter.
63. *OSA* for Alford.
64. *NSA* for Tough.

CHAPTER 4

1. Selkirk, *Observations on the present state of the Highlands*, 36–37.
2. Michie, *Deeside Tales*, 10.
3. Grant, *Legends*, 188.
4. Marjorie Harper, *Emigrants from North-East Scotland, Volume 1: Willing Exiles* (Aberdeen, 1988), 3.
5. Harper, *Emigrants*, vol. 1, ix, 4, 8.
6. Harper, *Emigrants*, vol. 1, 156.
7. Harper, *Emigrants*, vol. 1, 158.
8. Marjorie Harper, *Emigrants from North-East Scotland, Volume 2: Across the Broad Atlantic* (Aberdeen, 1988), ix.
9. Harper, *Emigrants*, vol. 2, 56.
10. Harper, *Emigrants*, vol. 2, 1, 13, 34, 36, 167.
11. Harper, *Emigrants* vol. 2, 62, 109, 111, 118–19.
12. Harper, *Emigrants*, vol. 2, 199–200.
13. Fouin, *Valley of Echoes*, 223.
14. R.W. Billings, *The Baronial and Ecclesiastical Antiquities of Scotland*, ed. Ian Gow (Edinburgh, 2008 [1845–52]), vol. 2, 127.
15. Grant, *Legends*, 187.
16. Mackintosh, *History*, 136.
17. Henderson, *Annals of Lower Deeside*, 119–20.
18. Forbes of Foveran, 'Description of Aberdeenshire', 35.
19. All details and quotations are taken from the first (York, 1757) edition of Williamson's book.
20. *ODNB*.
21. *NSA* for Kincardine O'Neil.
22. Grant, *Legends*, 59.
23. Henderson, *Annals of Lower Deeside*, 204.
24. Henderson, *Annals of Lower Deeside*, 205.
25. Henderson, *Annals of Lower Deeside*, 167.
26. Henderson, *Annals of Lower Deeside*, 179.
27. Quoted in Albert E. Sanders, 'Alexander Garden (1730–91), Pioneer Naturalist in Colonial America', in *Collection Building in Icthyology and Herpetology* (n.p., 1997), 409–37, 415.
28. Sanders, 'Alexander Garden', 409.
29. Buchan-Watt, *Book of Banchory*, 163.
30. Quoted in Charles Turner, *The Old Flying Days* (n.p., 1972), 136.
31. 'The Davidson Gyropter. First Appearance of the Gyroscope in the Air', *Progress* 4:11, 1 September 1909, 381.
32. Quoted in *ibid*.
33. 'The Davidson Gyropter', *Flight*, 5 November 1910, 910.
34. McConnochie, *Royal Dee*, 37.
35. Elizabeth Grant of Rothiemurchus, *Memoirs of a Highland Lady* (n.p., 1911), 219–220.
36. *NSA* for Logie-Coldstone and Drumoak.
37. Michie, *Deeside Tales*, xvii.
38. Mackintosh, *History*, 144–45.
39. W. McCombie Smith, *The Romance of Poaching in the Highlands of Scotland* (n.p., 2008 [1904]), 140.
40. Susan Wilkinson, *Mimosa: the life and times of the ship that sailed to Patagonia* (Talybont, 2007), 49.
41. Michie, *Deeside Tales*, 207.
42. Quoted in Farr, *Royal Deeside Line*, 15.
43. Wilkinson, *Mimosa*, 51.
44. Mackintosh, *History*, 89.
45. William C. Wonders, *The 'Sawdust Fusiliers': the Canadian Forestry Corps in the Scottish Highlands in World War Two* (Montreal, 1991), 2.
46. Wonders, *Sawdust Fusiliers*, 53.
47. Wonders, *Sawdust Fusiliers*, 83.
48. Quoted in Wonders, *Sawdust Fusiliers*, 38.
49. O'Dell *et al.*, *North-East of Scotland*, 119.
50. Wonders, *Sawdust Fusiliers*, xii.
51. First Minister Salmond opposes the single-force proposal, but favours some reduction in the existing number of forces.
52. Gardyne, *Gordon Highlanders from 1816 to 1898*, 24.
53. Scottish North East Counties Constabulary (SNECC), *Silver Jubilee Brochure* (n.p., 1977), 43.
54. SNECC, *Silver Jubilee Brochure*, 55.
55. Fouin, *Valley of Echoes*, 103.
56. Michie, *Deeside Tales*, vi.
57. Henderson, *Annals of Lower Deeside*, 42.
58. Fr. Thomas Meany, MS of 1888–1899, quoted in Smith, *Land of the Lost*, 56.
59. Michie, *Deeside Tales*, 52, 55, quotation at 52.
60. William Roughead, *Twelve Scots Trials* (Edinburgh and London, 1913), 249.
61. https://secure.bebo.com/c/photos/view?MemberId=1857982767&PhotoAlbumId=1966716349&PhotoId=4619988415#photoId=1966716715, accessed 22 July 2010.
62. Michie, *Deeside Tales*, 78.
63. Michie, *Deeside Tales*, 61.
64. Timothy J.S. Wilkinson, *Banchory Cricket Club: A History* (n.p., 1987), 19.
65. Wilkinson, *Banchory Cricket Club*, 33.
66. Wilkinson, *Banchory Cricket Club*, 46.
67. A.R.B. Haldane, *The Drove Roads of Scotland* (Colonsay, 1995 [1952]), 3.
68. Haldane, *Drove Roads*, 10, 20, quotation at 20.
69. Haldane, *Drove Roads*, 23.
70. Haldane, *Drove Roads*, 48.
71. C. Greenhill Gardyne, *The Life of a Regiment: The History of the Gordon Highlanders from 1816 to 1898* (London, 1929), 3.
72. Chrissie Gibson, *Auld Bill's Granddaughter* (n.p., 1998), 48.
73. Haldane, *Drove Roads*, 204.
74. Haldane, *Drove Roads*, 207.
75. Haldane, *Drove Roads*, 212–213.
76. *OSA* for Towie.
77. Grant, *Legends*, 167.

CHAPTER 5

1. Fraser, *Old Deeside Road*, 185.
2. *NSA* for Aboyne.
3. *NSA* for Kincardine O'Neil.
4. Fraser, *Old Deeside Road*, 142n.
5. MacGillivray, *Natural History*, 296.
6. Fraser, *Old Deeside Road*, 182.
7. P.D. Baird and V.W. Lewis, 'The Cairngorm Floods, 1956', *Scottish Geographical Magazine* 73:2 (1956), 91–100, 92.
8. Baird and Lewis, 'Floods', 92.
9. In Fraser, *Old Deeside Road*, 161n.
10. *OSA* for Kildrummy.
11. Wyness, *Royal Valley*, 28.
12. Fraser, *Old Deeside Road*, 130.
13. McConnochie, *Royal Dee*, 75.
14. Fraser, *Old Deeside Road*, 169.
15. O'Dell *et al.*, *North-East of Scotland*, 32.
16. Wyness, *Royal Valley*, 89.
17. Fraser, *Old Deeside Road*, 178.
18. http://canmore.rcahms.gov.uk/en/site/232301/contribution/banchory+burnett+park+market+cross/?add_image=true
19. Buchan-Watt, *Book of Banchory*, 156, 157.
20. Wyness, *Royal Valley*, 80, 91, quotations at 80.
21. Fraser, *Old Deeside Road*, 140.
22. John Patrick, *The Coming of Turnpikes to Aberdeenshire* (Aberdeen, n.d. after 1976), 6, 10, 11, 16, quotation at 16.
23. Fraser, *Old Deeside Road*, 252.
24. Ballater Turnpike Road Act 1855.
25. McConnochie, *Royal Dee*, 25, 121.
26. MacGillivray, *Natural History*, 151.
27. Michie, *Deeside Tales*, ix.
28. Bruce Walker, *Clay Buildings in North East Scotland* (Dundee and Edinburgh, 1977), 5–29, quotation at 6.
29. Michie, *Deeside Tales*, ix.
30. Philip Rollo, 1660, quoted in RCAHMS site report.
31. Taylor, *Pennyles Pilgrimage*, sigs. [E4]v–F.
32. Wyness, *Royal Valley*, 276.
33. Quoted in *Balmoral . . . Guide to the Castle and Estate* (Wymondham, 2009), 18.
34. Wyness, *Royal Valley*, 279.
35. Mackintosh, *History*, 125.
36. Fouin, *Valley of Echoes*, 185.
37. Farquharson-Lang, *The Manse and the Mansion*, 121.
38. Andrew Jervise, *Epitaphs and inscriptions from burial grounds and old buildings in the north-east of Scotland* (Edinburgh, 1875), 30.
39. Buchan-Watt, *Book of Banchory*, 11–12.
40. MacGillivray, *Natural History*, 35, 199.
41. Friends of the Earth (Aberdeen), *A Promise to Move Mountains* (Aberdeen, 1977), 7, 18.
42. Farr, *Royal Deeside Line*, 33.
43. Farr, *Royal Deeside Line*, 39.
44. Dick Jackson, *Royal Deeside's Railway: Aberdeen–Ballater* (n.p., 1999), 60.
45. Most of the information and all quotations in this section are drawn from G.J. Barclay's 'The Cowie Line: a Second World War "stop line" west of Stonehaven, Aberdeenshire', *Proceedings of the Society of Antiquaries of Scotland* 135 (2005), 119–61.
46. The 9th division was a 'clone' of the 51st, and accordingly were renamed on 7 August 1940, after the original 51st division was captured in France.
47. http://www.roe.ac.uk/roe/library/crawford/index.html.
48. Except between Aberdeen and Park, 1899–1951, when double track was used. The re-conversion to all single track, in 1951, led immediately to one of the line's few accidents, a non-fatal derailment at Culter. The line's three confirmed fatalities, only one of which involved a passenger, all occurred before 1864.
49. Farr, *Royal Deeside Line*, 65, 67.
50. O'Dell *et al.*, *The North-East of Scotland*, 1.
51. A lost community on the Old Deeside Road, halfway between Drum and Peterculter.
52. Mackintosh, *History*, 30.
53. McConnochie, *Royal Dee*, 122.
54. Jackson, *Royal Deeside's Railway*, 43.
55. Farr, *Royal Deeside Line*, 133.
56. P.R.O. AN 169/142, from which all quotations in the remainder of this section.
57. Geddes, *Deeside and the Mearns*, 83.
58. MacGillivray, *Natural History*, 23.

INDEX

Page references presented in italics refer to illustrations.